Relevant Topics in Athletic Training

Edited by
Kent Scriber, M.S., R.P.T., A.T.C.
Head Athletic Trainer
School of Health, Physical Education
and Recreation
Ithaca College
Ithaca, New York 14850

Edmund J. Burke, Ph.D.
Associate Professor
School of Health, Physical Education
and Recreation
Ithaca College
Ithaca, New York 14850

Mouvement Publications
102 Irving Place
Ithaca, New York 14850

Box 26 Torquay
Victoria 3228
Australia

18 Kilmorey Park
Chester CH23QS
United Kingdom

Copyright©. 1978 by Mouvement Publications
Art work by: Tom Stearns
Typeset by Wilcox Press, Inc.
Printed in the United States of America
by Wilcox Press, Inc.

ISBN 0-932392-02-4

LIST OF CONTRIBUTORS

Ed Abramowski, M.S., A.T.C.
Head Athletic Trainer
Buffalo Bills Football Club
Buffalo, New York

Marge Albohm, M.S., A.T.C.
Head Women's Athletic Trainer
Indiana University
Bloomington, Indiana

Dennis Aten, M.S., R.P.T., A.T.C.
Head Athletic Trainer
Eastern Illinois University
Charleston, Illinois

Susan K. Borowicz, M.S., A.T.C.
Athletic Trainer
Cornell University
Ithaca, New York

Edmund J. Burke, Ph.D.
Associate Professor
Ithaca College
Ithaca, New York

Michael J. Cappeto, M.S., A.T.C.
Head Athletic Trainer
Columbia University
New York, New York

Garret P. Caffrey, Ph.D.
Director, Human Performance Laboratory
Syracuse University
Syracuse, New York

Jeff Fair, M.S., C.C.T., A.T.C.
Head Athletic Trainer
Oklahoma State University
Stillwater, Oklahoma

James Garrick, M.D.
Orthopedic Surgeon
Phoenix, Arizona

Joseph Godfrey, M.D.
Team Physician
Buffalo Bills Football Club
Buffalo, New York

Robert Grant, M.P.E., L.P.T.
Associate Professor
Ithaca College
Ithaca, New York

Marc Gruder, M.A., A.T.C. (M.S.)
Athletic Trainer
Cornell University
Ithaca, New York

Institute of Sports Medicine and Athletic
  Trauma
Lenox Hill Hospital
New York, New York

E. James Kelley, Ed. D.
Assistant Dean, College of Health,
  Physical Education and Recreation
The Pennsylvania State University
University Park, Pennsylvania

Charles "Chuck" Kerr, M.S., A.T.C.
Chairman, Department of Athletics
Ithaca College
Ithaca, New York

Karl K. Klein, M.S., C.C.T.
Professor of Health, Physical Education and
  Recreation
University of Texas, Austin

Kenneth L. Knight, Ph.D., A.T.C.
Sports Medicine Research Laboratory
State University of New York at Brockport
Brockport, New York

Frederick Kriss, M.D.
Section of Neurosurgery, Department of
  Surgery
University of Michigan Medical Center
Ann Arbor, Michigan

Donald D. Lowe, M.A., A.T.C.
Coordinator of Sports Medicine
Syracuse University
Syracuse, New York

Donald Maron, D.P.M.
Sports Podiatrist
Syracuse, New York

Sayers "Bud" Miller, M.S., R.P.T., A.T.C.
Athletic Training Program Director
The Pennsylvania State University
University Park, Pennsylvania

George Moss, J.D.
Attorney at Law
Flushing, New York

National Dairy Council
111 North Canal Street
Chicago, Illinois

William "Pinky" Newell, M.S., R.P.T., A.T.C.
Chief Physical Therapist, Assistant Professor
Purdue University Student Hospital
Lafayette, Indiana

John P. O'Shea, Ed.D.
School of Physical Education
Oregon State University
Corvallis, Oregon

Theodore C. Quedenfeld, M.Ed., A.T.C.
Associate Director of the Temple
  University for Sports Medicine and Science
Temple University
Philadelphia, Pennsylvania

Charles J. Redmond, M.S., A.T.C.
Head Athletic Trainer
Springfield College
Springfield, Massachusetts

Bob Reese, A.T.C.
Head Athletic Trainer
New York Jets Football Club
New York, New York

Michael Rielly, M.S., A.T.C.
Head Athletic Trainer
University of Buffalo
Buffalo, New York

Ralph Requa, A.T.C.
Division of Sports Medicine
University of Washington
Seattle, Washington

Richard C. Schneider, M.D.
Section of Neurosurgery, Department of
  Surgery
University of Michigan Medical Center
Ann Arbor, Michigan

John Sciera, M.S., L.P.T., A.T.C.
Head Athletic Trainer
State University of New York at Cortland
Cortland, New York

Kent Scriber, M.S., R.P.T., A.T.C.
Head Athletic Trainer
Ithaca College
Ithaca, New York

Bob Spackman, M.S., R.P.T., A.T.C.
Head Athletic Trainer, Associate Professor
Southern Illinois University
Carbondale, Illinois

Williard "Bud" Tice, M.S., A.T.C.
Athletic Trainer
Buffalo Bills Football Club
Buffalo, New York

Joseph S. Torg, M.D.
Director, Temple University Center
  for Sports Medicine and Science
Temple University
Philadelphia, PA

CONTENTS

PREFACE

As the athlete extends human potential to its limit in sport, injuries commonly ensue. The discipline of sports medicine has evolved in recent years with the goal of assisting the athlete through a conscious effort to prevent and efficiently manage the sports injury. Practitioners of sports medicine include the physician, athletic trainer and the coach. Each has his/her special duties in providing for the physical well-being of the athlete but to a greater degree their roles overlap and should combine to form an effective team in the battle against injury.

Thanks to greater research and improved communication between practitioners, sports medicine has taken significant strides in recent years. The modern athlete has many advantages over his/her predecessor of an earlier era. Athletic trainers were almost unknown in the 1930's. Few were competent; most were relatively uneducated "massage men." In the 1940's the true fathers of modern athletic training first began working with physicians and exercise physiologists to train and rehabilitate our armed forces in World War II.

Much of the credit for our improved modern sports medicine practices (at least in non-physicians) must go to the National Athletic Trainers Association (NATA). Since 1950, this organization has been a leader in the concern for the health care of athletes. Largely through the efforts of the NATA, the professional status of athletic trainers has been greatly enhanced. In the early 1970's, NATA began a certification process for trainers, leading to the degree A.T.C., (athletic trainer, certified). Required educational guidelines have been developed by the association's professional educational committee. Three different approaches may be taken toward certification: (1) apprenticeship as a trainer (2) through a physical therapy curriculum or (3) through an athletic training curriculum. When all educational and practical requirements are met, an individual becomes eligible to take the NATA certification examination.

These certification procedures help to insure a modern athletic trainer capable of devising sophisticated training programs for improving performance, as well as providing safeguards against injury. He/she is familiar with the latest technology in protective equipment in each sport. And when the athlete is injured, rehabilitation is managed under the direction of the physician to quickly bring the athlete back to the field consistent with his/her personal health and safety.

Lest we paint too rosey a picture, we should point out that deficiencies, particularly at the secondary and junior high school level, still exist. While it is true that certified athletic trainers are usually found at the college or university level, in a state such as New York, there are nearly 1000 high schools with less than 10 schools actually served by certified athletic trainers. This situation, coupled with the shortage of high school team physicians leaves much of the responsibility for the prevention and management of athletic injuries solely in the hands of the coach. It is our belief, based on experience in clinics and in "courses for the coach" that coaches want to learn everything they can in dealing with sports injuries. Unfortunately, few authoritative, non technical sources, exclusively designed for the coach are presently available. With this in mind, we have attempted to assimilate a collection of readings in sports medicine which are of particular relevance to the coach in the field.

The book is also designed to meet certain demands of the student athletic trainer. Several of the authors, rich in experience, have attempted to relay to the reader the essence of what "athletic training is all about." The student will also find many of the latest and most effective methods in preventing and managing athletic injuries. In addition, the student is provided with many references in order that he/she can "go from here."

We believe that the book may be arbitrarily divided into 9 areas: (1) an introduction to basic anatomy with the most common injuries described (2) an overview of the role of the athletic trainer (3) an analysis of life-threatening situations in sport (4) a review of injuries to selected parts of the body (5) the rehabilitation and treatment of selected injuries (6) topics related to the role of the athletic trainer as a counselor of athletes such as nutrition, development of the components of physical fitness and ergogenic aids to human performance (7) an analysis of the need for athletic trainers in the public schools (8) legal implications in sport and (9) appendices to provide practical source material for the day to day prevention and care of athletic injuries.

In summary, it may be accurately stated that both the coach and trainer are called upon to make daily paramedical decisions in attempting to maximally preserve the health and well-being of his/her athlete. These involve decisions concerning the optimal training of the athlete, forming an optimal environment for sport performance, and of course the inevitable acute and chronic care of injuries. In the optimal situation these decisions are formed with maximal communication between the coach, trainer, physician and athlete. It is to facilitate this communication process that this book is devoted.

The editors would like to express their gratitude to each author without whose effort this volume could not have come to fruition. Thanks also go to the various journals in the field of sports medicine which do such an outstanding job in communicating the latest advances in the field. Special acknowledgement goes to *Athletic Training, Emergency Product News, Medicine and Science in Sports* and *The Physician and Sports Medicine* for their contributions to the present volume. Finally we would like to thank Cornell University, Cooper Products, Futura Publications, Ithaca College, the Ithaca Journal, Johnson and Johnson Company, the Journal of the American Medical Association, Kay Laboratories, Kramer Products, Lea and Febiger Company and the National Federation of State High School Associations for making available some of the illustrations used herein.

A Review of Musculo-Skeletal Anatomy with Special Reference to Common Athletic Injuries

Kent Scriber, M.S., R.P.T., A.T.C.
Edmund J. Burke, Ph.D.

Both the public school and college coach are frequently called upon to provide the initial care for an injured athlete. Similarly, and possibly more importantly, the coach should be able to provide the athlete with a training regimen which will minimize the potential for injury occurrence. In order for the coach to effectively perform these functions it is most important that there be a sound understanding of human anatomy.

A complete course in anatomy involves an acquaintance with literally thousands of anatomical structures. Such in-depth knowledge is a necessity for future physicians and paramedical personnel such as physical therapists; and certainly an advantage for the future coach or athletic trainer. However, the actual number of anatomical terms used in everyday trainer – coach – athlete – physician parlance is quite manageable. We are not so brave as to offer this brief paper as a substitute for a quality college course in anatomy but rather as a remedial measure for the coach or trainer who is not "going back" for an anatomy course and wants to master some of the basics needed to improve his/her ability in preventing and caring for athletic injuries.

Anatomy and Its Subdisciplines: A Systems Approach

The study of gross anatomy is primarily a memorization process. Most of the parts (structures) of the body have been named and we might add have been named for a long time. Actually, the ancient Egyptians, Greeks and Romans provided most of the names we will be studying in this paper. Anatomy then, is a study of the names of body structures. An important subdiscipline of anatomy is the study of how the body moves, *kinesiology*. *Physiology* is another subdiscipline of anatomy in which we study how the body functions. *Exercise physiology* is a further subdiscipline of anatomy in which body function is examined during and as a result of exercise.

Anatomy can be studied in two distinct ways. We can study body regions and analyze each of the structures in, for example, the shoulder region. This is called regional anatomy. Alternatively, it is possible to study the anatomy of the body, system by system. The system approach is the method used for the present paper. And since this book is primarily concerned with the prevention and management of athletic injuries we will concentrate on the two systems which are of the greatest significance to human movement: the skeletal and muscular systems. But before we do so perhaps we should briefly review the systems we are not going to concentrate upon.

In order to function, the muscle must be provided with fuels for energy and must be signalled when to contract. The *circulatory system* provides the first function. This closed loop set of canals filled will blood pumped by the powerful heart muscle provides the skeletal muscle with food and oxygen and a means of removing the muscle's waste products. The *nervous system* provides the muscles with the proper integration needed for the immensely complex movement patterns for sport. As a matter of fact, the central nervous system integrates and controls twelve billion neurons — a complex process which we probably won't fully understand for centuries to come.

We must also be cognizant of the interaction of other systems on human movement. The kidneys together with the rest of the *renal system* provide an important waste removal function as well as helping in the regulation of the acidity and alkalinity of the body fluids. The *digestive system* is in essence a long coiled tube which functions in breaking down complex foods into a form which can be used by the body. This system also provides another waste removal function. Some of the functions of the skin or *integumentary system* include protection of the body and the maintenance of a normal body temperature. The *respiratory system* consists of a series of progressively narrower canals which function in transporting O_2 rich air to and removing waste products from the blood. The *endocrine system* provides a series of chemicals which assist the nervous system in regulating the body. Hormones such as epinephrine and glucagon have a profound effect on the body's ability to get ready for exercise. Finally, the *reproductive system* functions in providing each generation with a succeeding generation. Let's now examine the two most crucial systems for those interested in the prevention and care of athletic injuries.

Skeletal System

When the skeletal system is referred to, one should be able to picture the basic bony structure of the human body. This can be done by reviewing figures 1 and 2. With this perspective for the structure of the skeletal system the coach is able to easily locate the major bones of the body.

Bone is made up of two layers, a hard ivorylike outer layer called compact bone and an internal layer called cancellous bone. Except for joint surfaces, the external surfaces of bone are covered by a dense connective tissue sheath called periosteum. Tendons, ligaments, and cartilage are firmly attached to the periosteum.

It is not difficult to see that each bone has a different size and structural configuration. Because of these varying characteristics they are able to serve different functions. Some bones act as long levers to generate a great amount of force (e.g., long bones of the arms and legs); some are grouped together and though they allow very little movement by themselves, as a group they allow for much overall motion (e.g., wrist bones or the vertebral column); some act as pulleys to provide for a better line of pull for the muscle (e.g., patella); and some serve mainly to support and protect important internal structures (e.g., the cranium or skull, the pelvis, or the ribs).

The coach with limited background in this area should spend time becoming familiar with the names of the major bones of the upper and lower extremities. Most athletic injuries occur to the extremities and this should be an important consideration when a limited amount of anatomy is studied. In the upper extremity the scapula, clavicle, humerus, ulna, radius, carpals, and phalanges are all bones that the coach should be familiar with because they are common injury sites. In the lower extremity the femur, patella, tibia, fibula, metatarsals, and phalanges are the bones most often injured.

The most significant injury to a bone is a fracture or a break in the continuity of that bone. This type of injury generally takes at least six to eight weeks to heal. A coach should be aware of the soft tissue damage that may occur along with a fracture such as damage to muscles, tendons, blood vessels, or nerves.

Closely related to the bones of the skeletal system are the various joints of the body which are frequently injured in athletics. A *joint* or *articulation* is a place of union between two or more bones of the skeleton. There are several different types of joints and they serve several functions depending on their structure. Some are much more mobile than others. For example, the glenohumeral joint of the shoulder is much more mobile than the hip

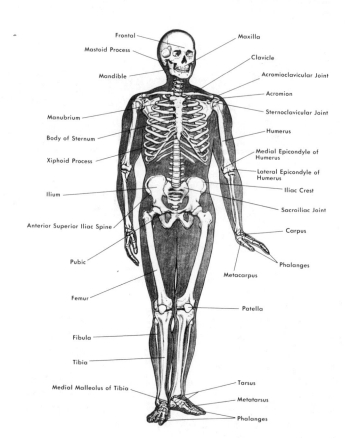

Figure 1. *The skeletal system—anterior view. Reprinted with permission of Cramer Products, Inc., Gardner, Kansas.*

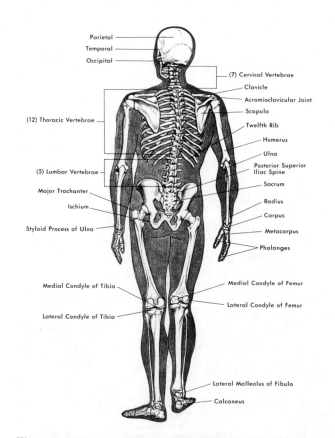

Figure 2. *The skeletal system—posterior view. Reprinted with permission of Cramer Products, Inc., Gardner, Kansas.*

joint. This is because the hip must provide a stable support for weight bearing whereas the shoulder must be mobile for the many activities carried out by the upper extremity. Many joints are known by their common names and most people are quite familiar with them. Some of the joints which are most commonly injured are the hip, knee, ankle, elbow, and wrist. Other joints are named for the anatomical structures that make up that particular joint. Examples here are the acromioclavicular and glenohumeral joints of the shoulder. The acromioclavicular joint is the articulation between the acromion process of the scapula ("shoulder blade") and the distal end of the clavicle ("collarbone"). The glenohumeral joint is formed by the meeting of the glenoid fossa of the scapula and the head of the humerus. The coach should be familiar with the location of all of these joints as well as the amount of movement or range of motion (ROM) that is normal at each of these joints. As the coach becomes more familiar with the movement of which each joint is capable he/she may have a more accurate picture of the extent of damage that has been caused by an injury.

A *ligament* is a fibrous band of tissue that usually connects the bones that form a joint. In some cases ligaments function to support the viscera (internal organs). There are several ligaments, referred to in subsequent articles, with which the coach should become familiar. In the ankle the two ligaments most often sprained are the anterior talofibular and calcanofibular ligaments which give support to the lateral (outside) portion of the ankle joint. The deltoid ligament is thick and strong giving the major support to the medial (inside) portion of the ankle joint. At the knee the collateral ligaments (medial and lateral) give support to the inside and outside aspects of the knee. The cruciate ligaments are located inside the knee joint and assist in giving the joint anterior and posterior stability. If any of these ligaments are torn the joint becomes unstable and the athlete should not participate. The cartilages or menisci of the knee lie on top of the tibial plateau and can often be injured. Though these cartilages are not ligaments they are worth mentioning at this point as they are significant when referring to injuries at the knee joint. In the shoulder joint (glenohumeral) the major ligament anteriorly is the glenohumeral ligament and this helps prevent dislocation or complete displacement of the humerus from its normal articulation. When referring to the acromioclavicular joint of the shoulder there are acromioclavicular ligaments and coracoclavicular ligaments that are of importance in regards to joint stability. If these ligaments are torn and there is a deformity of the distal clavicle it is often referred to as a "separation." The reader should review the diagrams of the ligamentous structure of the major joints that are included in other portions of this book. (See pp. 36/40/47).

A *sprain* of a ligament is the most frequently occurring injury involving joints. Everyone associated with sport knows of the numerous practices and games missed by athletes each season due to knee or ankle sprains. Sprains are categorized according to their severity. A mild or *first degree sprain* involves stretching of the ligaments beyond the normal range of movement allowed by the ligaments. A moderate or *second degree sprain* is a stretching and partial tearing of ligaments and a severe or *third degree sprain* refers to a complete tearing or rupture of the ligaments. The range of disability from each type of injury varies greatly depending on the severity of the injury, the joint involved, and the functions that the involved athlete is expected to perform. For example, a football lineman may not miss a play with a sprained thumb and forefinger, whereas a quarterback with the same injury on his throwing hand might be completely disabled. Similarly, a basketball player may miss three weeks with a moderate ankle sprain, whereas a hockey player with the same injury may only miss a few days. This is simply because the nature of the game is different and there is less stress on the joint.

The Muscular System and Human Movement

If someone with a limited anatomical background takes even a cursory view of Figures 3 and 4, he/she could be discouraged with the number of names of the muscles. As with most other anatomical structures some of these muscles are named for their size, some for their shape, some for their attachments, some for their position, and some are named for their function. When viewing these diagrams one should be aware of the fact that muscles are often layered and some of the superficial muscles are "cut" away to illustrate the deeper muscles.

The nature of human movement is such that muscular contraction has to take place. Most muscles are anchored at one end (origin) and are freely moveable at their other attachment (insertion). Strictly defined, a *muscle* is an organ that produces movement by contracting. A *tendon* is defined as the nonelastic tissue bundle that connects muscle to its bony attachment. As a muscle contracts it grows shorter and thicker and the bone at the insertion will usually move.

If the position of various muscles is viewed along with the attachments of these muscles, one can often figure out what movements will result when a particular muscle contracts. Look at the large pectoralis major muscle as an example. It has a broad origin on the sternum and clavicle and inserts on the humerus. When it contracts the arm has to move toward the center of the body (adduction). In contrast, the deltoid works as an antagonistic muscle by controlling the opposite movement which is abduction of the shoulder. Knowing the function of the muscle can be of great importance to anyone when evaluating an injury.

Some muscles are commonly injured in athletics. Although there are several types of injuries that may occur to muscles, the two most common injuries are strains ("pulls") and contusions (bruises). The names, actions and types of injuries in the commonly injured muscles are so important that

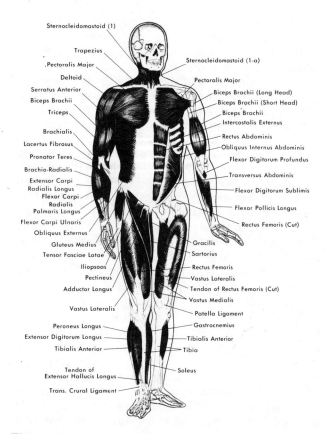

Sternocleidomastoid (1)
Trapezius
Pectoralis Major
Deltoid
Serratus Anterior
Biceps Brachii
Triceps
Brachialis
Lacertus Fibrosus
Pronator Teres
Brachio-Radialis
Extensor Carpi Radialis Longus
Flexor Carpi Radialis
Palmaris Longus
Flexor Carpi Ulnaris
Obliquus Externus
Gluteus Medius
Tensor Fasciae Latae
Iliopsoas
Pectineus
Adductor Longus
Vastus Lateralis
Peroneus Longus
Extensor Digitorum Longus
Tibialis Anterior
Tendon of Extensor Hallucis Longus
Trans. Crural Ligament

Sternocleidomastoid (1-a)
Pectoralis Major
Biceps Brachii (Long Head)
Biceps Brachii (Short Head)
Biceps Brachii
Intercostalis Externus
Rectus Abdominis
Obliquus Internus Abdominis
Flexor Digitorum Profundus
Transversus Abdominis
Flexor Digitorum Sublimis
Flexor Pollicis Longus
Rectus Femoris (Cut)
Gracilis
Sartorius
Rectus Femoris
Vastus Lateralis
Tendon of Rectus Femoris (Cut)
Vastus Medialis
Patella Ligament
Gastrocnemius
Tibialis Anterior
Tibia
Soleus

Figure 3. *The muscular system — anterior view. Reprinted with permission of Cramer Products, Inc., Gardner, Kansas.*

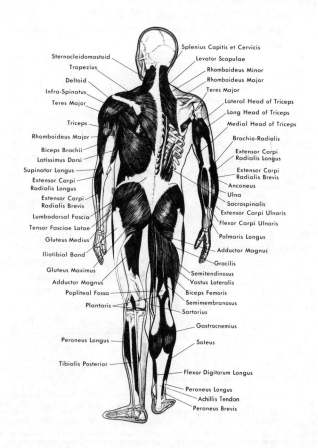

Sternocleidomastoid
Trapezius
Deltoid
Infra-Spinatus
Teres Major
Triceps
Rhomboideus Major
Biceps Brachii
Latissimus Dorsi
Supinator Longus
Extensor Carpi Radialis Longus
Extensor Carpi Radialis Brevis
Lumbodorsal Fascia
Tensor Fasciae Latae
Gluteus Medius
Iliotibial Band
Gluteus Maximus
Adductor Magnus
Popliteal Fossa
Plantaris
Peroneus Longus
Tibialis Posterior

Splenius Capitis et Cervicis
Levator Scapulae
Rhomboideus Minor
Rhomboideus Major
Teres Major
Lateral Head of Triceps
Long Head of Triceps
Medial Head of Triceps
Brachio-Radialis
Extensor Carpi Radialis Longus
Extensor Carpi Radialis Brevis
Anconeus
Ulna
Sacrospinalis
Extensor Carpi Ulnaris
Flexor Carpi Ulnaris
Palmaris Longus
Adductor Magnus
Gracilis
Semitendinosus
Vastus Lateralis
Biceps Femoris
Semimembranosus
Sartorius
Gastrocnemius
Soleus
Flexor Digitorum Longus
Peroneus Longus
Achillis Tendon
Peroneus Brevis

Figure 4. *The muscular system — posterior view. Reprinted with permission of Cramer Products, Inc., Gardner, Kansas.*

they should become secondhand information to anyone interested in the prevention and care of athletic injuries. A summary of some of these important muscles follows. For the purpose of sequence we will begin with the lower extremity.

In the lower-leg there are three muscle compartments. The posterior compartment is composed of the gastrocnemius, the soleus, and the plantaris which all insert into the calcaneus as the achilles tendon. The lateral compartment is made up of the peroneal muscles which evert or move the foot outward. The anterior compartment contains the tibialis anterior muscle along with other muscles that dorsiflex or lift the foot toward the body. Muscle strains or contusions may occur to all three compartments. *Tendonitis* or an inflammation of the achilles or peroneal tendons are not unusual problems. Any of these types of lower leg problems may be very disabling to an athlete involved in running or jumping activities.

The musculature of the upper leg is also significant with regard to athletic injury. *Muscle strains* occur frequently to the quadriceps (anterior thigh) muscles which extend the knee joint and the hamstrings (posterior thigh) muscles which flex the knee joint. The quadriceps muscle is also particularly prone to contusions in contact sports. Regardless of the type of leg injury, there may be enough disability to prevent an athlete from participating effectively.

Injuries around the hip often involve two groups of muscles that may be subjected to excessive strain. These are the hip flexors and the hip adductors. The hip flexors (rectus femoris and iliopsoas) lift the leg upward at the hip joint. The adductors (adductor magnus, adductor longus, and gracilis) function to move the leg toward the midline of the body. Strains to any of these muscles are often referred to as *"groin pulls."* A *"hip pointer"* is a contusion to the iliac crest which may be painful and incapacitate an athlete. Not only is the iliac crest contused but some of the sheet-like oblique muscles may be sheared off their attachments resulting in a functional loss.

Important muscles of the back include the erector spinae, the latissimus dorsi, and the trapezius. The erector spinae is a group of muscles that extend from the low back region to the base of the skull. These muscles function to extend, laterally flex and rotate the vertebral column. The lower portion is often strained when improper lifting, rowing, or blocking techniques take place. The latissimus dorsi ("rowing" muscle) adducts, extends and medially rotates the humerus. The trapezius functions to adduct the scapula and helps control the head. When either of these muscles are involved, impairment of movement and strength result in the upper extremity.

The pectoralis major muscle is important in shoulder girdle function because it adducts, flexes and medially rotates the arm. Other muscles of the shoulder that are especially prone to contusion and strain type injuries are the deltoid and a group of muscles known as the rotator cuff. The deltoid abducts the arm and the rotators (supraspinatus, infraspinatus, teres minor, and supscapularis) internally and externally rotate the arm. An athlete involved in a throwing sport such as baseball or involved in a racquet sport such as tennis is virtually paralyzed with an injury to these areas.

The muscles of the upper arm and forearm are also subjected to overuse and muscular strain type injuries in the throwing or racquet sports. The biceps which flex the elbow and the triceps which extend the elbow are often involved. So are the forearm flexors (little league elbow) and extensors ("Tennis elbow") which are groups of muscles extending from the medial and lateral aspects of the elbow to the hand and fingers.

As stated earlier the authors have not attempted to develop all aspects of human anatomy in this paper. Instead, they have attempted to point out several of the major aspects of this field of study to make it more understandable from a practical point of view for the coach. When an injury occurs it is important for the coach to be familiar with the structures that are involved and the loss of function resulting from these injuries. Only when the coach is familiar with what disability an athlete has as a result from injury can he begin to make intelligent and effective decisions as to whether the athlete must be sent to medical attention immediately or whether returned to competition. A coach who is responsible for injury care should find a knowledge of basic anatomy an important step in successful injury management.

Glossary
OF SELECTED TERMS

The reader is referred to this list of terms when confronted with unfamiliar terms in the articles to follow.

ABDUCTION. movement away from the midline of the body.

ABRASION. wearing or rubbing of the skin that results in an open wound.

ACUTE INJURY. an injury in its initial phase.

ADDUCTION. movement toward the midline of the body.

ANTERIOR. (VENTRAL) referring to the front surface or forward part.

APNEA. breath holding.

ARTHROCENTESIS. the puncture and subsequent aspiration of fluid in the joint.

ASPIRATION. a process in which gases or fluids are suctioned out of a cavity.

ATP. (adenosine tri phosphate) this is the "energy currency" of the body; by splitting ATP into ADP (adenosine di phosphate) and Pi (inorganic phosphate) great amounts of energy are made available for the work of the cell.

BRUISE. see contusion.

BURSA. connective tissue sacs with slippery surfaces for the reduction of friction in various tissues.

BURSITIS. inflammation of a bursa.

CARTILAGE. a tough, resilient connective tissue; there are three types: hyaline, fibrocartilage, and elastic.

CHRONIC INJURY. an injury that persists over a long period of time.

CIRCUMDUCTION. circular (actually in the shape of a cone) movements of limb.

CONCUSSION OF THE BRAIN. a violent blow to the head, sometimes accompanied by loss of consciousness, nausea, vertigo, weak pulse and slow respiration.

CONTUSION. a bruise or superficial injury produced by impact without lacerating the skin.

CRICOTHYROID CANNULA. a tube for insertion into the trachea in the area of the cricoid and thyroid cartilages (throat).

CYROTHERAPY. use of cold in the treatment of injuries.

CYANOTIC. a condition characterized by a bluish discoloration of skin and mucous membranes due to excessive concentration of reduced hemoglobin in the blood.

DEEP. situated far beneath the surface.

DEHYDRATION. a condition characterized by loss of fluids in the tissues.

DISLOCATION. a displacement of a bone from its normal articulation.

DISTAL. designates a part farther from a point of reference.

DIURETIC. an agent that increases the production and secretion of urine.

DORSIFLEX. bending of the foot such that the toes point upward.

DURA. (dura mater) the outermost, toughest, and most fibrous of the three membranes (meninges) covering the central nervous system (brain and spinal cord).

ECCHYMOSIS. a discoloration below the skin caused by escaped blood.

EDEMA. abnormally great quantities of fluid distributed in the intercellular spaces; usually accumulated in the tissues

(Continued on page 140)

The Physician and Trainer: A Team

Michael J. Cappeto, M.S., A.T.C.

The purpose of this paper is to discuss the relationship between the physician and the trainer. At Columbia University we are fortunate to have more than adequate coverage of athletics by physicians. We constantly work with two surgeons, an internist and an orthopedic specialist. Recently we were fortunate to acquire the services of a second orthopedist, an alumnus of Columbia University and a former athlete who has returned to New York City.

Different physicians are responsible for the care of different teams, but almost all of them wind up seeing an injured athlete at one stage or another during the full circle of recovery from an injury. Establishing relationships with each of them and attempting to coordinate their efforts is at times quite a job. However, they all give of themselves and are very generous with their time. Each has a great deal of empathy and respect for the athletes at Columbia and for athletics in general. This, along with their competence in the field of medicine, make them an enjoyable group with which to work.

The team physician and the trainer have the same goals. They are working to better the situation of the athlete. In most instances, the trainer works with the doctor and adds his insight into the problems at hand, helping the doctor to arrive at decisions with regard to the prevention and management of athletic injuries.

In order for the trainer and the doctor to work together, they must understand each other. The trainer must be aware of the fact that a team physician is often paid at a minimal rate, or volunteers his services. Figured on an hourly basis, most doctors could obtain much more money for an equal investment of time in almost any other aspect of medicine. Therefore, one must assume that the doctor is involved because of a genuine interest in the well-being of the athlete, and an enjoyment in being involved with athletics.

The trainer should also be aware of the physician's limitations. Since athletics are rarely the doctor's prime concern, he cannot be expected to be on call 24-hours-a-day, seven-days-a-week. Some of us are fortunate enough to work with physicians who are involved to this extent. Others have to realize that availability will have to be arranged according to the schedules of everyone involved. The trainer should be wary of the doctor who never needs to consult another physician. A team physician is called upon to make decisions touching on all areas of medicine, and no one can be an expert in every field. When special problems arise, an opportunity for outside consultations should be arranged by the team physician. This could mean that a trainer will need to deal with dermatologists, neurologists, orthopedists, internists and others from time to time. These individuals cannot be expected to be as generous with their time or in their scheduling as the team physician.

We recently had a problem with a wrestler who had torn the extensor tendon in a finger. Our orthopedist attended to the immediate problem. This type of injury is usually splinted for six weeks so that the tendon can reattach itself. In similar cases in the past we had no problems and complete function had been recovered. However, the athlete usually has to be held out of contact sports while healing. The wrestler, in this case, wanted to return to competition immediately. It was decided that a hand specialist should evaluate the situation and decide on the advisability of the boy's wrestling. If the tendon did not reattach, functional control of the finger could be lost and surgery might be necessary to correct the problem. This particular operation does not have a great history of success. In any case, the appointment was scheduled, but it was not going to be for at least two weeks. The specialist was busy and had only limited office hours.

The wrestler involved was quite upset and felt that each day missed could never be regained. He was not worried about his finger and felt that whatever damage was done could be fixed at the end of the season. We were not as anxious to expose him to further injury. When our team physician was advised of the date of the appointment, he contacted the hand specialist personally and set up a visit for the next day. The wrestler subsequently was not allowed to wrestle for two weeks and then was returned to full competition with proper splinting and padding.

One has to keep in mind that the specialist will not always be aware of the importance of the passage of time to the athlete. Usually, however, if a brief explanation of the situation is offered, needed care can be obtained within a reasonable period of time.

On the other side of the coin, a doctor should have an understanding of just who and what an athletic trainer is. He should be aware of the background and education of the trainer. The National

Athletic Trainers' Association has been working for over 25 years to improve and upgrade the capabilities and credentials of its member trainers. Many of the organization's members hold degrees in physical education, physical therapy, or health education. These disciplines are probably the most directly related to athletic training. Some trainers, of course, hold degrees in other disciplines. The N.A.T.A. has also helped in the organization of graduate and undergraduate curricula in athletic training at several colleges and universities across the country. After a close look at the background of the certified trainer, the doctor will realize that the trainer is a professional. With this understanding in mind, he, as well as the trainer, should strive for a close working relationship.

I think you should keep in mind that I am a trainer and that I make statements from my point of view. Each doctor-trainer relationship is different and may hinge on varied factors. Because of this, the trainer and team physician should work out a method of handling as many types of situations as possible, before problems actually arise. Perhaps a brief case history will help illustrate the need for an effective plan of action which will cover a wide spectrum of possible situations.

While we were out of the city at football camp this fall we were faced with a serious problem. During an inter-squad scrimmage one of our players struck his head on the ground in the course of making a tackle. We found out later that he was dazed on the play. However, he remained on the field for two additional plays. He finally came to the sideline complaining of dizziness. We suspected a concussion and treated him accordingly. He started to become incoherent and lost consciousness. Fortunately we had taken the precaution of setting up our school station wagon as an emergency vehicle.

We moved him from the field on a spine board into the wagon, and started for the hospital. One of my assistants called the hospital and alerted the emergency room. In this way, necessary care could be expedited. Our team physician was immediately contacted and notified of a possible emergency. He had earlier made sure that he had a list of specialists to contact within the vicinity of the football camp. He was thus able to contact a neurologist whom he might not otherwise have been able to obtain, and have him at the hospital when we arrived. During the ride to the hospital it became rather obvious that the concussion was severe. The athlete was stabilized at the emergency room of one hospital and then transferred to another hospital where more complete facilities were available. He was admitted to neurological intensive care and in the course of the next 36 hours regained most of his faculties. Today he is fine, in excellent health, and has no limitations in his normal life style.

Outlining courses of action for specific situations saves time and lives. In this instance, the team physician's knowledge of the facilities near camp and of specialists saved time and eliminated needless phone calls. Knowing what our team physician wanted us to do allowed us to respond quickly to this emergency. Procedures for this type of emergency or any other major accident should be set up. These plans of action should also be subject to review, and updated on a regular basis. Doing things the way they were done in the past or at another institution might not be the best way to handle problems as they occur.

There are other areas of the medical program that can also be planned in advance. The pre-participation physical examination is something the doctor and the trainer must discuss. Different items may have to be checked depending on the age group involved, the type of activity they are competing in, and the physical demands of the particular sport. For example, should physicals given to the golf team differ from those administered to football teams? Should physicals be given once a year? Should a fall physical carry over to the winter and spring seasons? Should men and women receive the same basic physical? What will be the basis for limiting activity or declaring someone ineligible at your institution? These questions must be answered in advance and not left for last-minute decisions.

Medical histories can be very helpful when the physical examination is conducted. These can help the doctor become aware of pre-existing problems. However, it must be kept in mind that athletes do not always recall their illnesses and injuries. They may not remember, or since in their minds they are fully recovered, may think an injury or illness is not worth mentioning. The athlete must be questioned carefully so that the medical team is confident that the information given is complete. This questioning should be done prior to and during the physical exam.

Any major problems that a prospective athlete has had should be gone over by both the doctor and the trainer. Initially this is done to make sure that he or she is fully recovered. Depending on the findings, necessary special padding or braces can be made, and exercise programs may be planned to prevent re-injury, and to strengthen the injured body part. This medical history process assures that there is no secondhand information. I realize that this type of physical is time-consuming, and doctors are often under pressure from several sources to give a quick cursory physical. If this is done, or if histories are taken and never read, the pre-season physical becomes a waste of time for all concerned.

I'll admit that I was sorely embarrassed to find out that we had a diabetic playing football one year. I realize it is possible to have a diabetic play. The embarrassing part was that we found out that he was a diabetic when he requested that the trainer on the field carry some chocolate bars in case he needed sugar in a hurry. The athlete had played football in the past and anticipated no problem. He did not think it was worth mentioning. We might have been confronted with a serious medical problem that could have been avoided. Fortunately, no problem ever arose.

On August 11, 1976, an article appeared in *Newsday,* a Long Island newspaper. The article was titled "Death Puts Physicals on Trial." It was concerned with the manner in which physicals were given to high school football players. It was written after the second death of a high school player in less than a month on Long Island. Though the boys had had physicals, they had been members of groups receiving a fast physical exam. Even though they may have received adequate exams, the hurried procedure is a source of concern to parents. In many cases athletes will joke and laugh about physicals, representing the athlete's attitude toward the fast shuffle some of them get. Their lack of seriousness can lead to problems. The physical is for the protection of the athlete and not simply to absolve the institution of responsibility.

Once he is past his physical exam, the athlete's medical care should continue. When he is injured, he is fortunate if a trainer is there to attend him. The trainer is usually the first person on the scene when an injury occurs in a game or practice, that is, if the injured athlete's institution had the forethought to employ a trainer in the first place. Most institutions cannot possibly have a doctor on the field or in the gymnasium for each athletic event, let alone for every practice. Even if the arrangements for handling injured athletes are made at the particular institution's health service, doctor's office or local hospital, someone will have to give immediate care. This could range from cleaning and washing a minor abrasion, or putting a compression bandage on a bruise, to maintaining an open airway or assuring that an athlete with a possible cervical spine fracture is immobilized until the proper method of transportation is available.

It is important that the doctor realize the potential of the trainer. There are some physicians who think the trainer should do only exactly what he is told to do, that the trainer should not be allowed to make decisions regarding practice status or exercise programs. There are other physicians who will simply diagnose an injury and then turn the entire matter over to the trainer. Both these extremes fall short of an ideal situation. The trainer is there to recognize injuries and to administer primary care. Then, if necessary, the trainer should refer the athlete to the doctor for whatever further care is required. The trainer can help minimize the athlete's injury through proper immediate care. He can also spot the incidental injuries that an athlete might not think worth mentioning. For example, the pain associated with a navicular fracture, a commonly fractured bone in the wrist, is not incapacitating by any means. Since the trainer is aware of the implications of pain in this area, he can refer the athlete to the doctor for further diagnosis and to check on this potentially severe injury.

If the proper primary care is administered the athlete is often able to return to full participation sooner. In most athletic activities, the types of injuries that can and will arise are predictable to some extent. Aware of the probable injuries, the doctor and the trainer can discuss what should be done so that at the moment of injury no time is wasted. This will give the trainer a good idea of how far the doctor wants him to go in administering primary care. At the same time, the doctor should be able to assess the trainer's capabilities, by going over what the trainer would like to do for specific injuries. A problem that can develop here is that many doctors are so busy that they cannot keep up with the changes made in the care of the suddenly injured athlete. The trainer should be well versed in this area, as it is central to his profession.

The doctor and the trainer must communicate effectively. If the doctor, or for that matter, the trainer, is not open-minded, they may come to disagreements. This type of situation can arise very easily when the trainer is working with a doctor who has had little experience with athletics. It can also be a problem for the trainer who has to deal with several different team physicians, or a health service staff. All of these set-ups have their advantages and disadvantages. The main problem is that it can be tough for a trainer to establish rapport with each individual.

The physician has the final say in any matter concerning the medical care of the athlete, and all concerned will certainly want to offer the best care possible. This gets into another sore spot. Just what is the best possible care? I have seen physicians attending to athletes immediately after the incidence of injury, diagnose a first to second degree sprained ankle, and then turn around and promptly tell the trainer to use hot soaks or a warm-to-hot whirlpool on it right away. Although this procedure often results in a soothing warm feeling for the athlete, it also may result in a swollen ankle the size of a grapefruit. This increased swelling can set the athlete back for weeks. The average trainer would probably have trouble following these directions. As most trainers, medical personnel, the majority of coaches, and even most grandmothers today know, ice, compression and elevation are the preferred treatments until the immediate swelling has subsided. This is usually for the first 24 to 48 hours. Then a different course of treatment can be discussed.

The types of exercise programs and the methods used in them can be another awkward point for the doctor and the trainer. Usually the trainer is more aggressive than the doctor in this area. More and more trainers are turning to active exercise as the quickest way to get athletes back into action after injuries. Range of motion work, partial weight bearing, isokinetic, isometric, isotonic and flexibility exercises are combined with various modes of treatment in a total exercise program. The doctor who sees the athlete once a week and tells him to immobilize an injured limb for a week or two at a time is not taking full advantage of the athlete's recuperative powers. This is an issue that the trainer must try to work out with the doctor. Although the athlete will recover in time just by going through his normal daily activities, he may recover faster and better on a specific exercise program.

Unless an injury is severe enough to sideline a player for the remainder of the season, there is concern as to when he may return to full activity, particularly from the point of view of the coach. Once again, it is important for the doctor and trainer to work together. The actual diagnosis of the injury is made by the doctor. When the extent of the injury is established, estimation as to the date of the player's return to competition becomes feasible. Typical time limits for the player's return to competition can be based on experience with similar injuries. Insight into individual athletes, how hard each will work, and how much tolerance for discomfort he possesses, will help in making an accurate estimate. Still, these are areas that always hold surprises. You never know how an athlete will handle an injury. Each case is different, and there may even be variations in recuperative powers of an individual athlete who is faced with different injuries.

The athlete needs to be physically able to participate fully before being allowed to return to play following an injury. Assessing full recovery is a problem with which some physicians and trainers become entrapped. When confronted by a seemingly recovered athlete trying to get permission to resume play, a doctor should always make himself aware of the total picture. What will this athlete be required to do? When this question is answered, the decision to let him compete can be made, and not before. This is a situation in which the doctor should rely heavily on the trainer. Through direct observation and from information supplied by coaches and teammates, the trainer can establish what the athlete's capabilities were prior to the injury. He can also determine what will be required of the athlete by analyzing his sport and position.

With this information a better decision can be made. To clear an individual for full activity on the basis of lack of pain, full range of motion or what seems to be adequate strength is not really enough. One should go a step further. Different functional tests, such as running figure eights, or obstacle or agility courses, should be formulated. Specific strength measures can be made through the use of weights or isokinetic machinery. Speeds for covering distances such as the 40- and 100-yard dashes can be checked against previous performances, or team averages. Cardiovascular endurance can also be evaluated in various ways. Other testing can be as simple as taking the athlete out and making him go through the drills that he would normally have to perform. If he meets the criteria set by the trainer and the doctor, he is allowed to participate. If not, areas of weakness can be pinpointed and exercise programs to

strengthen those areas established. These functional measures should be appropriate for the activity involved, and not arbitrary. They can be arranged for most common situations well in advance of when they will be needed. Coaches can also be involved in choosing content for these tests.

The trainer is also responsible for providing the doctor with progress reports on injured athletes. By discussing progress toward recovery prior to the examination by the physician, the doctor and the trainer can avoid the pitfall of being misled by the athlete anxious to return to competition. The doctor can develop awareness of the difference between the subjective opinion of the athlete and the objective evaluation of the trainer concerning the athlete's recovery from injury. At times, our team physician will see an athlete at the Health Service without a trainer present. This creates problems. We had a freshman basketball player who had undergone a knee operation due to an injury over the summer. He came under our care upon his arrival to Columbia in September. After he saw our doctor we started him on the customary exercise program for his injury. At the start of the basketball season the player had made progress but was still not ready to play. He had recovered some strength and mobility, but still had not fully recovered. At the Health Service, he told the orthopedic specialist that he was ready to play. The athlete said that he had regained his strength and could do all the running and agility work that we had wanted him to do. Since the doctor was familiar with what that consisted of, he gave the athlete permission to play. He assumed that the boy had been sent over to him by the trainers. We found this out at practice and checked with the doctor. We explained that although the boy did most of what was asked of him, he was still somewhat limited. He had yet to complete the final stages of the rehabilitation program. The doctor then decided that since the youngster seemed to be all right we might as well allow him to try playing. He was to be watched closely for any problems.

The first day was uneventful. The second day it became obvious that the boy could not keep up with the pace of his teammates. We pulled him out of practice and put him back on the exercise program. He could do some team work, but the amount and degree had to be controlled. At least at this point, he too realized that he was unable to fully participate.

There are some instances in which the athlete must be protected from himself. Due to an athlete's desire to compete he may weigh athletics too heavily. At times the immediate rewards associated with competition may seem more desirable and real than the possible negative consequences. Although the individual athlete has a certain right to decide what he or she may or may not do, there is a larger issue at stake. It is the responsibility of the trainer and the team physician to keep the athletes from making errors and risking damage to their health. Authority may have to be exerted to prevent an athlete from exposing himself to unnecessary danger. This is not always a pleasant task.

There is another person from whom an athlete may need to be protected, and that is his coach. We are lucky to have as many knowledgeable coaches as we do working in the field today. However, there is the possibility of the coach overemphasizing the importance of his sport. An athlete's physical and mental well-being should always be placed above all else. The doctor should remain independent of the coaching staff. He should not allow winning and losing to affect his medical decisions. He should work with and through the trainer to make sure that the athletes receive whatever care is required.

There should be no medical situation in which a coach can override a doctor's decision. It is important that the medical decisions are made and enforced by the doctor and trainer as a team. At times this can be difficult. Not every athlete can handle being sidelined or held out of practice, no matter how short the time span. At the same time, not every coach is willing to accept the decision of a doctor that removes his players from competition. The more the physician is involved with the total program, the more readily his decisions are accepted.

Our wrestling team had more than its share of injuries one year. In one instance a wrestler suffered an injury to his elbow. The joint had been hyper-extended and the wrestler cried out. The referee stopped the match and let the doctor examine the athlete. The doctor diagnosed the injury as a hyper-extended elbow with possible torn ligaments. He also said the wrestler could not continue with the match. The boy was upset and tried to demonstrate that he had no lasting impairment from the injury. With some supportive taping he might have been able to continue. However, the doctor forbade it. We treated the elbow with ice and a pressure bandage. The athlete was sore but had good strength and range of motion. He returned to wrestling the next day and had no further problems. In this case, and it's much easier to see with hindsight, the doctor could have let the boy continue.

The decision had been made well before the allowed injury time had expired. It might have been better to wait until more of the three minutes had passed. Then the athlete would have had a chance to get over the initial shock of the injury and a more objective evaluation might have been possible. It is awkward to support a point when it becomes fairly obvious that the grounds for support are not very solid. All of the circumstances involved should be weighed before a decision of this sort is made.

During another team meet, one of our other wrestlers was brought down very hard. He struck his head as he came down to the mat. The referee saw that he was dazed and although the maneuver had been legal, he stopped the match. After examination of the wrestler, the doctor thought the young man had suffered a minor concussion and would not allow him to risk further injury. At first I was surprised. I didn't think the boy was too seriously hurt and he wanted to continue. Our coach was mad, and compared the situation to "getting your bells rung" in football.

Our doctor explained that in any head injury there is a certain amount of hemorrhaging in the brain. In most sports a minor head injury is not too great a problem. However, in wrestling, a great deal of the muscular contractions that take place are isometric in nature. This means that there is no movement, but that the muscles exert tremendous force upon an immovable object, usually the opposing wrestler. The result of this exertion is a large increase in the wrestler's blood pressure. Knowing this, the doctor decided that it would be risky to let the wrestler continue. The build-up in blood pressure could have caused increased hemorrhaging and turned a minor injury into a major one. In this case it was easy to understand the doctor, and we realized his decision was based on sound medical judgment.

While it is important for the doctor to be thorough and correct in his decisions, he must also be able to deal with a certain amount of questioning and criticism. Some of the people the doctor has to work with might not understand his decisions, or may want him to change them. If the doctor has made a decision and then is easily swayed, the trainer who was enforcing his orders may look foolish. This is especially apparent during a contest. The sidelines of a football game, for instance, can become very busy. When athletes are hurt they are usually examined by the doctor and then treated for immediate injuries by the trainer. If the doctor removes the player from competition, he and the trainer must see to it that the athlete is not inadvertently put into the game. If the physician reevaluates a player's status, he should advise the trainer of this so that they both are working within the same guidelines. Otherwise the trainer may try to restrict someone from playing who has been cleared by the doctor. At the same time, a doctor should not give in to the pressures of an anxious coach, parent or player if the athlete's condition has not really improved. If youngsters think that the doctor is an easy mark for coaches or others, they will try to go over the trainer's head when they want to get things their own way.

It is important that medical personnel have a sound basis for what they do. Above all, the doctor should be available to discuss problems and the rationale for his recommended course of action. If the doctor spends only seconds on his examination, if he evaluates only the most obvious symptoms, if he exercises poor judgment, if he is conservative beyond necessity, if he fails to tailor decisions to specific situations and individual athletes, he can expect a lot of disagreement and friction from the trainer and other members of the athletic staff. A doctor who is aware of changes in his profession and the world of athletics, and who is willing to try new techniques, is likely to be a more competent team physician.

The trainer is normally involved with a certain amount of experimentation, if for no other reason than that few athletes are willing to wait for time to do all the healing necessary. In order to satisfy an injured athlete on a daily basis, the trainer has to do something for him; otherwise the athlete starts to think he is being neglected. Even if it's the same set of exercises that have worked in the past, numbers of repetitions differ, weights differ, speeds of recovery differ. Every athlete is an individual and should be treated as such.

Specific training techniques differ throughout the country. The underlying theory is usually consistent. It's the application that may vary. Different trainers can try the same techniques on their athletes. Each set will have its own responses to deal with. These must be interpreted, and the course for additional action must be plotted.

It is important that doctors involved with sports medicine work to practice good aggressive medicine. They should be unwilling to wait until the body has had unlimited time to recover its losses. They should want to help the bodies of our athletes to be as strong and as fit as they possibly can be in a minimum amount of time. This does not mean that the health and well-being of the athlete should in any way be endangered. A healthy 18-year-old is not to be treated in the same manner as someone in his 30's, 40's or 50's. The 18-year-old is often treated the same as older patients. If he is an athlete he is usually more resilient and durable than many of his non-athletic peers. A doctor should guide the trainer in doing all that can and must be done to get the athlete back to his former capabilities, and as soon as possible. The doctor, too, must keep up with what is happening around him.

Adjustments have to be made in established guidelines as new methods of treatment arise. New techniques have to be learned, and traditional ideas must occasionally be abandoned. In general, a doctor must not sit back and rest on what he learned in medical school. As soon as he does, the athletes he treats will wonder if they are getting the best care possible. Some of them will always question a decision or try to get things their own way. The more a doctor knows about what is going on in the profession, the less he will be questioned. He will have the confidence of the athletes he treats.

Everything I have discussed thus far has been involved with the medical well-being of the student athlete. It is fairly obvious that I think the doctor and trainer should work together. Each possesses certain strengths and weaknesses. The balance of the two should yield an effective medical team for combating the problems that confront athletes. There are many places, unfortunately, where this team is incomplete. Regardless of the level of competition, most teams will at some point have the services of a doctor. The amount of contact might not always be ideal. The same doctor might not always be involved. However, somewhere in the organization, a doctor is present.

The trainer is the part of the team that most schools find that they can live without. For whatever the reasons, from budget to lack of concern, schools do not seem to think that the trainer is vital to an athletic program. This is wrong. The institutions which don't provide a trainer to cover the athletic program are cheating their athletes. Those which call on an unqualified individual to perform the duties of a trainer may be creating problems so serious that they cannot be imagined. There are many important ways in which a doctor, trainer, and athletic department work together and interact. Most of the situations I have discussed are common to all levels of competition. Many institutions have excellent athletic programs and employ highly skilled coaches to work for and with their youngsters. An appalling few have certified trainers on their athletic staffs.

This is an area in which many administrators are deficient. They don't know what a trainer really is, what kind of background he or she has, or what the trainer's responsibilities are. Many have antiquated ideas of a trainer being the old time rubber, who massaged athletes; the taper who did not know much else; the laundry-equipment man who branched out a little. Today the certified trainer has a diversified background and is a professional. Often he is an educator qualified to instruct at a school or university in a subject area, and who can be employed as a teacher/trainer similar to the teacher/coaches at many institutions.

Whether one is involved in the athletic program as an administrator, doctor, trainer or coach, he should realize the importance of the doctor-trainer relationship. A good working relationship can make a good program better. A poor relationship can destroy confidence in an athletic program and endanger the health of the youngsters involved.

This paper has attempted to point out some situations concerning the physician and the trainer that are common to most athletic programs. Hopefully, it has helped to increase the reader's knowledge on some of the elements in that relationship.

The Female and Athletic Training: A Coach's Key

Susan K. Borowicz, M.S., A.T.C.

INTRODUCTION

With the recent upsurge in sports participation by the American woman, it is often difficult for the new coach to master the techniques of coaching as well as the prevention and care of injuries to her athletes. As the only female athletic trainer in a large university, I can greatly sympathize with the coach in these matters.

Athletic training is a growing field for both the male as well as the female, but for the female, its growth has been slower. At the present time, there are approximately 150 certified female athletic trainers in the United States, and most of them are located at the larger colleges and universities. Because high school female athletes are often forced to go without adequate coverage from a qualified athletic trainer, injuries and their prevention become the duty of the coach. However, when the coach has an athletic trainer available to her, the two should have a close working relationship so that similar goals can be attained.

Athletic training as a profession for a female is no different than that of a male. Our responsibilities concern the prevention and care of athletic injuries, and the return of the injured athlete to playing condition in the shortest amount of time. These responsibilities should also be part of the coach's responsibility to each athlete, especially if there is no trainer available. According to Neal (5), the coach's responsibilities in the high school should be:

1. To prevent injuries. This is the key!
2. To prevent further injury when an injury has occurred.
3. To be concerned with returning your athlete back into playing condition in the shortest amount of time. Dealing with the athlete not only involves the physical injury; it is just as important to relieve tensions and frustrations over injuries by reassuring your athlete, besides encouraging her by setting goals for rehabilitation.

INCIDENCE OF INJURY

Every person involved in coaching or training the female athlete, no matter what level, should have a basic understanding of the incidence of injury involving the female athlete. Klafs and Arn-

Figure 1. *Ice hockey. "The rise of women in contact sports such as ice hockey has given rise to incidence of injury." Courtesy of Cornell University.*

heim (3:166) have reported that "injuries involving conditions of overstrain (periosteal, bursae, or tendinous, in nature) are reported to occur almost four times as much among women athletes as among men." According to deVries (1), in studies involving comparable groups of men and women, "the overall incidence of athletic injuries in women is almost double that in men" and that the greatest percentage of all injuries is found in sports that require explosive efforts.

There have been two studies done recently involving incidence of injury and/or susceptibility of the female athlete to injury. Haycock and Gillette (2) studied the susceptibility of women athletes to injury by combining the results of three independent studies. From the first survey, the researchers found that the greatest number of injuries occurred in basketball, volleyball, field hockey, and gymnastics while the fewest injuries occurred in golf, swimming, squash, and archery. The data was compiled from respondents covering 19 major sports.

Types of injuries were compiled by Gillette from a second survey sent to 300 certified trainers in the United States who were asked about specific injuries recorded in each sport. Haycock also sent a third survey to the same 300 trainers to determine if the injuries from Gillette's survey occurred primarily because the athlete was female. Haycock asked for opinions concerning the participation

12

of the female in contact sports including football, soccer, and ice hockey.

Results from Gillette's survey on types of injury showed that the more serious injuries such as major fractures, head injuries, and dislocations occurred in basketball, field hockey, softball, and gymnastics. The most common types of injuries to female athletes are depicted by the following table.

TABLE 1
Most Common Injuries to Female Athletes*

Injury

	No. of Positive Responses	Total Responses, %
Sprained ankles	96	100
Knee	59	61
Contusions	53	55
Lower back	25	26
Muscle pulls and strains	23	24
Shin splints	20	21
Fractures	15	16
Hand and finger	13	14
Lacerations	10	10
Dislocations	10	10
Blisters	8	8
Soft tissue	7	7
Concussions	7	8
Wrist	6	6
Eye	3	3

*Table reprinted with permission from *JAMA*, July 12, 1976, Volume 236, pp. 163-165. "Copyright 1976, American Medical Association."

The researchers received 96 (32%) of the replies from the 300 surveys sent to trainers. The most common types of injuries were sprained ankles followed by knee injuries and contusions. Quite low on the list were concussions, wrist, and eye injuries. Breast injuries were not specifically listed under this table, however the authors considered breast contusions as a rare occurrence.

Concerning the involvement of the female athlete in contact sports among themselves, the authors found only 17 of 125 trainers opposed. At the present time, women's ice hockey has generated much interest at the university where I work, and would in all probability, rank equally high in incidence of injury to basketball with a greater severity of injury, however there is no objective data to support this premise at the present time.

The other study involving incidence of injury was reported by Whiteside (9). She conducted a study of injuries to female athletes using the National Athletic Injury Report System (NAIRS) involving reports from 29 states. The five sports used in the study were basketball, volleyball, field hockey, gymnastics, and softball. Basketball and field hockey were undoubtedly one and two respectively involving incidence of injury while softball was considered last. Gymnastics and volleyball were three and four respectively, then four and three when reported for

Figure 2. *Gymnast. "Note the flexibility, agility and balance of this athlete performing a gainer back handspring on the balance beam." Courtesy of Cornell University.*

a second time involving incidence.

Whiteside also reported several interesting facts. Under types of injury, burns, drugs, and illness had very few occurrences while sprains were considered a primary type of injury especially in basketball and field hockey. Strains and fractures had a higher incidence among men.

Among injuries occurring according to body part, there were four areas most frequently injured. In order, from greatest occurrence to least, the four areas reported were ankle-foot, hip-leg, knee, and finally forearm-hand.

Whiteside (9) also reported on incidence of injury relative to time of the game. For purposes of the study only, basketball and field hockey were divided into quarters rather than the official halves which are used in game play. It was reported that in basketball, the highest incidence of injury occurred in the fourth quarter of a game. In field hockey, injury was reported to occur most frequently in the first quarter which Whiteside conjectured to be caused by lack of adequate warm-up and cold weather. Also reported for field hockey was a higher rate of incidence during the second half of practice. Highest frequency of injuries was reported in gymnastics on the second event of the day (usually the uneven parallel bars), in softball after the first two innings, and in volleyball, during the middle game.

INJURY PREVENTION

For coaches, injury prevention is the key to a successful sport season. For the female athlete, who is not used to preventive taping and wrapping as well as sound conditioning and weight training, the coach and trainer must take the time to work out a program. Each athlete involved should be educated as to what is available to her from athletic trainers when injuries do occur.

First and foremost, each participating athlete should have a sport physical and an orthopedic joint screening *before* the season begins, to weed out the potential athletes subject to injuries. The coach should then work out a conditioning program along with her athletic trainer, if one is available.

Klafs and Arnheim (3:82) have reported that some of the causes of improper physical conditioning are muscular imbalance, improper timing because of poor neuromuscular coordination, lack of ligamentous or tendinous strength, lack of flexibility, and inadequate muscle bulk. Inadequate nutrition and psychological readiness can also be considered part of improper conditioning. According to Stoedefalke (8:334), women athletes need much more training and conditioning for participation in team sports than there is at the present time. He cites the following reasons:

1. To acquire fewer athletic or orthopedic injuries.
2. The athlete who is conditioned for the activity has a greater tolerance for fatigue.
3. A conditioned athlete recovers more rapidly from fatigue.

Ideally, a sound conditioning program would include off-season conditioning, pre-season conditioning, and in-season warm-up. An athlete should be able to start a sport in relatively good condition if a pre-season program was started 6 to 8 weeks prior to the season. A conditioned group of athletes will be able to do more work more efficiently and with better performance. The coach would then be better able to concentrate on strategy, skill, and refinement of skill. For the coach, it is highly important to keep injuries to a minimum by teaching and coaching proper technique *specific* to the sport being coached.

A few words also need to be said concerning weight training for women. Coaches of female athletes should be encouraged to start using weights as part of their athletes' conditioning repertoire, if they have not already done so. Weight training will *not* produce bulky, unsightly muscles in females! Women benefit not only from an identifiable loss of adipose tissue, but also an improvement in strength, from which follows speed and endurance. Weight training can develop muscles in need of growth, improve tonicity, and bring about aesthetic and coordinated movement.

Women should follow the same general weight training procedures as men, however it may be appropriate for progressive resistance increments to be in units of 2½ and 5 pounds rather than 5 and 10 pounds. If the individual is capable of lifting the heavier increments, she should be encouraged to do so.

PROCEDURE FOR HANDLING ATHLETIC INJURIES

A standard procedure for handling athletic injuries should be made a part of every coach's program before her season begins. If a trainer is available, the coach and trainer should work together to establish a set policy. Furthermore, the team physician and school administration should also carry joint responsibility along with the coach and trainer.

Klafs and Arnheim (3:34) have established a suggested procedure for on-the-spot injuries if no physician is present.

1. First, make a preliminary examination to assess the seriousness, type, and extent of the injury.
2. If the injury is beyond your scope, immediately send for a physician. *Always* know where to get hold of a doctor or the school nurse.
3. Administer first aid, if indicated. Keep ice on hand at all times during both practices and games.
   - I: Apply ice.
   - C: Compress with an elastic bandage.
   - E: Elevate the affected body part.
4. Determine whether the player is in a condition to be moved from the playing area. If the player is unconscious, do *not* move her. Wait for trained assistance.
5. Have an ambulance on call for all games involving contact.
6. Report any accidents and give all pertinent information on a standard report form including such details as date, time, place of the accident, sport being played, extent of injury, emergency procedures used, and names of two witnesses, if possible.

CONCLUSIONS

With the gradual fading of myths generated from the past about female injuries, has come the exciting reality that the female athlete is truly a competitor in today's sports world. It is encouraging to observe the upgraded performance each year of America's athletes, yet we still have many more goals to achieve.

There is a growing need for qualified professional female athletic trainers to serve in public school systems, local communities, and colleges. If our athletes are going to receive the best possible care, it should begin when they are young, as injuries oftentimes become chronic over the years.

For the coach that has no trainer available at the present time, there are several alternatives.

1. Take a Cramer workshop during the summer or attend a clinic on athletic training any time one is available in your area to familiarize yourself with training techniques.
2. Set up an area for first aid and taping if you do not already have one. This can be begun

very simply and inexpensively.

3. Encourage students interested in becoming athletic trainers. They could be your greatest asset! Finally, your enthusiasm as a coach for improving the health care of your athletes can generate much positive action toward achieving a truly successful program in your community.

REFERENCES

1. deVries, H. A. *Physiology of Exercise for Physical Education and Athletics.* Dubuque: Wm. C. Brown Company, 1966.
2. Haycock, C. E., and J. V. Gillette. "Susceptibility of Women Athletes to Injury: Myths vs. Reality," *Journal of the American Medical Association,* 236:163-165, July 12, 1976.
3. Klafs, C. E., and D. D. Arnheim. *Modern Principles of Athletic Training.* Saint Louis: C. V. Mosby Company, 1977.
4. Martin, J. "Women Trainers: A Growing Field," *The Physician and Sportsmedicine,* 4:93-97, August, 1976.
5. Neal, P. *Coaching Methods for Women.* Massachusetts: Addison Wesley Publishing Company, 1969.
6. Ryan, A. J., and others. "Are Athletic Trainers a Luxury or a Necessity?" (Part 1), *The Physician and Sportsmedicine,* 5:50-64, October, 1977.
7. _____. "Are Athletic Trainers a Luxury or a Necessity?" (Part 2), *The Physician and Sportsmedicine,* 5:76-87, November, 1977.
8. Stoedefalke, K. "Training and Conditioning Techniques for the Female Athlete," in *Women and Sport: A National Research Conference,* Dorothy V. Harris (ed.). Pennsylvania State University, August, 1972.
9. Whiteside, Patti. "Incidence of Injury in Female Athletes." Paper presented at the Eastern Athletic Trainers Association Convention, January 23, 1978.
10. Wilmore, J. H. "Inferiority of Female Athletes: Myth or Reality," *Journal of Sports Medicine,* 3:1-6, 1975.

When the Athlete's Life is Threatened*

Joseph S. Torg, M.D.
Theodore C. Quedenfeld, M.Ed., A.T.C.
William Newell, M.S., R.P.T., A.T.C.

Life-threatening situations in competitive and recreational athletics are by no means epidemic; however, they can occur. In 1970, 43 deaths resulted as either a direct or an indirect result of playing football. Reliable mortality data report the annual incidence to range from 25 to 35. Because of the large number of participants, the actual mortality rate for tackle football in this country is on the order of two deaths per 100,000 participants. Mortality rates for the numerous other athletic activities are not available. It appears that the team physician, trainer, and coach are dealing with the possibility of death, despite the fact that the probability is low. However, when a life-threatening condition does occur and if you are the responsible physician involved, it becomes a very significant episode in your life. Therefore, anyone involved in sports medicine and responsible for the care of athletes should be able to recognize and deal effectively with the various life-threatening conditions.

Basically, six situations can immediately threaten the life of an athlete: airway obstruction, respiratory failure, cardiac arrest, heat injury, craniocerebral injury, and cervical spine injury.

Airway Obstruction

Airway obstruction can occur in the unconscious athlete. The unconscious player may experience a transient apneic episode. When in the supine position, relaxation of the oropharyngeal musculature can allow the tongue to fall back and occlude the oropharyngeal airway. In this instance, immediate action must be taken to reestablish the airway. This may be effected by simply supporting the neck with one hand and tilting the head back with the other. Such a maneuver pulls the retropharyngeal musculature forward, thus opening the oropharyngeal airway. If this maneuver does not work, the next step is to grasp the mandible firmly and pull it forward, again with the head tilted backwards. When a cervical spine injury is suspected, care should be taken not to forcibly manipulate the cervical spine.

Conceivably, a foreign body could be aspirated, become lodged in the larynx or trachea, and obstruct the airway. Such a sequence occurring in the athlete is exceedingly rare. Obstruction can result from a direct blow to the larynx that fractures or deforms the structure in such a way as to impede the free flow of air. Again, this is quite unusual. In that airway obstruction secondary to foreign bodies or traumatic deformation of the air passages is so unusual, as a general rule, we feel that there is no place for performance of the emergency tracheostomy by the sports medicine practitioner. In the long run, more problems will be created than solved by this procedure. However, in experienced hands, the use of the cricothyroid cannula may be considered in a desperate situation.

Respiratory Failure

The most common type of acute respiratory failure is simple syncopal apnea. This usually occurs in the physician's office when the husky, body-conscious athlete is threatened by some diagnostic or therapeutic procedure such as an arthrocentesis. The athlete has a psychophysiological reaction and becomes hypotensive, pale, nauseated, and loses consciousness, with an associated period of apnea. Occasionally, the patient will also have a convulsion. To the inexperienced physician, such an episode can be quite frightening. If not prepared, he may not know whether to lift the jaw forward to establish an airway or to check on the status of his malpractice insurance. Such patients usually start breathing again on their own, however. If they don't, the physician should simply pull the jaw forward, making sure that the airway isn't obstructed, and, if necessary, initiate rescue breathing.

As already mentioned, players with craniocerebral injuries may have apneic episodes complicated by obstruction to the airway from transient paralysis of the oropharyngeal musculature. Of course, respiratory arrest can be caused by other factors.

Initial management of acute respiratory failure is the same as that for airway obstruction. An airway should be established immediately, and if spontaneous breathing fails to occur, mouth-to-mouth rescue breathing should be initiated. A plastic oropharyngeal airway should be available to maintain the airway once it has been established in an unconscious patient. Another emergency instrument is the oral screw that may be necessary to establish an airway in a hypoxic patient who is either convulsing or has developed trismus. An Ambu bag should also be available, in case respiration must be supported for a prolonged period.

A basic rule for dealing with the unconscious

*An article published in *The Physician and Sportsmedicine*, March, 1975. Reprinted with permission of the publisher.

football player is that the helmet should not be removed. Head injuries are often associated with injuries to the cervical spine, and this possibility must be considered until the patient regains consciousness or until an x-ray proves otherwise. Forced manipulation of the cervical spine to remove the helmet may cause irreversible damage to the spinal cord. Thus, if the unconscious football player has respiratory problems, his face mask should be removed with a No. 1 bolt cutter and the helmet left in place.

Cardiac Arrest

Cardiac arrest can result from cardiovascular collapse, ventricular fibrillation, or ventricular standstill. If cardiac arrest occurs on the playing field, a precise diagnosis is immaterial. Regardless of the cause, if the heart has stopped, as determined by the absence of the carotid pulse, cardiopulmonary resuscitation should be initiated immediately. The important principles of cardiopulmonary resuscitation,[1] although beyond the scope of this paper, are a must for every physician, trainer, and coach. The appropriate standards for cardiopulmonary resuscitation are available from the American Heart Association, 44 East 23rd Street, New York 10010.

Heat Injuries

Of the three types of heat injury — heat cramps, heat exhaustion, and heat stroke — only the last two are life-threatening. Signs of heat injury include muscle cramps, excessive fatigue or weakness or both, loss of coordination, a slowing of reaction time, headache, decreased comprehension, nausea and vomiting, and dizziness. Heat cramps occur when an individual sweats excessively and doesn't have adequate salt replacement. He may drink water, but he doesn't take salt with it. A relative sodium chloride deficiency develops with subsequent spasm and cramps of voluntary muscles, usually in the calf. Emergency management of heat cramps involves stretching the involved muscles and then giving salt, fluids, and rest. Salt can be given as tablets or in commercially available electrolyte preparations.

Heat fatigue or exhaustion occurs when an individual is exposed to a high environmental temperature and sweats excessively without salt or fluid replacement. This is followed by collapse and circulatory insufficiency. The patient will usually respond to fluids, salt, rest, and cooling, but death may result if the condition isn't recognized and treated immediately. The patient should be laid in a cool, shaded spot, undressed, and given fluids and salt. If he doesn't respond promptly, he should be moved to a hospital *immediately*.

Heat stroke occurs when an unacclimatized individual is suddenly exposed to a high environmental temperature. The thermal regulatory mechanism fails, sweating stops, and body temperature rises. Above 107 F, brain damage occurs and death follows if heroic measures are not instituted. This is a serious medical emergency. The diagnostic key in this situation is the high body temperature in the absence of sweating. The athlete with these signs should be packed in ice and hospitalized immediately. Note that heat cramps and heat exhaustion are not necessarily a prelude to heat stroke, but they can be.

To prevent heat injuries, the athlete fresh from vacation in a cool climate should be allowed 14 to 21 days of acclimatization before exposure to a competitive situation where he must perform regardless of temperature. Initial practices should be arranged for the cooler hours of the day — early morning or late afternoon or early evening — rather than at high noon. Practice clothing should permit moisture to evaporate. Above all, players should be given adequate salt and fluid replacement. Weight charts are a good way to monitor the daily weight loss. Since one quart of water weighs 2 lb, the exact fluid loss can be determined. It is not unusual for an athlete to lose 8 lb, or one gallon of fluid, in several hours. Fluid losses must be replaced!

To prevent heat injury, several basic rules should be followed. First, unlimited fluids should be provided before, during, and after practices and games. Conditioning by dehydration is not only an antiquated practice, but is almost criminal. Second, on hot days when they sweat excessively, players should be given four to eight 10-grain salt tablets daily and allowed liberal use of table salt as well. Salt supplements shouldn't be overdone, however, recent studies at the Naval Laboratories in Bethesda[2] indicate that too much salt replacement in the form of salt tablets can be dangerous in itself. With an intake of more than 15 g daily, there is a danger of rhabdomyolysis.

Intracranial Injury

Intracranial injuries in athletics include concussion, skull fracture, subdural and epidural hematoma, and intracerebral hemorrhage.

Cerebral concussion is classified by Schneider[3] as first, second, and third degree. First-degree concussion is characterized by a transient aberration in the electrophysiology of the brain substance as a result of impact. The athlete does not lose consciousness, but he may have slight mental confusion and possibly memory loss, tinnitus, and dizziness, but no unsteadiness or lack of coordination. The recovery rate is generally rapid. The point to remember is that even though an individual is not knocked unconscious, he may suffer a concussion.

In second-degree, or moderate, concussion, there is transient loss of consciousness (up to three or four minutes), momentary mental confusion, definite mild retrograde amnesia, and moderate tinnitus, dizziness, and unsteadiness. These individuals generally recover in five minutes.

In third-degree, or severe, concussion, there is prolonged loss of consciousness (over five minutes) with mental confusion, prolonged retrograde amnesia, severe tinnitus and dizziness, and marked unsteadiness. The general recovery rate is slow — well over five minutes.

When can an athlete who has had a concussion return to play? This depends on the sport. The high school football player who has any degree of concussion should not be allowed to go on playing, but the situation is different in college or professional football. If an experienced team physician can evaluate the player and keep an eye on him, a player with a mild concussion can return. In the case of a moderate concussion, we believe that if there is any loss of consciousness, a player — whether high school or college — should not return that game. Professional football is a different matter, however, and no one can make a generalized rule. A player at any level of play who has had a third-degree concussion should be moved to a hospital where he can be adequately evaluated.

A skull fracture can be linear or depressed. It is often difficult to determine clinically whether a skull fracture is depressed or whether there is only a subgaleal hematoma, just as it can be difficult to determine whether there is a linear fracture. When ever a player receives a severe blow to the unprotected head, a skull fracture should be suspected and roentgenograms taken.

Signs and symptoms that demand emergency action in any athlete who has sustained a blow to the head are increasing headache, nausea and vomiting, inequality of the pupils, disorientation, progressive impairment of consciousness, a gradual rise in the blood pressure, and finally a diminution of pulse rate. Any of these signs means the individual has a problem and should be moved to a hospital.

An epidural hematoma may occur in an athlete who receives a severe blow to the head; for example, a batter who has been struck by a pitched ball. If there is a fracture across the groove through which the middle meningeal artery runs, that artery may be severed with subsequent formation of a "high pressure" hematoma. The player may do well for a short period of time — he may get to first base, for example — and perhaps 10 to 20 minutes later first demonstrates the danger signs. Such a player will need surgical intervention to decompress the hematoma, and he should be hospitalized immediately.

Subdural hematoma occurs when the brain is thrust against the point of impact by the force of a blow and the subdural cerebral vessels opposite the point of impact are torn loose. Low-pressure venous bleeding occurs, and clot formation is slow, so that the signs and symptoms may not be evident for hours, days, or even weeks after the injury. Schneider[3] points out that about 65% of the patients he has studied do show some signs of the problem within three to six hours. Thus, the physician should be suspicious of a blow to the head and watch the patient carefully. Again, neurosurgical intervention is required to evacuate the hematoma and decompress the brain.

Cervical Spine Injuries

Injury to the cervical spine — fracture, dislocation, or fracture-dislocation — is potentially the most disastrous traumatic insult that can occur to the athlete. It may be fatal or there may be irreversible spinal cord injury that results in para- or quadriplegia. When such an injury occurs or is suspected, it is imperative that the responsible individual on the scene make certain that the victim is protected from further injury to the neural elements. Specifically, a lesion without neurologic involvement must not be converted to one with irreversible cord or peripheral nerve damage by ill-advised examination or manipulation in transportation.

Significant injury to the bony, articular, and ligamentous supporting structures of the cervical spine should be suspected in any unconscious athlete, because head and neck injuries go hand in glove. Neck trauma precautions should also be taken with those who have severe, unremitting neck pain, with or without paralysis, after trauma. All athletes suspected of a cervical spine lesion who cannot actively perform a full range of cervical spine motion without pain or spasm should be withdrawn from competition. Appropriate roentgenograms — anteroposterior, lateral, and both oblique views of C1 through C7, as well as an open-mouth view to demonstrate the first cervical vertebra — are mandatory. If the results of roentgenographic study and neurologic examination are normal, the athlete should not be permitted to return to activity until full range of motion of the cervical spine without pain or spasm returns.

The basic principle in moving an unconscious player or one suspected of having a significant cervical spine injury is that he or she be "rolled like a log" (figures 1 through 8). One person must

Figure 1. *Initial evaluation of the unconscious player should first determine whether he is breathing and has a pulse. Next, consideration should be given to the possibility of an associated neck injury. Head and neck injuries often occur together. Care must be taken not to complicate a cervical spine fracture or dislocation.*

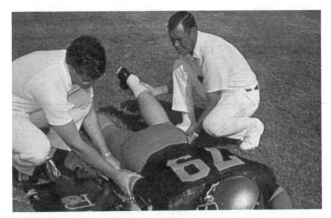

Figure 2. *The basic principle to remember in moving an individual with a suspected cervical spine injury is to "roll him like a log." First the extremities should be carefully placed in axial alignment with the torso. Preferably, the injured athlete should be moved on a fracture board when the possibility of cervical spine injury exists.*

Figure 3. *Proper technique in rolling the injured athlete requires a team of five. The "captain" of the team is responsible for protecting the head and neck during the transfer to the stretcher. Care must be taken to prevent the neck from being flexed, extended, laterally bent, or rotated.*

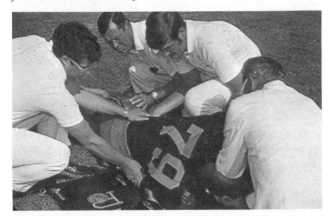

Figure 4. *On the command of the team leader, the patient is carefully rolled onto the fracture board, again with the head and neck being protected at all times.*

assume command of the situation and instruct four assistants in the transfer to a fracture board so that a loglike alignment of the head and neck with the axial skeleton is maintained. The football helmet should never be removed, and a pillow should never

Figure 5. *After the patient has been rolled onto the fracture board, the head and neck must still be protected.*

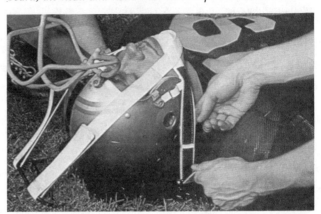

Figure 6. *DO NOT REMOVE THE HELMET in those who are unconscious or suspected of having an injury to the cervical spine. Should it be necessary to get to the face, the face mask should be removed from the helmet. The Purdue University fracture board is outfitted with an outrigger and buckles for a four-tailed chin strap. Other methods of spine immobilization may be used when such an apparatus is not available. The head and neck may be supported with sandbags, wet towels, adhesive tape, or simply by having someone hold it.*

Figure 7. *After having been secured on the fracture board, the injured player is transferred to a stretcher.*

be used. Once on the fracture board, the head and neck must be maintained in position by sandbags, tape, wet towels, or outrigger traction. Absolute immobilization must be maintained until appropriate roentgenograms are taken. Although the canvas stretcher is commonplace and suitable for evacu-

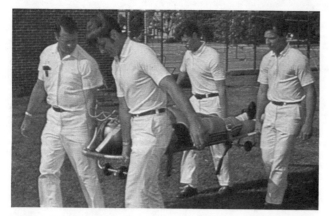

Figure 8. *Evacuation then proceeds with the head and spine adequately immobilized, thus avoiding the possibility of compounding an existing injury. Constant attention must be given to the maintenance of a patent airway.*

ation of the vast majority of injured patients, a fracture board is preferable when spine injuries are suspected. A simple device that can be constructed in any institution woodshop has been designed by the staff at Purdue University (figure 9).

References

1. American Heart Association Committee on CPR and ECC: Standards for cardiopulmonary resuscitation and emergency cardiac care. JAMA 227-837-868, 1974.
2. Brodine C: The Adverse Effects of Salt Loading: A Potential Problem of Salt Supplementation. Ramsay B. Thomas Symposium, May 4, 1974.
3. Schneider R: Head and Neck Injuries in Football. Baltimore, The Williams & Wilkins Co., 1973, p. 165.

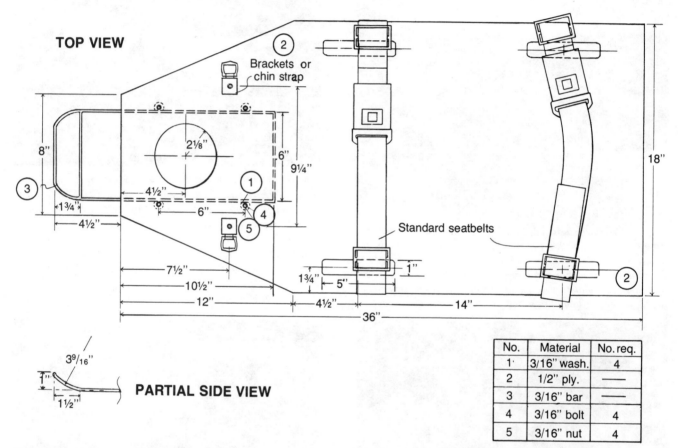

No.	Material	No. req.
1	3/16" wash.	4
2	1/2" ply.	—
3	3/16" bar	—
4	3/16" bolt	4
5	3/16" nut	4

Figure 9. *The Purdue University spine board can be constructed in any school wood shop. The board is cut from a piece of 18"×36" piece of 1/2" outdoor plywood. The outrigger is made from a 3/16" metal bar with a cross brace welded on. This is anchored to the board with four 3/16" bolts, washers, and nuts. Body straps are standard seat belts. The four-tailed chin strap is fashioned from helmet suspension webbing with Velcro fasteners added.*

Decisions Concerning Cerebral Concussions in Football Players*

Richard C. Schneider, M.D.
Frederick C. Kriss, M.D.

ABSTRACT. Three grades of cerebral concussion have been presented with suggestions as to management of players with such problems. It should be emphasized that the greatest concern is whether there is an expanding lesion within the cranium. Since the *initial* symptoms and signs of cerebral concussion are reversible and are identical with those of an expanding hemorrhage a few simple neurologic tests have been presented which may stress, at a field level, the urgency of the situation. There cannot be any simple compartmentalization for all head injuries. Since a physician cannot always be present at the athletic contests continued efforts must be made to keep coaches and trainers better informed about such problems. These are the people who frequently may have to make very vital decisions.

For many years the term cerebral concussion, which has been used in the diagnosis of the patient with a head injury, has implied to most neurosurgeons the occurrence of a state of unconsciousness which might have varied in its duration from a few transient seconds to prolonged periods of minutes. Usually the length of this interval, including recovery, was regarded as an index of the severity of the head injury. However, the use of such terminology appears unrealistic because the patient with a head injury may suffer from other symptoms of equal significance without having lost consciousness. In fact, the diagnosis of concussion has been so confusing that the British neurosurgeons recently have recommended abandoning its use. However, it will be difficult to expurgate a term which is so firmly entrenched in the medical literature.

In 1964 the Congress of Neurological Surgeons designated a Committee to study Head Injury Nomenclature and to clarify and classify types of head trauma endeavoring to standardize terms wherever possible. The definition which this group decided upon was:

"Concussion, brain: a clinical syndrome characterized by immediate and transient impairment of neural function, such as alteration of consciousness, disturbance of vision, equilibrium, etc., due to mechanical forces" (3).

While this nomenclature committee was discussing this problem, the Subcommittee on the Classification of Sports Injuries of the Committee on the Medical Aspects of Sports of the American Medical Association was in session attempting to clarify the terminology used in athletics. In order to promote the standardization of definitions the Nomenclature Committee of the Congress of Neurological Surgeons was requested to permit the use of their definition of "cerebral concussion." This request was kindly granted.

Thus, the patient with uncomplicated cerebral concussion has a **transient** or **reversible** physiological condition which is caused by a temporary interruption of the neural transmission of electrical impulses within the brain.

However, it seemed expedient to establish within this definition of concussion three subdivisions based upon the duration and severity of the symptoms in order to enhance its practical applicability to injuries of football players. These definitions have been published by the AMA in the Standard Nomenclature of Athletic Injuries (10). The revised current terminology is shown in Table 1 (4). *The classification is arbitrary, however, and must be subject to the changes dictated by experience.*

The football player who has sustained a mild or 1st degree cerebral concussion usually may be returned to the game after a play or two, but should be carefully watched for symptoms of fatigue, signs of disorientation, or for any peculiar behavior. Such vague symptoms may first be observed by an alert teammate. Thus it may be wise to take one of the stable players, such as the quarterback, aside and advise him to watch his friend for any unusual signs of physical behavior.

The second degree or moderate concussion victim should be removed from the game for at least 2 quarters and kept under observation. In this instance, there might have been a period of 3 to 4 minutes of unconsciousness. In both 2nd and 3rd degrees of concussion retrograde amnesia means a loss of memory for events immediately preceding the injury. If the player recovers *completely* after a sufficient period of rest, as noted above, he may be returned to action for the rest of the game. A repeated check for abnormal signs is essential.

The player with a third degree or severe concussion should be sent directly to the hospital for observation for the possibility of expanding intracranial bleeding. Originally, convulsions were listed as a possible symptom of severe concussion in the Stan-

Presented at the Ninth National Conference on the Medical Aspects of Sports of the American Medical Association, November 26, 1967, Houston, Texas. This work was supported by a grant from Alvin M. Bentley to the Richard C. Schneider Neurosurgical Research Fund.
* From *Medicine and Science In Sports* 1:112-115, 1969. Reprinted with permission of the publisher.

TABLE 1. SYMPTOMS OF CEREBRAL CONCUSSION

	1st Degree Mild	2nd Degree Moderate	3rd Degree Severe
CONSCIOUSNESS	No loss	Transitory loss (up to 3-4 minutes)	Prolonged loss (over 5 minutes)
MENTAL CONFUSION	Slight	Momentary	Present for 5 or more minutes
MEMORY LOSS	None or very transient	Definite mild retrograde amnesia	Prolonged retrograde amnesia
TINNITUS	Mild	Moderate	Severe
DIZZINESS	Mild	Moderate	Severe
UNSTEADINESS	Usually none	Moderate (up to 5-10 minutes)	Marked (over 10 minutes)

dard Nomenclature of Athletic Injuries (10), but subsequently have been deleted.

Quigley (7) has stated that three concussions sustained in football during one season automatically should remove the player permanently from the sport. The author agrees, but often circumstances are such that it will be wise to exclude the player permanently from any further play after only **one severe** concussion.

An incident is recalled which occurred some years ago. The football player, a nephew of a famous All-American, was trying to emulate his uncle. However, he obviously lacked the athletic ability to attain similar fame. He found that he received a great deal of attention, sympathy and understanding from his teammates, the coaches, and news media whenever he sustained a head injury. Consequently, when the scrimmages became a bit too rough, he would develop a headache and would roll around on the ground, holding his head. Sometimes he had to be restrained because he was throwing himself about too vigorously. After removal from the scrimmage his headache would last six or seven days and then he would return to practice. After this had occurred on four or five occasions he was sent to a neurosurgeon for evaluation. The player seemed to fit into the hysterical or psychological problem group. This reaction appeared to occur subconsciously, indirectly expressing the fact that the severe contact was repugnant to this player, or indicating that it was displayed to acquire attention or personal status. The player's father was consulted and the situation was explained to both father and son. The neurosurgeon suggested that the boy give up football, which he did. The player's headaches subsided and he eventually became a fine competitor in another sport. Needless to say, there is scarcely a physician, coach, or trainer who hasn't seen an occasional case of this type in which a player supposedly had a "concussion," and rolled, moaned, or thrashed about incoherently. It has been the author's experience that a patient with an acute head injury does not carry on in this manner unless he is hysterical, or unless there is some degree of cerebral hypoxia, i.e. deprivation of oxygen to the brain, usually due

to an obstructed airway. Most players with head injuries don't shake a severely aching head but tend to lie rather still and perhaps hold their head.

The failure of a physician or a member of a coaching staff to recognize this pattern may not only have a devastating and permanent effect on the player, but also have a demoralizing influence on the remainder of the squad. However, the most obvious difficulty in diagnosis is the problem of differentiating cerebral concussion, which is *transient* and *reversible,* from a more severe injury, such as cerebral contusion or an expanding hemorrhage; the initial symptoms for these conditions may be identical. For this reason brief mention must be made of the nature of expanding lesions and their symptoms and signs.

Cerebral contusion is a pathologic condition, that is, a "black and blue mark" on the brain itself. This may cause some definite brain damage from which the patient apparently may recover or have some residual neurologic disability. The semisolid cerebral hemispheres are supported on the brain stem in the cerebrospinal fluid within the intracranial cavity. If the player strikes the back of his head in a fall the brain rebounds forward, impinging the tips of the frontal and temporal lobes against the bony protuberances of the frontotemporal junction. In the contusion against the sharp sphenoid ridge of the skull a laceration of the brain may occur (4). Perhaps an extradural hemorrhage, a blood clot between the dura and the skull or a subdural hemorrhage between the dura and arachnoid may develop. Either one of these conditions may be successfully treated by the neurosurgeon. If perchance there is bleeding within the brain itself, an intracerebral hemorrhage, the chances of recovery even after surgical intervention is markedly diminished.

Ideally, injured players should be observed, on the bench and in the locker room, by a team physician. If one is unavailable, a well-informed coach or trainer is indispensable. There are a few relatively simple examinations which may be of benefit in evaluating the severity of the head injury. The symptoms of cerebral concussion, that is, what the patient feels, have already been presented. It may be recalled by definition these are reversible. *If there is a progression of the symptoms it suggests an expanding intracranial lesion which demands hospitalization and an emergency neurosurgical consultation is deemed essential.*

The signs of expanding intracranial lesion are listed in Table 2. These are simple fundamental tests for which the player should be examined.

TABLE 2. EXPANDING LESION

STATE OF CONSCIOUSNESS	Degree of impairment
PUPILS	Inequality
HEART	Unusual slowing
EYE MOVEMENTS	Nystagmus ("dancing eyes")
OUTSTRETCHED ARMS	Drift unilaterally
FINGER TO NOSE TEST (with eyes closed)	Asymmetry
HEEL TO KNEE TEST (with eyes closed)	Asymmetry
ROMBERG TEST (standing with eyes closed)	Falling
TANDEM WALK (heel to toe walking on a straight line)	Inability to perform

The state of consciousness should be determined. If the player had been alert for a time but finally became progressively drowsy, this period of temporary lucidity . . . the so-called "lucid interval" . . . suggests the presence of an expanding intracranial hemorrhage. Eliciting pain by pressure on the supraorbital nerve (on the bony ridge above the eye just an inch lateral to the nose), pressure on the Achilles tendon, or testicular pressure will rouse the semicomatose. In the 1967 football season the authors for the first time saw a trainer on the field shade a football player's eyes with his hands checking the equality of the pupils. If there is an inequality this is frequently an ominous sign, one of impending disaster. Observing the eye movement to see whether they are coordinated or track properly and testing for nystagmus can be simply performed. The development of a very slow heart rate after a lucid interval serves as a simple sign of imminent danger. Checking the outstretched arms with the fingers spread and the eyes closed may be very important. If there is a tendency for one of the arms to drift downward and outward there is evidence of a brain contusion or blood clot formation on the side of the head opposite to the weak arm. A simple checking of coordination by the finger to nose test or the heel to knee test may be readily performed. A tendency of the player to sway or fall toward one side when he puts his feet together and closes his eyes (a positive Romberg test) suggests the possibility of an expanding clot.

This cursory examination can be roughly done near the bench. Again if there is any progression of these signs the presence of a hemorrhage within the head should be suspected (4). Thus repetitive checks are very important, and changes in the neurologic status call for emergency action.

This paper is not an attempt to make a neurologist of the physician, coach or trainer, but to re-emphasize a few fundamental tests which will indicate the urgency of the situation. There were 69 subdural hematomas in our five-year study of serious and fatal neurosurgical football injuries reported in 1965 with a total of 28 deaths (8). Since 24 of these players died within six hours after injury, many of them within sixty minutes, time becomes a very important factor. To combat this mortality rate it is necessary for all of the medical team and the coaching staff to "beat the clock." The three cardinal points to be stressed for successful emergency treatment are: 1. **Communication:** A "non-pay" telephone with a direct outside line must be available at all times close to the sports arena for quick calls for help (for a physician, an ambulance, or both). 2. **Transportation:** An ambulance, station wagon or some other vehicle must be available at the site of competition to move the patient to the hospital. 3. **Notification:** The hospital to which the patient is being directed must be informed of the patient's status so that a neurosurgeon, other medical and nursing personnel and the proper facilities will be available on his arrival. This 3-point plan must be put into action immediately at a playing field where a serious head injury may be anticipated. It requires an informed and educated team response by all of the individuals concerned.

Considering the athlete with **chronic** headache and dizziness (9) after recurrent concussions: is there any test which will decide whether he should or should not continue to play football? The electroencephalogram or brain wave examination is often cited as a possible method of evaluating such problems (1). A normal electroencephalogram does not exclude brain damage (2). Another difficulty lies in the fact that between 12 and 15 percent of all supposedly normal individuals have an abnormal brain wave pattern. Thus, unless a player has had a previous test, the electroencephalogram is of little value to judge a single episode of concussion. However, repeated serial EEGs may disclose a progressive abnormality suggesting the presence of an expanding blood clot or a subclinical convulsive seizure (5,6). When this occurs we are no longer dealing with an uncomplicated cerebral concussion.

REFERENCES:

1. Dow, R. S., G. Ulett and J. Raff. Electroencephalographic studies immediately following head injury. *Amer. J. Psychiat.* 101:174, 1944.
2. Frantzen, E., B. Harvald and H. Haugsted. Fresh head injuries: clinical and electroencephalographic studies on 399 patients. *Acta Psychiat. Neurol. Scand.* 33:417, 1958.
3. Glossary of Head Injury including some definitions of injury of the cervical spine. *Clin. Neurosurg.* 12:388, 1966. The Williams & Wilkins Co., Baltimore, Md.
4. Kahn, E. A., E. C. Crosby, R. C. Schneider and J. A. Taren. *Correlative Neurosurgery.* C. C. Thomas, Ft. Lauderdale, Fla., p. 693, 1969.
5. O'Leary, J. L. Electroencephalography in head trauma. *Clin. Neurosurg.* 12:171, 1966. The Williams & Wilkins Co., Baltimore, Md.
6. Pampus, F. Früh und Spätmanifestationen Bedeckte Schädel-Hirnverletzungen in Electroencephalogram. *Chirurg.* 29:484, 1958.
7. Quigley, Thomas B. Personal communication.
8. Schneider, R. C. Serious and fatal neurosurgical football injuries. *Clin. Neurosurg.* 12:226, 1965.
9. Schneider, R. C., H. D. Calhoun and E. C. Crosby. Vertigo and rotational movements in cortical and subcortical lesions. *J. Neurol Sci.* 6:493, 1968.
10. Standard Nomenclature of Athletic Injuries, AMA, Chicago, Ill., p. 157, 1966.

Heat Illnesses: Prevention, Symptoms and First Aid Care

Donald D. Lowe, M.A., A.T.C.
Garret P. Caffrey, Ph.D.

Life-threatening situations are rare in athletics and when they do occur, they are frequently the result of a head or neck injury. However, occasionally there are deaths resulting from heat stroke. Approximately four such football deaths occur each year in the United States. This is very disturbing because each of these deaths resulting from heat stroke could have been prevented.

When a death occurs due to heat stroke, the causes are either extreme exertion or exercise in an environment with high temperature and associated high humidity. Heat-related deaths are preventable if people are made aware of the causes, the appropriate preventive measures, the symptoms of heat illness, and the first aid care to be used in the event an emergency does arise.

Most discussions about heat illness related to athletics center around football players. This is partly due to the wide media exposure of football. However, it must be noted that participants in other sports are also potential victims of heat stroke. For example, the cross-country runner on a calm day where the temperature and humidity are high, a wrestler cutting weight in a very hot workout room, and the lightweight crew man on a hot, humid day are potential heat illness victims. In sports such as soccer and lacrosse, the potential is not as great, but it still exists.

Swimming and ice hockey are sports where heat stroke seldom occurs. However, athletes in these sports can suffer from heat illness. The swimmer working very hard loses unnoticed body fluids in the pool and can become rapidly dehydrated. A very active ice hockey player with the traditional bulky uniform may also suffer heat stress.

The American College of Sports Medicine recently has published very strong statements concerning the danger of heat stress in long-distance runners. This group has established recommended guidelines for race sponsors. Participants in these long-distance races as well as the sponsors should be aware of these guidelines.

First, when a race is scheduled during a period when there is a chance for extremely hot weather, the race should be scheduled so the runners perform either early in the day or late in the day.

Second, it is recommended that athletes prehydrate themselves prior to the race. It is also advisable to have water available for consumption by the entrants along the route, especially at points after the 2½-mile mark.

Third, some form of external cooling along the route is advised. Either have a water sprinkler set up where the contestants run through the stream of water or have someone squirt the contestants with a hose.

Finally, coaches should educate runners to make them aware of the symptoms of heat stress so that they can remove themselves from the contest if necessary and secure first aid assistance.

The symptoms are: pilo erection on the chest and arms ("goose pimples"), a chilling sensation, headaches, weakness and stomachache. When these symptoms occur, the runner should stop and seek first aid care. It also seems advisable for sponsors to post people along the race route to closely observe the participants and remove them if they exhibit heat stress symptoms.[1]

In the sport of wrestling, we find athletes who use various methods to "cut" weight. Many such methods should be discontinued for the well-being of the athletes. Such practices as the use of rubber suits, diuretics, steam rooms, and hot whirlpool baths should be eliminated. An athlete who is losing weight by restricting body fluids and "sweating it out" in a rubber suit is over stressing his body and could suffer heat exhaustion or heat stroke or even kidney failure. Weight loss should be a slow, gradual process, not a rapid, dangerous procedure.

In football, during early fall, it is quite common to have strenuous exercise bouts in an environment with high temperature and high humidity. Each player is usually wearing a heavy, bulky uniform which compounds the problem. There are, however, certain preventive measures which coaches and/or trainers can take to greatly reduce the risk of heat illness.

Initially, let us examine the three types of heat illness:
1. **heat cramps.**
2. **heat exhaustion.**
3. **heat stroke.**

Heat cramps, although painful, are not serious. Heat exhaustion is frightening but usually not serious. Heat stroke is a very serious MEDICAL EMERGENCY and if not detected and properly cared for, death is imminent. Let us examine the causes, symptoms and treatment for heat cramps, heat exhaustion and heat stroke.

1. **Heat Cramps**

   Causes: Sweating, dehydration, salt and potassium deficiency.

   Symptoms: Painful contraction of voluntary muscles (usually calves and abdomen).

   Treatment: Direct pressure to the area; increase electrolyte and/or water intake. Rest.

2. **Heat Exhaustion**

   Causes: Salt, electrolyte and/or water intake depletion and overexertion.

   Symptoms:
   a. the skin is *always* moist.
   b. the victim is tired and glassy-eyed.
   c. the skin is either hot or cold. Body temperature undergoes little or no change.
   d. pulse is rapid, but strong.
   e. cramping, nausea, vomiting and weakness are possible.
   f. person could be hysterical or unconscious.

   Treatment:
   a. move the victim to cool spot.
   b. remove clothing.
   c. lower body temperature (ice towels, cool water, fans, air-conditioned room, etc.).
   d. hydrate with water, salt solution, electrolyte drink, ice, soda, etc.
   e. if rapid improvement is not seen, summon medical attention.

3. **Heat Stroke**

   Causes: Cessation of sweating, shock and cell death due to overexertion, water and electrolyte depletion.

   Symptoms:
   a. skin is DRY (there is no sweating).
   b. skin is hot and red.
   c. pulse is rapid and very weak.
   d. temperature is high (105°F or more).
   e. respiration is usually shallow.
   f. unconsciousness may occur.

   Treatment: MEDICAL EMERGENCY
   a. cool the victim as rapidly and efficiently as possible. (Figure 1)
   b. telephone emergency squad.
   c. notify a hospital.
   d. hydrate if victim is conscious.
   The victim needs care at a hospital as soon as possible. Lowering the body temperature while waiting for transportation and during transport can save the individual's life.

Prevention is the key in our discussion of heat-related problems in athletics. To prevent heat illness,

Figure 1. *The removal of uniform and external cooling using iced towels as the care for heat exhaustion and or heat stroke.*

consider the following areas:
1. Acclimatization of the athlete.
2. Proper conditioning of team members.
3. The wearing of appropriate clothing.
4. Maintenance of fluid and electrolyte balance.
5. Diet and health factors.[2]

Acclimatization — This is the most effective method of prevention. The athlete must be acclimated to the climate (heat conditions) and to the exercise involved. Heat problems occur when it is hot and humid. Athletes, therefore, should work out and allow the body to become accustomed (acclimated) to strenuous work in the hot environment. The body must adapt to sweat properly and retain fluids and electrolytes. Therefore, advise athletes to perform off-season exercises in the heat to acclimate their bodies for the work they will do in practice when they return to school for two-a-day football sessions in the early fall. Problems develop when one lives in an air-conditioned world (home, office, automobile) and conducts his workout routine in the cool of the evening or early morning and never acclimates to exercise in the heat. On return to school and football practice he is thrust into strenuous exercises in climatic conditions he is unaccustomed to. Hence, a crisis can develop.

Conditioning — It is wise to become as physically fit as possible in the off-season. Start at a low level of exercise and gradually increase the level of work and the length of performance. As fitness increases, continue to overload the body by increasing the intensity and the length of time of the workout. Total conditioning is a must. Concentrate on strength, cardiovascular endurance, flexibility, muscular endurance, speed, quickness, agility and coordination. Athletes in "top" condition are not as susceptible to heat illness as players who are less fit. Therefore, hard work in the off-season will help protect the athlete from heat stroke.

Proper Clothing — In football, the clothing worn in a hot climate can play a tremendous role in preventing heat illness. For example, the use of a mesh jersey allows for cooling of the body by radiation, convection and evaporation. (Figure 2) Everything must be done to ensure that the body

Figure 2. *A mesh jersey and half T-shirt exposes the athletes midsection to the air for cooling by radiation, convection and evaporation.*

is able to cool itself most efficiently by normal processes. The use of long sleeves and long stockings should be avoided in early fall. Long stockings covering the calf as well as bulky forearm pads should be discouraged since they cover parts of the body which should be exposed to the air to allow heat to leave the body. Lightweight clothing is preferred over heavier materials. Light colored clothing will reflect heat while darker jerseys retain heat and should be avoided during practice sessions.

The practice of using a short ½ T-shirt is advisable for it leaves the abdomen and lower back open for dissipation of heat from the body. (Figure 7) By using the ½ T-shirt and a mesh jersey, the surface area for dissipation of heat is twice that normally available. If mesh jerseys are not available, instruct each player to tie the jersey up onto the shoulder pad in the front and back to allow for exposure of the mid-section. (Figure 3) It is also advisable to have clean dry clothing available for the second practice session during two-a-days in football.

Fluid and Electrolyte Replacement — The single most important factor in prevention of heat stress

Figure 3. *Tying the jersey up onto the shoulder pad exposes the midsection to the air for cooling as does the mesh jersey.*

in athletes is fluid replacement. (Figure 4) The great myth in athletics is to restrict water. The old philosophy that "no water" will make you tough is absolutely contra-indicated. We have all heard the

Figure 4. *Fluid intake is vital for the prevention of heat stress.*

statement by a coach, "I didn't get water breaks when I played and it didn't kill me." In looking at this statement we can drift back a few years and recall practice sessions. First, there were fewer coaches involved with teams, hence, less active participation by the players. This is not to say that practices weren't tough. There was simply more time to recuperate. Organization was not as elaborate then as it is today. Currently, the good teams are busy and hustling every minute on the field. Today, practices are planned where all units are participating continually. This would then indicate today's athletes are under more stress than those of yesterday.

Finally, we live in a world of growing research and recent studies of environmental heat stress have yielded a large source of information and knowledge, useful in athletics. We cannot ignore the knowledge available regarding heat illness prevention. If we hydrate players, performance will increase with a reduction in the possibility of heat stroke. Smart coaches utilize this knowledge to get the "winning edge."

Prehydration is useful for preventing heat illness and should be practiced by trainers and coaches. Prior to the event, athletes should be encouraged to drink several 10-oz. glasses of fluid.

Breaks are a necessity to keep players "sharp" and to prevent an emergency situation from developing. Here are some suggestions that may be employed:

1. Schedule breaks according to the temperature and humidity and not on a regular routine. More breaks are needed as the temperature and humidity rises.
2. Provide plenty of fluids, either electrolyte drinks or plain water. The use of 10–12-oz. cups is a good practice. (Figure 5)

Figure 5. *Fluid replacement with 10-ounce cups of water or electrolyte drink. Also external cooling with towels soaked in tubs of ice water.*

3. Provide for some form of external cooling via cold ice towels or the spraying of players with a stream of water from a hose. (Figure 6)
4. Allow players five minutes or so on one knee with their helmets off to relax and cool off. A shade tree is excellent. If no shade is available, build a lean-to against the fence around your practice area.

Note: *To prevent the spread of communicable diseases do not allow more than one player to drink from the same cup.*

Diet — For many years it was the custom for athletes to consume numerous salt tablets before, during and after each practice. Today, this is not the accepted method of preventing heat stroke. The indiscriminate use of salt tablets is not recommended. One current philosophy is to request that

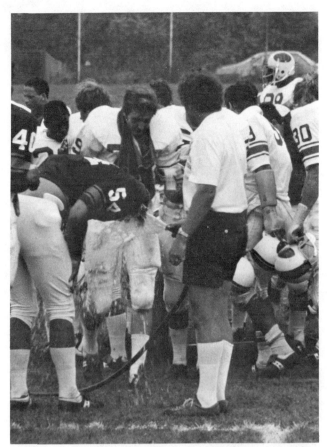

Figure 6. *A form of external cooling whereby players are sprayed with a stream of water, usually about the head and neck, to cool them.*

players do the following:

1. Drink plenty of fluids.
2. Put a little extra salt on their food at meals.
3. Eat foods or drink liquids high in potassium. Such things as oranges, ketchup, broccoli, orange juice and legumes are high in potassium which serves as an important electrolyte for muscular contraction and the prevention of heat illness.

The use of salt tablets compounds the dehydration problem since the body is forced to send fluids from the body's cells to where the salt is; thereby further removing fluids from the cells. If salt tablets are used, ½ pint of water should be consumed with each tablet taken.

The goal is to provide and encourage adequate intake of fluids. Try to educate and encourage young athletes to utilize natural foods high in potassium to combat fatigue and heat illness.

(Note: *Commercial electrolyte drinks are expensive and coaches and trainers can make their own by using water, flavoring, salt and a potassium supplement with ice added.*)

Health Factors — Be advised that a label of "high risk" must be tagged to an athlete who recently has suffered diarrhea or vomiting or one who, for some reason, has elected to lose weight. An illness resulting in diarrhea and vomiting greatly alters one's electrolyte balance and most surely dehydrates an individual. These "recently ill" people

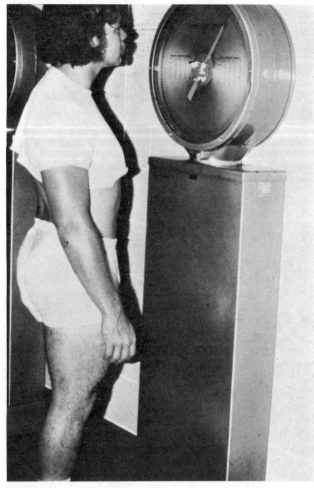

Figure 7. *The practice of weighing in and out for each practice will enable coaches or trainers to check the weight chart and learn which players are loosing too great a percentage of body weight (fluids). Also it is easy to determine those players who are not rehydrating themselves from one practice session to the next. NOTE: The ½ T-Shirt.*

either should not practice or they should practice under very close supervision and be encouraged to take copious amounts of water.

The overweight athlete should be placed on a sound diet and under a physician's supervision to lose weight. No athlete should be allowed to drop weight by dehydration. The use of a rubber suit should never be allowed. An important factor to remember is that people who have suffered heat exhaustion or heat stroke tend to be repeaters. The "100 percenter," the one who goes all-out and never loafs or paces himself must be considered a candidate for heat stroke.

Another practice used to prevent heat stroke is to require athletes to weigh in and out at practice. A scale and weight chart is needed. The scales and weight chart must be located in an easily accessible area. Weight should be determined with the athlete in shorts and T-shirt. Extreme weight loss reflecting dehydration should be reported to the head trainer, team physician or head coach. Any athlete with a marked weight loss should be evaluated and possibly kept from the next practice unless hydration following practice is such that the athlete replaces

water to bring his weight back to normal after 3-4 hours.

Weight charts are useless unless the athlete is weighed and recordings made regularly. The coach or trainer must look at these recordings to determine if some players have, indeed, lost such a percentage of body weight that precautions must be taken. Losses of over 3% of body weight during practice indicates dehydration. A return weigh-in before the next practice should find a near normal body weight. If a return to normal is not the case, the athlete should not practice or be closely supervised.[2]

Special attention must be paid to female athletes. Because of body composition, females begin to sweat at a higher body temperature than their male counterparts. This presents a special problem since perspiration is one mechanism which the body uses to cool itself. Women, with perspiration beginning at a higher body temperature are therefore inherently developing a higher core temperature and thus are potential candidates for problems when exercising in hot, humid environments. Add to this that the sweat rate is lower in the female and a situation develops where extra care and added precautions are necessary.[3]

To determine temperature and relative humidity, consider the following:

1. A telephone call to your nearest U.S. Weather Bureau.
2. A telephone call to your local airport for current readings.
3. The use of a sling psychrometer to obtain a dry bulb and wet bulb reading to determine relative humidity. (Figure 8)

Method three (use of the sling psychrometer) is the most effective, providing you with information relative to your actual location. The recordings should be collected from your practice or game area during the actual practice time. The wet and dry bulb readings then enable you to alter practice, add more breaks, or take other appropriate action.

Note: A day when it is calm (no breeze) is much more dangerous than a day when there is a good breeze blowing. The breeze helps cool the players through convection by removing the warm air around a player and replacing it with cooler air.

Once the temperature and humidity is known, keep in mind the following guidelines:

Precautions — Wet Bulb Thermometer —

60°F — No precautions necessary.
61-66°F — Alert observation of all squad members particularly those overweight or suffering from exercise weight loss.
67-72°F — Insist that water be given on the field frequently.
73-77°F — Alter practice schedule to provide a lighter routine in addition to precautions above.
78°F and above — POSTPONE PRACTICE or conduct in shorts.

Figure 8. *A Taylor 1328 Sling Psychrometer to detect wet bulb and dry bulb readings. Readings should be taken at practice time and on or near the practice area.*

If relative humidity is 95% or higher, extreme caution should be observed.

Note: Practice or games on artificial surfaces pose added problems. Temperatures on artificial turf are 6-10° higher than those in surrounding areas.

Precautions — Temperature and Humidity —

1. When the temperature is 80-90 degrees and the humidity is under 70%, observe carefully the athletes susceptible to heat problems.
2. When the temperature is 80-90 degrees and the humidity is over 70%, or the temperature is 90-100 degrees and humidity is under 70%, players should be given a ten-minute rest period every hour, T-shirts changed when soaked and observe all players very carefully for heat stress symptoms.
3. When the temperature is 90-100 degrees with the humidity over 70% or anytime the temperature is over 100 degrees, practice should be postponed or a shortened program conducted in shorts and T-shirts.[4]

SUMMARY OF HEAT ILLNESSES

TYPE	SYMPTOMS	FIRST AID CARE
1. Heat Cramps	Painful contraction of voluntary muscles.	Direct pressure, increase fluid and electrolyte intake. Rest.
2. Heat Exhaustion	The skin is wet. Victim is nauseated, glassy-eyed and tired. Pulse is rapid, but strong. Athlete may be unconscious or exhibit cramping.	Move to cool spot, remove clothing, cool victim, give fluids if conscious. If rapid improvement is not seen, seek medical assistance.
3. Heat Stroke MEDICAL EMERGENCY	The skin is dry. Victim is not sweating. Skin is hot and red. Pulse is rapid and weak. Body temperature is high (105° +), respiration is shallow and victim is often unconscious.	Maintain breathing. Cool victim. Seek medical assistance. Transport to hospital quickly. Hydrate if victim is conscious.

REFERENCES

1. The American College of Sports Medicine, Guidelines, "Heat Peril in Distance Runs Spurs ACSM Guidelines Alert," *The Physician and Sports Medicine,* July, 1975.
2. Murphy, Robert J., M.D., Team Physician — The Ohio State University, "Heat Illness," Presentation — Thirteenth National Conference on the Medical Aspects of Sports of the American Medical Association, New Orleans, La., Nov. 28, 1971.
3. Klafs, Carl and M. Joan Lyon, *The Female Athlete.* St. Louis, C.V. Mosby Co., 1973, P. 44.
4. Klafs, Carl E. and Daniel D. Arnheim, *Modern Principles of Athletic Training.* St. Louis, C.V. Mosby Co., 1969, P. 394.

Evaluation of the Injured Athlete

Kent Scriber, M.S., R.P.T., A.T.C.

During the past several years it has become apparent that, for the most part, athletes at the secondary school level need better health care than they are presently receiving. The National Athletic Trainers Association has a lofty goal of someday having a certified athletic trainer in every high school participating in interscholastic athletics. Realistically, this goal can not be met for some time and until each school does have a certified athletic trainer to help give our young athletes better care, the coach will usually have to bear much of the burden for the immediate care of athletic injuries. The initial evaluation and recognition of injury can be of great importance in assisting a physician to determine a diagnosis and the correct follow-up care for a particular injury. The intent of this paper is to give the coach who must also be his team's "athletic trainer" information that will better prepare him or her to deal with the initial management of athletic injuries.

After an injury occurs the coach should have some sort of organized routine for examining the injured body part. Though each injury is unique, it is usually easier to do an evaluation by following a basic and organized sequence. The coach should not be too aggressive in his handling of an injury or he may risk aggravating the existing problem.

There are five major questions that a coach should consider with regard to any athletic injury. First, *"What is the anatomy of the area that is injured and must be evaluated?"* It is quite obvious that if the coach doesn't have a good understanding of the underlying anatomical structures it will be difficult to examine any injury. Second, *"How did the injury happen or what was the mechanism of that injury?"* Knowing the mechanism of injury can give helpful clues to determine what structures may be injured or what limitations this could put on the athlete. Third, *"What do I suspect is wrong?"* Is this a minor injury that I can deal with or is it a more severe injury that should receive immediate medical attention? This is closely related to the first two questions and it is again obvious that a sound background anatomically is important for an evaluation to be useful for the coach. The fourth question the coach must ask is, *"Can the athlete safely return to full participation in athletics or is the athlete handicapped to the point where the return to the activity may risk further injury?"* Making this determination may be quite difficult to do and will be discussed in more detail later in this paper. The last consideration that a coach must

make is, *"What should I do for immediate care of the injury if this athlete can not return to participation?"* Without exception the immediate care should consist of basic or standard first aid procedures. A coach or trainer is not a doctor and should realize the limitations of his position. For example, a dislocated elbow should never be reduced by anyone except a doctor. If the coach applies cold or ice, immobilizes the affected body part, then calls for medical attention he should be carrying out proper first aid and should not be exposing himself to any subsequent legal difficulties.

To assist in determining the answers to these five questions it is very helpful for the coach to use an ordered sequence as a guideline for evaluation. One sequence that should be helpful for both slight and severe injuries is as follows:

History It is important for a person evaluating an injury to obtain a good history to help determine the extent of that injury. Many athletic injuries occur with no one witnessing them. Therefore, it is important to ask the athlete what happened. Did the ankle turn inward or outward? Did the athlete hear a pop or snap? Has this ankle ever been injured before? Did the knee just buckle or was the knee hit from the side? Where were you hit? Was the foot planted or free? Is there pain? If so, where is the pain and what elicits this pain? What other symptoms or changes in an athlete's bodily state are described to you that may be indicative of a certain injury? For example, headache, nausea, or loss of recent memory may be indicative of a cerebral concussion as a result of a head injury. In short, the more information a coach can obtain from taking a history from the athlete the more accurately the specific problem can be identified.

Observation Closely associated with taking a good history of an injury is observing the results of that injury. What signs or objective evidence of injury are apparent? Is there swelling, redness, discoloration or ecchymosis, muscle spasm, or any other physical changes that may give a clue to the extent of the injury? Is there joint instability or is there a visible deformity? Usually, severe injuries such as a major fracture or dislocation are quite easily identified even by those with limited background in the area of athletic injuries. One of the simplest tests of observation is to compare the injured body part to the same part on the opposite side of the body. Swelling of an ankle, instability of a knee ligament, or a bony deformity caused by a dislocated finger or elbow can often be seen and more easily determined when a comparison to the symmetrical body part is made. Most athletic injuries do occur to the extremities so these simple tests of comparison are no trouble for most people to make. If there is a head injury one may observe a glazed look in the athlete's eyes; there may be unequal pupil size; or there might be an unsteady walking pattern which may all be indications that a cerebral concussion has occurred. Profuse sweating, a pale face, a weak, rapid pulse, or leg cramps may be indications of heat exhaustion and should be seen by an observant coach.

Palpation Once the history has been taken and the observations have been made, the coach can palpate or touch the injured body part with light pressure from the fingers for the purpose of determining the physical signs and/or symptoms of the injury. When carrying out this procedure some of the signs the coach is looking for are: swelling, joint instability, point tenderness, abnormal muscle tightness or spasm, bony deformity, or crepitus which is a rubbing or grating sound caused by certain structures rubbing against each other. Swelling or edema is an increased amount of fluid in the intercellular tissue spaces in the body and is a normal response to injury. Joint instability may be caused by tearing of the ligamentous or muscletendonous structures. Point tenderness refers to a specific area that is more painful to touch than other body parts. It is usually found at the injury site regardless of whether the injury is of a bony, ligamentous, or muscle-tendonous nature. Muscle spasm is defined as an involuntary contraction of a muscle or muscle group and is often a result of a muscular strain ("pull") or a contusion (bruise). Bony deformity may be a result of a dislocation or fracture with displacement. This may result in crepitus or a grating sound upon movement of the injured part.

Active Range of Motion (AROM) Active range of motion refers to the amount of movement at a joint that a person can move through actively or without any assistance. For example, if an athlete has injured an elbow, the coach should ask him/her to straighten (extend) or bend (flex) the elbow to see if there is any limitation. Any limitation in the normal range of motion when compared to the non-injured side may be an indication of a number of problems. Pain will most often be apparent and may be caused by injury to the ligaments of the elbow, the muscles surrounding the joint, the bones that make up the joint, or other soft tissue around the elbow that may be swollen. Joints such as the shoulder, allow for movement in many directions and the athlete with an injury here should be asked to demonstrate active movements in all directions.

Resistive Range of Motion Once an athlete has demonstrated normal movement around an injury site with minimal discomfort, he/she should go through the same ranges of motion with the examiner giving resistance to that motion. This will give the examiner a good idea as to whether the athlete has retained "close to normal" strength. This testing should be done bilaterally. If the athlete can perform these movements against resistance it may be possible for a return to full participation, assuming the ability is retained to carry out the tasks needed for effective competition. Functional testing should precede the return of the athlete because demonstrating full strength may not always mean the athlete can compete effectively. Occasionally athletes with knee injuries will have full muscular strength around the knee joint but are unable to cut or change directions due to joint pain or ligament instability. Therefore, this athlete should demonstrate the ability to perform such activities before being allowed to return to full participation.

The intent of this article is to make it evident that athletic injuries should not be passed over too lightly and to give the coach a step-by-step approach for evaluation of injuries. There is much more to evaluation and recognition of injuries than most people, including coaches, are aware of. Minor injuries may become more serious if they are ignored or not properly evaluated and recognized. It is every athlete's right to receive proper care after an injury and the initial evaluation of that injury is the first part of this proper care. Coaches probably should not be burdened with this responsibility, but until changes are made at the secondary school level, it is apparent that coaches will continue to be responsible for the primary care of the athletes on their athletic teams. Therefore, the coach should have a reasonably sound and organized approach when evaluating the injuries with which he/she will be confronted.

Role of External Support in the Prevention of Ankle Sprains*

James G. Garrick, M.D.
Ralph K. Requa, A.T.C.

ABSTRACT

Two thousand five hundred and sixty-two participants in a college intramural basketball program were studied during two successive intramural "seasons" with regard to the frequency of ankle and knee sprains, as related to the use of external ankle support. The influence of injury rates of high- and low-top shoes and the use of prophylactic ankle taping were examined, and an additional group of players was supported with a disposable elastic material during the second season of study. The use of both high-top shoes and prophylactic ankle taping appeared to decrease the frequency of ankle sprains. This decrease was particularly marked in those subjects who had suffered previous ankle sprains. The size of the additional group was too small to permit valid comparisons.

No increase in the frequency of occurrence of knee sprains was observed to result from the use of high-top shoes and/or prophylactic ankle taping.

INTRODUCTION

The practice of prophylactic ankle taping is almost traditional in many athletic endeavors. Published research dealing with this practice has dealt with comparisons of taping and strapping techniques, changes in athletic performance resulting from taping and strapping, and the effectiveness of taping on the limitation of physiologic ranges of motion (1,2,3,4). The authors have been unable to find any published studies relating the incidence of ankle and knee sprains to the practice of prophylactic taping/strapping. This study is an attempt at defining this relationship.

METHOD

This study was carried out during January and February of 1972 and 1973 at the University of Washington. Intramural basketball was selected as the test sport because first aid facilities reports indicated that ankle sprains were more commonly encountered in this activity than in any other organized athletic endeavor available for study. Two methods of case/control selection were employed. During the first year of study participants in scheduled intramural basketball games, played during specified hours on three basketball courts, were utilized as subjects. Intramural league scheduling of games and courts was allowed to randomize the likelihood of any specific individual or team being included in the study. As a result, some participants were studied on more than one occasion. During the second year of study the teams and participants were allowed to participate in the study only if they agreed to be randomly assigned to experimental groups, and in this year a third experimental group was added, those supported with a new disposable elastic material. During the first year, prior to each game studied a team was selected as the "case group" with their opponent serving as a simultaneous control. Selection of case and study teams was carried out in a random fashion, except in instances when entire teams agreed to cooperate only if they could be included in a specific group. This group of player-games was examined with respect to frequency of previous knee and ankle injury and shoe type, and was not found to differ; hence they were included in the study. In any case, this group makes up less than 20% of the first year's population.

During the second year of study the random assignments to experimental groups were maintained throughout the season. In the first year, prior to the beginning of each game, and during the second year prior to the season as well, members of all teams were identified and queried regarding the presence and frequency of previous ankle and knee injuries. They were thus divided into the following groups for analysis: 1) those recalling no prior ankle or knee sprains; 2) those suffering "occasional" prior knee or ankle sprains[1]; and 3) those suffering "frequent" ankle or knee sprains.[2]

The participants' footwear was also identified and coded to record brand and height of shoe (e.g., high-top or low-top). All members of the taped group then had both ankles prophylactically taped utilizing a foam underwrap (J-wrap[R]) and white, perforated zinc oxide adhesive tape (Zonas[R]), and in the case of the new group, the disposable elastic material (J-Flex[R]) was applied according to man-

*An article published in *Medicine and Science in Sports* 5, 200-203, 1973. Reprinted with permission of the publisher.

ufacturer's specifications.[3] The taping procedure utilized initial placement of anchor strips followed by stirrups and horseshoe strips finished with a figure-8 lock supporting the lateral structures. This is the taping technique routinely utilized at the University of Washington as prophylaxis primarily aimed at the prevention of inversion sprains.

The games were observed by study investigators (trainers and student trainers at the University of Washington), and the occurrence of any ankle or knee injury necessitating stoppage of play, substitution or obvious disability was noted. At the conclusion of the game all participants were again questioned regarding the occurrence of ankle or knee injury during the game.

Ankle and knee sprains were classified according to the following criteria:
1. *Mild:* The occurrence of a sprain fulfilling the above criteria for injury but that was essentially asymptomatic at the conclusion of the game.
2. *Moderate:* Occurrence of a sprain fulfilling the criteria for injury that had resulted in swelling on examination, and/or pain with weight bearing or motion, and/or a detectable limp, but allowing the subject to walk unaided.
3. *Severe:* Moderate plus the inability to walk unaided (crutch) or assistance from another individual required).

All information was then entered on punch cards, verified and subjected to computerized analysis.

RESULTS

There were 2562 player games[4] studied. One thousand one hundred and sixty-three games were designated as "taped," e.g., had ankles prophylactically taped, and 1107 player games designated as "untaped" or controls. Of this group 132 used some method of external support (for example, self-applied prophylactic taping or wrapping) and, while not theoretically unsupported, they were included as such since there was no control, quality or otherwise, over their application. Any bias resulting from this decision would, in any case, tend to be a conservative one. Finally, 292 player games were included in the elastic wrap group.

A total of 66 ankle and knee sprains were sustained during the investigation, although the focus will be primarily upon ankle sprains. Table 1 provides a breakdown of the ankle sprains by study group and by shoe type. Table 2 provides the same information for knee sprains.

A very small number of bruises were sustained about the knee and ankle but are excluded from the analysis.

Tables 3 and 4 indicate the frequency with which cases and controls and those wearing high- and low-top shoes suffered ankle sprains. It is also worthwhile noting that the taped group (Table 3) and the high-top group include higher proportions of those previously injured than did the untaped and low-top groups, 68% vs. 39% and 66% vs. 51% respectively.

Of the eleven subjects sustaining knee sprains, six had previously sustained similar injuries. Four of these were in the control, or untaped, group and the remaining two were in the taped group. The elastic material group sustained no knee sprains.

Most ankle sprains were mild. Of the taped group, 16 of 17 were mild, and the remaining injury was moderate. The control or untaped group sustained both of the severe ankle sprains, and about a fifth of their sprains were moderate. The J-Flex group had two ankle sprains, one of which was mild and one moderate.

DISCUSSION

The theoretical aim of prophylactic ankle taping is to support externally a ligamentous structure

TABLE 1. Ankle sprains.

	High-Top Shoes			Low-Top Shoes			Total		
	Subjects	Injuries	Rate*	Subjects	Injuries	Rate*	Subjects	Injuries	Rate*
Taped	307	2	6.5	852	15	17.6	1159	17	14.7
Untaped	230	7	30.4	867	29	33.4	1097	36	32.8
J-Flex	93	1	10.8	195	1	5.1	288	2	6.9
Totals	630	10	15.9	1914	45	23.5	2544**	55	21.6

*Rate expressed /1000 participant-games.
**Missing data were encountered on shoe height for 18 player-games.

TABLE 2. Knee sprains.

	High-Top Shoes			Low-Top Shoes			Total		
	Subjects	Injuries	Rate*	Subjects	Injuries	Rate*	Subjects	Injuries	Rate*
Taped	307	2	6.5	852	2	2.3	1159	4	3.5
Untaped	230	2	8.7	867	5	5.8	1097	7	6.4
J-Flex	93	—	—	195	—	—	288	—	—
Totals	630	4	6.3	1914	7	3.7	2544	11	4.3

*Rate expressed /1000 participant-games.

without limiting normal range of motion or function. This support of ligaments need be present only when the physiologic or normal ranges of motion have been exceeded. The achievement of this goal, however, is virtually impossible.

In a pragmatic sense, taping is accomplished in such a way as to provide increasing support or restriction as the extremes of normal range of motion are approached, hopefully providing maximal restriction (support) at a point just prior to rupture of the ligamentous fibers. Assuming this to be true, some authors have indirectly evaluated efficacy of taping by measuring restriction of motion within the non-injurious range. However, for such an evaluation to be valid, one must establish that restriction of normal motion is an adequate indicator of the protective influence of the method of support and has no other deleterious effects.

Other studies have reported the concomitant incidence of ankle taping and knee and/or ankle sprains. However, without information regarding the frequency of ankle taping in the uninjured population, one is unable to draw any conclusion regarding the efficacy of taping as a prophylactic measure.

The frequency of ankle sprains in this study is about 1 per 50 exposures (player games) or a rate of 22 ankle sprains per 1000 player games. Rates differed substantially with regard to the type of external support utilized (shoes and taping). If one assumes that higher rates of injury may be the re-

sult of a lesser degree of protective influence (e.g., shoe height and prophylactic taping) then one is able to rank the efficacy of these influences.

The combination of circumstances studied theoretically offering the most external support to the ankle would be prophylactic taping plus a high-topped shoe. This group exhibited the lowest incidence of ankle sprains (6.5 ankle sprains per 1000 player games). The opposite end of the spectrum of external support (e.g., low-topped shoes, untaped group) exhibited a frequency of ankle sprains of 33.4 per 1000 — greater than 5 times the rate of the former group.

Further examination reveals that the high-topped untaped (30.4/1000) and the low-topped taped (17.6/1000) groups fall between the two extremes with regard to incidence of ankle sprains. Thus, ranked by degree of protective influence from most to least, the combinations would be as follows:

1. High-top/taped rate 6.5/1000
2. Low-top/taped rate 17.6/1000
3. High-top/untaped rate 30.4/1000
4. Low-top/untaped rate 33.4/1000

A Chi-square test applied to the frequency distribution underlying these rates yields statistical significance at the .025 level.

A history of the presence of previous ankle sprains also appeared to influence the likelihood of sustaining a similar injury during the study. The participants giving a history of previous ankle sprains were about twice as likely to be injured as

TABLE 3. History of previous ankle sprain.

	Taped			Untaped			J-Flex			Totals		
	Subj.	Inj.	Rate*	Subj.	Inj.	Rate*	Subj.	Inj.	Rate*	Subj.	Inj.	Rate*
No History	367	4	10.9	670	12	17.9	115	0	—	1152	16	13.9
Occasional	389	4	10.3	337	10	29.7	118	2	16.9	844	16	19.0
Frequent	407	9	22.1	100	14	140.0	59	2	—	566	23	40.6
Total	1163	17	14.6	1107	36	32.5	292	2	6.8	2562	55	21.5

*Rate expressed /1000 participant-games.

TABLE 4. History of previous ankle sprain by shoe type.

	High Top			Low Top			Total		
	Subjects	Injuries	Rate*	Subjects	Injuries	Rate*	Subjects	Injuries	Rate*
No History	211	4	19.0	932	12	12.9	1143	16	14.0
Occasional	229	4	17.5	607	12	19.8	836	16	19.1
Frequent	190	2	10.5	375	21	56.0	565	23	40.7
Total	630	10	15.9	1914	45	23.5	2544	55	21.6

*Rate expressed /1000 participant-games.

TABLE 5. Ankle sprains positive history of previous sprain.

	High Top			Low Top			Total		
	Subjects	Injuries	Rate*	Subjects	Injuries	Rate*	Subjects	Injuries	Rate*
Taped	242	2	8.3	552	11	19.9	794	13	16.4
Untaped	104	3	28.8	330	21	63.6	434	24	55.3
Total	346	5	14.5	882	32	36.2	1228	37	30.1

*Rate expressed /1000 participant-games.

their previously uninjured counterparts (27.7 vs. 13.9/1000). Those individuals reporting the presence of "frequent" prior ankle sprains were almost three times more likely to be reinjured than the previously uninjured. Both of these comparisons are significant under the Chi-square test at the .025 level.

The protective influence of external support for the previously sprained ankle can be observed in Table 5. For those wearing high- or low-top shoes, prophylactic taping reduced the likelihood of reinjury by about two thirds. The protective influence of the use of high-top shoes only appears to exist for those who had previously sprained their ankles, particularly those with frequent previous injury. For those with a positive history of ankle injury, the high-top group had an injury rate less than half that of their low-top counterparts. The utilization of prophylactic ankle taping, in addition to decreasing the likelihood of reinjury, may well also offer some protective influence to the previously uninjured (e.g., no history of prior ankle sprains) participant, although this was only observed for those wearing high-top shoes.

The small number of participants injured during the study prohibits in-depth analysis of the relationship of the severity of injury to various types of external support. It is interesting to note, however, that of the eleven moderate and severe ankle sprains only one was sustained by a taped subject and only three by subjects wearing high-topped shoes.

The paucity of knee sprains also prohibits statistical analysis. It can be pointed out, however, that any increased likelihood of knee sprains in individuals utilizing some form of external ankle support is appreciably overshadowed by the protection these means offer to the ankle. There is no evidence that an increase in knee sprains results from the use of external ankle support.

REFERENCES

1. Juvenal, J. P. The Effects of Ankle Taping on Vertical Jumping Ability. *Athletic Training* 7:146-149, 1972.
2. Libera, D. Ankle Taping, Wrapping, and Injury Prevention: *Athletic Training* 7:73-75, 1972.
3. Mayhew, J. L. Effects of Ankle Taping on Motor Performance. *Athletic Training* 7:10-11, 1972.
4. Simon, J. E. Study of the Comparative Effectiveness of Ankle Taping and Ankle Wrapping on the Prevention of Ankle Injuries *J NATA* 4:6-7, 1969.

Ankle Injury Care: An Outline

Charles "Chuck" Kerr, M.Ed., A.T.C.

I. INTRODUCTION

Ankle injuries are among the most commonly treated conditions in the care of athletes. Of the various types of ankle injuries, sprains outnumber all others. The frequency of injury is due to the weight-bearing function of the ankle, its anatomical structure, and its subjection to violent forces and high speed movements. All sports participants, especially those involved in running and jumping activities, are susceptible to the possibility of sustaining some type of ankle injury.

There are several complications that can arise as a result of ankle injuries. Included are such occurrences as an avulsion fracture of a malleolus, a fibrous union of a malleolar fracture, calcification of the deltoid ligament, or spurring on the talus and fibula, all of which may possibly result in some degree of ankle abnormality. Therefore, it is necessary and important that coaches and athletic trainers alike understand the anatomy of the ankle joint, the mechanics of the ankle sprain and some methods through which it can be treated, protected, and prevented. The following outline is offered to the reader to help describe these factors.

II. ANATOMY OF THE ANKLE JOINT

  A. Muscle support to the ankle
    1. Invertors include
      a. Tibialis posterior
      b. Tibialis anterior
      c. Flexor digitorum longus
      d. Flexor hallicus longus
    2. Evertors include
      a. Peroneus longus
      b. Peroneus brevis
      c. Extensor digitorum longus
      d. Peroneus tertius
    3. Plantarflexors include
      a. Gastrocnemius
      b. Soleus
      c. Tibialis posterior
      d. Peroneus longus
      e. Peroneus brevis
      f. Flexor digitorium longus
      g. Flexor hallicus longus
      h. Plantaris
    4. Dorsiflexors include
      a. Tibialis anterior
      b. Extensor digitorum longus
      c. Extensor hallicus longus
  B. Ligamentous support of ankle (See Illustrations 1 and 2)

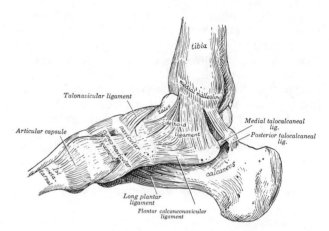

Illustration 1. *The ligaments of the right ankle. Medial aspect. From Gray's Anatomy of the Human Body, 29th edition, edited by Charles M. Goss, Philadelphia: Lea and Febiger, 1973. Reproduced with permission of the publisher.*

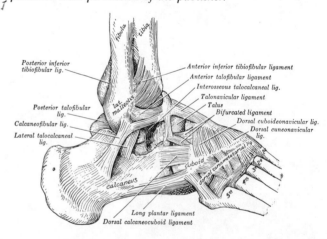

Illustration 2. *The ligaments of the right ankle. Lateral aspect. From Gray's Anatomy of the Human Body, 29th edition, edited by Charles M. Goss, Philadelphia: Lea and Febiger, 1973. Reproduced with permission of the publisher.*

    1. Medial collateral (deltoid)
      a. Four portions
      b. Strong, dense and fan shaped
    2. Lateral collateral ligaments—thinner and less dense
      a. Anterior talofibular
      b. Posterior talofibular
      c. Calcanofibular
  C. Boney Structure
    The distal ends of the tibia and fibula (medial and lateral malleoli) contain the

talus, forming a mortise joint where dorsiflexion and plantarflexion occur. These distal ends are bound by the anterior and posterior tibiofibular ligaments. The subtalar joint is where inversion and eversion of the foot occur.

III. HISTORY OF THE INJURY

A. Three important questions should be asked after the injury.
   1. Which way did the ankle turn?
      a. Most lateral sprains result from inversion injuries.
      b. These are often associated with plantarflexion as well.
   2. At the time of the injury, did the athlete hear or feel anything snap or pop?
      a. If yes, further examination must be completed to rule out fractures or torn ligaments.
      b. Bony and stress x-ray may be necessary.
   3. Has the athlete ever had problems with the injured ankle before?

IV. EXAMINATION OF THE ANKLE JOINT

A. Examination procedure
   1. Compare both ankles
   2. Look for deformity
   3. Location of swelling
   4. Ask athlete to move his foot through a range of motion
   5. Palpate to determine the degree of swelling, point tenderness, or crepitus
   6. Gently maneuver the foot through a range of motion
B. Testing procedure to see if the athlete may return to competition
   1. Toe and heel raises with both feet
   2. Injured ankle heel and toe raises
   3. Hopping on injured ankle
   4. Run figure eights
   5. Sprinting
   6. Cutting
   7. If the athlete can perform these without disability, the athlete may return to competition
C. Post initial examination
   1. If unable to perform previous tests
      a. Give crutches to athlete
      b. Apply ice, compression, and elevation
   2. Send to medical attention

V. VARIOUS TYPES OF ANKLE SPRAINS

A. In order to properly treat an ankle sprain, it is necessary to categorize the injury as to the structures involved and the degree of severity. Each category then will result in slightly different treatment. Each sprain is different, according to both its severity and its location.
B. Three categories of sprains.
   1. Mild Sprain (stretching injury to a ligament without a tear)

a. No loss of function
b. Mild point tenderness
c. Minimal swelling
d. Little or no pain on weight bearing
   2. Moderate sprain (partial tearing of ligaments)
      a. Possible that there will be a tear of the joint capsular ligaments
      b. Diffuse swelling with more swelling in the immediate ligament area
      c. Severe joint tenderness
      d. Pain on movement
      e. Ligament weakness
   3. Severe sprain (complete tear of one or more ligaments)
      a. There is extensive soft tissue damage and near complete loss of the ligament function
      b. Extreme pain and swelling
      c. Possibility of fracture
C. How the different ankle sprains may be difficult to determine
   1. A mild sprain often is considerably more painful than a severe sprain and often has a great amount of swelling.
   2. Some mild to severe sprains may have very little swelling

VI. FIRST AID FOR ANKLE SPRAINS

A. Ice—compression—elevation (ICE)
   1. Cold may be applied in the various methods
   2. Ice, coldpacks, or foot submersion in ice water (for at least the first 48 hours)
B. Compression
   1. Ace bandage—either with or without a felt horseshoe placed around the involved malleolus.
   2. Open Gibney boot or weave strapping
C. Elevation

VII. TREATMENT AFTER HEMORRHAGING HAS STOPPED

A. Heat — may be in the form of:
   1. Contrast baths
      a. Heat for 2 minutes (104°F)
      b. Ice water 1 minute (40–50°F)
      c. Alternate for a total of 20 minutes
   2. Whirlpool (104° to 106°) — 10 to 15 minutes
   3. Moist Heat — 10 to 15 minutes
B. Other modalities to use
   1. Short wave diathermy
   2. Ultrasound

VIII. RECONDITIONING OF THE ANKLE JOINT

A. It is important to begin reconditioning of the ankle to regain the integrity of the supportive structures involved in the initial injury
B. Suggested reconditioning program
   1. Cryokinetics (ice treatment with exercise)
      a. Plantarflexion—with ice massage or ice pack

b. Dorsiflexion—with ice massage or ice pack
c. Inversion—with ice massage or ice pack
d. Eversion—with ice massage or ice pack
e. The above exercises are done in ten repetitions for each exercise
2. After athlete can bear weight do the following
   a. Lift light weights to the above with ice
   b. Increase weight as soon as athlete can do each weight with ease
C. Rehabilitation exercises
   1. Walk short distances
   2. Toe raises—hold for 5 count—10 repeats
   3. Carrioca or serpentine (cross over step — figure eight)
   4. Light jogging—start with 10 yards and continue as athlete can tolerate
   5. Sprinting 10 yards at a time and continue as athlete can tolerate
   6. Light cutting
   7. The above is done every day until athlete can go full speed in all the above exercises. When he can, he may return to activity.
D. Alternate exercises to strengthen the ankle joint
   1. Rolling over the ankle—walk about 7 yards (reverse)
   2. Toe raises—hold to count of 5
   3. Jumping over an imaginary ball
      a. First on one foot
      b. Then both—10 repetitions
   4. Running through a rope maze—tire arrangement—etc.
   5. Partner exercises
      a. Resistive exercises
      b. Plantar- Dorsi-Flexion—hold 5 count —5 repeats
      c. Inversion—Eversion—hold 5 count —5 repeats

IX. SELECTED TECHNIQUES OF TAPING AND WRAPPING

The following illustrations (Figures 1–11) represent some taping and wrapping techniques which we have found successful at Ithaca College. It should be pointed out that there are probably several methods which can be used successfully to achieve the goals of most taping or wrapping procedures. Perhaps the most important considerations in evaluating a taping or wrapping procedure are that the technique is (1) anatomically sound (2) functional and (3) it offers adequate support to the intended area.

X. CONCLUSION

Ankle sprains are a common athletic injury and therefore deserve much attention in their care and prevention. Only if prompt and proper care is given; only if an effective program of rehabilitation is per-

formed; only if all steps are taken to prevent the injury from occurring; and only if additional research is completed to determine the most effective methods of protecting and predicting the ankle injury, will the statement coined by Thorndike in 1930, "Once a sprain, always a sprain" be proven wrong.

| Fig. 1 | Fig. 2 | Fig. 3 |

Tension maintained at all times should provide maximum support to the joint without having a tourniquet effect of stopping blood flow.

| Fig. 4 | Fig. 5 | Fig. 6 |

Continue the wrap with a heel lock [Fig. 4 and 5]. Keep the wrap snug. Use the remaining length of the material with figure eights around the foot. This heel lock must be applied carefully to avoid wrinkles in the back that could cause blisters.

| Fig. 7 | Fig. 8 | Fig. 9 |

One figure eight with this tape is made [Fig. 7]. Tape is torn and end is anchored over the instep. The final piece of tape applied [Fig. 8 and 9] is 2 inches wide and starts at the top of the ankle and angles at a 45° angle down the inside of the ankle, across the edge of the heel, which indicates that half of the tape width is on the bottom of the heel and the other half is on the back. This strip is pulled very tight and taken to the outside of the ankle and back to the top front as shown.

Figures 1-9. *Ankle wrap. From: The First Aider, December, 1975. Reprinted with permission of Cramer Products, Inc. Gardner, Kansas*

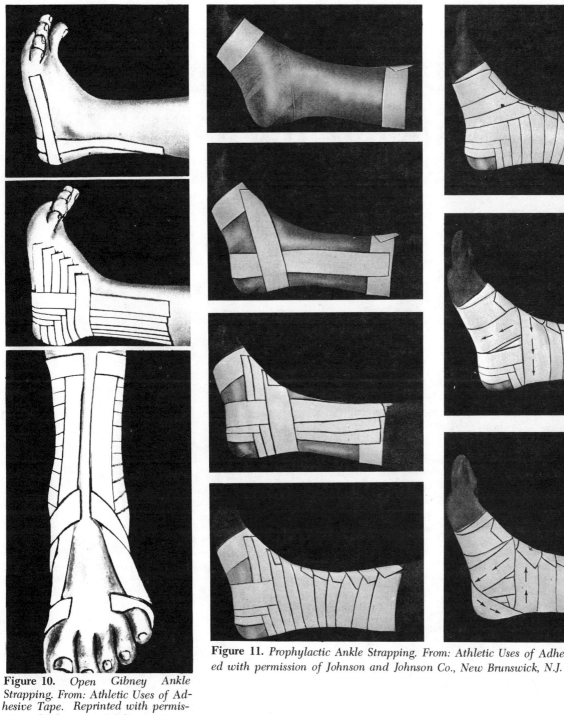

Figure 10. *Open Gibney Ankle Strapping. From: Athletic Uses of Adhesive Tape. Reprinted with permission of Johnson and Johnson Co., New Brunswick, N.J.*

Figure 11. *Prophylactic Ankle Strapping. From: Athletic Uses of Adhesive Tape. Reprinted with permission of Johnson and Johnson Co., New Brunswick, N.J.*

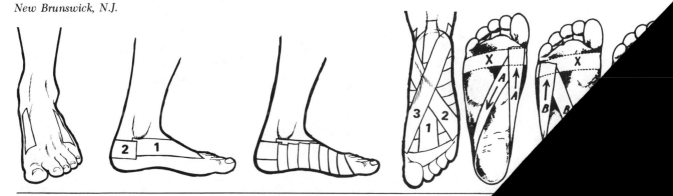

Figure 12. *Arch support. From The First Aider, December, 1974. Repirnted with permission of C*

Guidelines for Evaluating the Injured Athlete: The Knee Joint

Kent Scriber, M.S., R.P.T., A.T.C.

To better understand the principles of evaluating the injured athlete it is beneficial to discuss the evaluation of particular anatomical regions. Since reports dealing with high school, college, and professional football players show that the knee is injured more frequently than any other anatomical area, it is worthwhile to consider this joint individually.

The knee joint is formed by the distal end of the femur and the proximal end of the tibia (figures 1-3). The patella or kneecap lies anteriorly to the joint. Functionally, the knee joint is a hinge joint although there is some gliding of the femoral condyle on the tibial plateau. The medial (inside) collateral ligament and the lateral (outside) collateral ligament are two strong ligaments that give medial and lateral (side to side) stability to the knee. There are also capsular ligaments medially, laterally, and posteriorly which are thinner than the collateral ligaments. Though these are thin, the capsular ligaments are strong and add to the stability of the

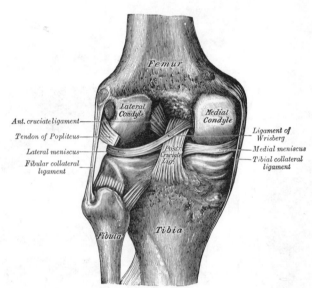

Figure 2. *Left knee joint, posterior aspect, showing interior ligaments. (From Gray's Anatomy of the Human Body, 29th edition, edited by Charles M. Goss, Philadelphia: Lea and Febiger, 1973. Reproduced with permission of the publisher.)*

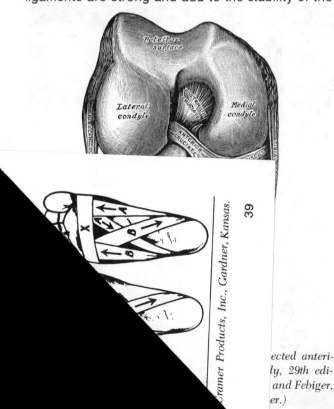

ected anteri-
ly, 29th edi-
and Febiger,
er.)

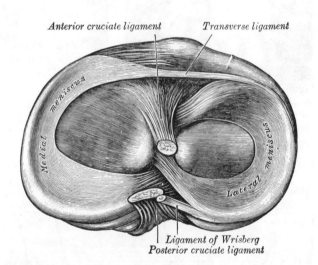

Figure 3. *Head of right tibia seen from above, showing menisci and attachments of ligaments. (From Gray's Anatomy of the Human Body, 29th edition, edited by Charles M. Goss, Philadelphia: Lea and Febiger, 1973. Reproduced with permission of the publisher.)*

joint. Inside the knee the anterior and posterior cruciate ligaments cross and prevent forward and backward displacement of the knee. Also inside the knee joint are the medial and lateral menisci or cartilages that lie on top of the tibial plateau.

There is strong musculature around the knee. Anteriorly is the quadriceps femoris muscle group (thigh) which surrounds the patella and inserts as the patellar tendon onto the tibial tuberosity. These muscles are primarily responsible for extension of the lower leg. The posterior muscle group (hamstrings) are primarily responsible for flexion of the lower leg. There are some muscle tendons that give minimal support medially and laterally, but side to side support of the knee is primarily given by the previously mentioned ligaments. Along with this brief anatomical review the reader should keep in mind this joint was more designed for movement in a straight ahead plane than for the stresses of cutting, twisting, and being hit that are applied in athletic activities. Though the knee joint is well supported for everyday activities it becomes particularly vulnerable in athletics.

Once the knee joint is injured the coach can use the guidelines set forth in my earlier article to make an initial evaluation. The coach should not by any means be expected to determine exactly what is wrong with the injured athlete, but he should be able to make an intelligent determination as to whether it is safe for an athlete to return to a contest or whether this athlete needs immediate medical attention. Many high school coaches are forced to make this type of decision with their athletes every day because of the shortage of medical coverage at practices and athletic contests. To be on the safe side, a coach in this situation should always take a conservative approach when he or she is responsible for the initial care of a knee injury. In other words, if there is any question in regards to the integrity of the injured area, the athlete should be held out of the activity and seen by a doctor. The coach should never ignore an injury or tell the athlete to "run it off" or he/she may then be found negligent in his or her duties.

If the coach has a basic knowledge of the knee joint he is much better able to deal with the initial management of an injury. The first thing the coach should find out is what was the mechanism or how did the injury happen. Was the injury caused by a direct blow? Which way did the knee move? Was the foot planted? If these questions can be answered this information may be valuable to the physician who will see the injuries that are more serious. At the same time that the history of the injury is taken the coach can observe the injured athlete and the injured body part. Did the athlete walk off the field? Did he limp? Is there any visible deformity or swelling around the joint? This is most easily determined by observing the non-injured extremity at the same time. The next step in the evaluation is for the examiner to palpate the injured area. The examiner may find an area of tenderness over a particular structure, such as a

ligament. This point tenderness stretching, tearing, or a contusion Range of motion testing should f athlete flex and extend the injured k Or is there pain and limitation or lock is attempted? A problem here should b tion for the coach to immobilize and the injured area and send the athlete to medical attention.

The coach should be aware of the fact that there are cases when an athlete may have suffered a complete ligament rupture and have very little pain or limitation initially. Pain, swelling, and discomfort will most likely occur within the next few hours. This athlete may describe to you that he heard a "pop" or "snap," or that his knee feels "funny" or "mushy," or that it "gives out" when he walks. In this case, if no doctor is available, the coach may want to carefully and passively test the stability of the ligaments. To test the collateral ligaments the athlete's knee should be flexed slightly and supported by the examiner. To test the medial collateral ligament, the examiner should support the lower leg above the ankle joint with one hand and gently push inward with the other hand just superior to the lateral joint line. (See figure 4). If there is a "giving way" or if pain is

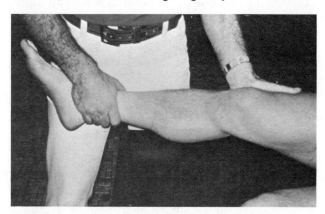

Figure 4. *Testing for stability of the medial collateral ligament. Note hand placement and slightly flexed knee for testing.*

elicited, the exam should end here as far as the coach is concerned. The lateral collateral ligament is tested in a similar fashion with the hands and force applied reversed. The anterior cruciate ligament can be tested by giving stabilization above the ankle joint and applying a forward pull from the posterior aspect of the knee joint. This is referred to as a drawer test. (See figure 5). The same tests should be done on the non-injured knee for comparison. If any joint instability is suspected the athlete should be referred for medical examination. Performing these tests correctly takes much practice and it is not recommended in the initial examination by the novice in the area. Though this author feels that ligament stability testing is not necessarily within the realm of the coach's responsibility, it is mentioned here because the coach who has no medical assistance immediately

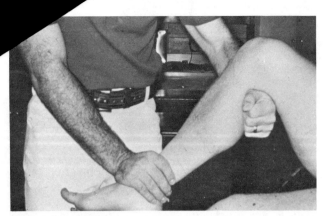

Figure 5. *The drawer test for stability of the anterior cruciate ligament.*

available may be able to ascertain information for the doctor if he properly completes an initial examination. It is much easier to test a joint's stability before pain, effusion, and muscle guarding become apparent. Many times a secondary school athlete is not seen by a doctor until several hours after an injury and these signs and symptoms may make the doctor's examination more difficult.

Even for the novice, it is usually not too difficult to identify a serious injury. As a rule its initial care consists of ice, compression, and elevation along with immobilization of the injured knee and transport to medical attention. What becomes a most difficult task for coaches, athletic trainers, and physicians alike is making the determination of when an athlete with a less than severe knee injury may safely return to a practice or contest. If we assume that we have taken an adequate history of the injury, observed the athlete and the injured knee, palpated on and around the joint over various structural landmarks, tested the active range of motion and found no limitation, and there is no joint instability we can then take the next step in our evaluation. Can the athlete go through a normal range of motion against a resistance? If the athlete can demonstrate full strength it is a good indication that he could return to athletics. However, this should not be the last criteria before the coach allows an athlete to return. The most important criteria is that an athlete be able to perform a series of functional tests for the lower extremity.

Whether an athlete has missed 6 months of practice after a knee injury or whether he has missed 6 minutes, he should be tested before he returns to full participation. There are many activities that an athlete may be asked to perform before returning. Among the author's favorite functional tests are jogging without a limp, running figure '8s,' hopping on the injured leg, carioca (cross-over running), and straight on sprinting. When an athlete can perform these tests without pain or limitation he can return to participation without greatly risking reinjury.

External support for the knee by means of taping or bracing is not as uniformly effective as coaches, athletic trainers, and physicians would like. There is no substitute for the development of muscular strength around the knee joint after an injury. Therefore, rehabilitation is the key to regaining full strength and the coach should not be misled into thinking that taping and bracing will solve all the problems of an athlete with an injured knee. If external support is used for the knee, it should be used as a supplement to rehabilitation and not as a substitute for it.

The knee joint is a very complex joint and is quite vulnerable to injury in athletics. Evaluation of knee injuries vary from a basic initial examination that a coach may perform in the absence of medical assistance, to the complex testing procedures performed by an orthopedic surgeon. This article has attempted to establish a basic guideline of evaluation for the knee for the coach. A basic initial examination is relatively simple and the coach should be familiar with it and well aware of the potential problems that may occur at the joint that is most frequently involved in athletics.

REFERENCES

1. Garrick, J. "Clues to Knee Injuries in Athletes," *AFP,* 8:128-133, Oct. 1973.
2. Hirata, I. *The Doctor and the Athlete,* Philadelphia: J.B. Lippincott Co., 1974.
3. Hoppenfield, S. *Physical Examination of the Spine and Extremities,* New York: Appleton-Century-Crofts, 1976.
4. Klafs, C., and D. Arnheim. *Modern Principles of Athletic Training,* St. Louis: C.V. Mosby Co., 1977.
5. Klein, K., and F. Allman, *The Knee in Sports,* Austin and New York: Jenkins Book Publishing Company, Inc., 1969.
6. Leach, R. "Knee-Ligament Injuries," *Skiing,* Spring, 1976.
7. Nicholas, J. "Injuries to Knee-Ligaments," *JAMA,* 212:2236-2239, June 29, 1970.
8. O'Donoghue, D. *Treatment of Injuries to Athletes,* Philadelphia: W.B. Saunders Co., 1977.
9. Ryan, A. "The Unstable Knee," *The Physician and Sports Medicine,* 3:46-52, Dec. 1975.

The Knee Injury in Athletics: An Outline

Bob Spackman, M.S., R.P.T., A.T.C.

Each year we see a higher incidence of knee injuries in sports. Many of these injuries could have been prevented. The following is a brief outline of possible causes and remedial measures to be taken in dealing with this important area of sports medicine.

1. Many of our athletes in the 8-15-year-age group are too weak to play sports due to our mechanized society.

2. When these young athletes are injured, prompt medical attention for diagnosis and treatment is rare.

3. There are very few certified athletic trainers in high schools. The 15-18-year-old athlete gets very little treatment or supervised strength and flexibility programs. Many high school injuries are never seen by the physician. These early untreated injuries lead to the surgical cases seen at the college level.

4. College, university and professional teams that I have observed may also injure many athletes with poorly supervised and incorrect methods of lifting weights. We need to sit down and write proper, standardized methods of how to lift weights, how to use isokinetic exercise equipment and how to use isometric exercise correctly so no one will be injured with progressive resistive exercise.

5. Too many athletes reinjure their knees, ankles and shoulders when they are permitted to go back on the playing or practice field before the injured area is as strong as the non-injured side. This is a major cause of knee surgery and many other serious injuries. We need methods of testing muscle strength to show that the injured areas are back to equal strength and range of motion (ROM) of the normal side.

6. Physical exams are often superficial on all levels of athletics, with the possible exception of professional athletics. Many physical exams consist of a questionnaire (did you have this, that, etc.), some lab work, chest x-ray blood pressure, etc. The physician often does not get much closer than a stethoscope to the athlete. One cannot hear a weak knee or ankle with a stethoscope. We must have an orthopedic exam including strength testing to find weak musculature around the knee joint. Weak athletes must be disqualified on all levels of athletics until the musculature around the knee joint is equal in strength with the contralateral side. Too many athletes are permitted to return to the practice field with the idea that running and practice will strengthen the knee musculature.

7. Most schools have no specific, daily exercises during the season to strengthen the muscles of the knee and ankle joints. Athletes do resistive exercises such as the toe raise, leg press or squat press for group muscle action but rarely do anything for inversion, eversion or dorsiflexion of the ankle. The usual conditioning program includes a few quad-hamstring exercises and other large muscle group exercises with weights and isokinetic exercises, but rarely do we see exercises done specifically for one leg with weak quadriceps or hamstrings.

8. *Exercises must be specific.* Exercise one leg at a time and every day during the regular season. Players and coaches spend too much time lifting or throwing heavy weights for the upper body and group exercises for the legs. The weak knee joint or ankle joint goes along for the ride and never returns to full strength.

9. We must also stretch every joint every day after resistive exercise to maintain and improve flexibility. Lack of flexibility is another causative factor of knee injuries. Many athletes are inflexible in the heel cords, hamstrings, hip flexors and back. Tightness in these areas may result in sprained and torn ligaments in the knees when forced beyond their inflexible ranges.

10. During the sport season, every athlete, male or female, should work at least ten minutes a day on resistive exercises for every muscle crossing the knee joint, preferably one leg at a time.

11. During the season, every athlete, male or female, should stretch every major joint in the

Editor's Note: The author had dealt with the knee injury in athletics for over twenty years. Based on his experience he has offered the reader an outline for the possible causes and methods prevention of the knee injury. His suggestions for isometric exercises are also found in his book: CONDITIONING FOR FITNESS, Schwebel Printing Co., P.O. Box 344 Murphysboro, Illinois, 62966 ($2.00).

body (shoulders, hip flexors, hamstrings, back and heel cords) at least ten minutes every day. They must stretch after every resistive exercise session to avoid losing flexibility. Working for extremes in flexibility will help prevent major musculoskeletal injuries.

12. We have found isometric exercise to be an effective method in strengthening a weak muscle group for both the prevention and rehabilitation of injuries.

Here is the *"Spackman Method"* of how to do isometric exercises correctly:

a. Push or pull only as hard as you can without pain against an immovable object.

b. Should you have pain — ease the contraction off, and push only as hard as you can without pain.

c. Ease the contraction on very slowly. Count and hold for six seconds, counting one thousand one, one thousand two, etc.

d. Ease the contraction off slowly at the end of six seconds.

e. *"Never hold your breath — breathe in and out normally."*

f. Exercise at least three different points through a complete range of motion.

g. Do at least three contractions for six seconds each at each point through a complete range of motion. Example — exercise the Quadriceps (muscles on the front of the thigh) at 90°, 135°, and 165° for 3 times for 6 seconds with each leg.

As an athletic trainer at Southern Illinois University, I have been using isometric exercise to re-strengthen athletic injuries and postoperative knee, ankle and shoulder injuries for 20 years. With this six-second isometric exercise method, I have been successful in getting athletes back playing much faster than using isotonic (weights) methods.

Everyone of any age can do isometric exercise, without danger, using the "Spackman Method," by not holding your breath while exercising. One can remain strong indefinitely by doing isometric exercise daily all your life. *Remember — Breathe in and out normally — Do not hold your breath while doing isometric exercise for six seconds.*

Developmental Asymmetry of the Weight Bearing Skeleton and its Implication on Knee Injury*

Karl K. Klein, M.S., C.C.T.

Major skeletal asymmetries developing during the period of growth may be recognized early in life and may eliminate young people with significant problems from participating in certain sports. Minor asymmetries are rarely recognized unless pain or structural fatigue syndromes call the problems to the attention of those concerned with the individual's health and welfare. The prevalence of minor asymmetries (short leg syndrome) was pointed out by Pearson (8) in an eight-year study of children's growth during the school years. Over that period of time 93 percent of the children x-rayed every two years showed evidence of lateral asymmetries and perpetuation of lateral imbalance in growth with no spontaneous correction. Beal (1) and Green (2) also contributed certain factual information concerning the incidence of the short leg syndrome. Previous to the work of Redler (9) it was mentioned by Strachan (10) that the use of heel lifts on children's shoes should compensate slightly less than the asymmetry shown by x-ray. The differences in leg length may decrease or disappear before the closing of the epiphyseal line and the child should be watched closely for changes calling for altering the thickness of the heel lift. Redler's (9) work strongly indicated that the use of the heel lift was a positive approach to the correction of minor lateral asymmetries and could be used to balance the pelvis and legs, for correcting awkward gait, and for relieving stress and pain. This technique for correction of body balance was reinvestigated by Klein and Buckley (3). Rose (11), reporting on the effects of lateral asymmetries on the injury potential in the field of sports, emphasized that abnormalities in the musculo-skeletal structure of young athletes should be "caught early." Those with significant asymmetries should be discouraged from continued participation, especially in the field of contact sports. An adequate rationale of the problem will be accepted by the sportsman.

But, where do minor lateral asymmetries begin? Reviewed studies (1,2,4,8,9,10) pointed out that the problem is evident in early childhood but stress

and pain factors are by-and-large non-existent at the early age levels. Minor asymmetries are not noticed unless a trained observer looks for them specifically. The high posterior iliac spine, high hip, and low shoulder on the same side torquing backward with a slight spinal curvature in the opposite direction are obvious signs. The Adam's test can also be used to provide further evidence of the short leg syndrome. The low posterior iliac spine will be on the side of the short leg. The high side of the back will be on the side of the high posterior iliac spine if the curve is functional.

In the erect standing position, placement of the heel wedge under the short leg side will level the posterior spines, and will straighten as well as derotate the functional lateral spinal curve. On forward bending it will maintain the level of the iliac and have a similar effect on the back. If lateral correction is made with a wedge a positive effect should result on the redevelopment of the symmetry of movement.

In observing gait patterns of people with lateral asymmetry, abnormalities may be noted in the movement of the leg, ankle and foot. Common observations are the "toeing outward" of the foot on the short leg side, an ankle pronation as the foot is placed on the ground as well and a valgus knee position as the leg is carried forward. On the opposite side the knee and the foot will be carried straight forward toward the foot's contact with the ground. These observations will be fairly consistent.

It may be surmised that there is a neurological basis for this action in that, as the short leg swings forward the toe will automatically point outward to balance the abnormal lateral sway of the body when the weight is shifted to the short leg side. A slight foot supination, ankle pronation and valgus knee commonly accompany this body action.

We have observed this lateral imbalance anomaly for a number of years in our work involving knee problems a program of measuring to the incidence of knee injury. Data were collected from the majority of cases coming to the Rehabilitation Labora-

*An article published in *Athletic Training*, 8:68-69, 86, June, 1973. Reprinted with permission of the publisher.

tory for specific exercise programming.

Measurement procedures for determining the body asymmetry known as the "short leg syndrome" have been described in the literature (4).

PROCEDURES:

During a five-year period data were collected on 200 cases, college age level, 165 post operative and 35 post injury. Standing measurements were made of the posterior iliac spines for symmetry or asymmetry, the general lateral curvature of the spine and the position of the shoulder were determined. The Adam's test (forward bending) was used as a part of the evaluation procedures to validate the standing test findings. Calibrated blocks, ranging from ¼ to 1 inch were used as a heel wedge for determining the exact amount of lateral imbalance and amount of lift necessary to level the posterior iliac spines in both test positions.

RESULTS:

The yearly data evaluation revealed a consistent pattern of injury relationship to the short leg syndrome injury, i.e., 82.2%, 80.7%, 83% and 82% of the cases studied each year.

Table I illustrates the composite findings for the 200 cases evaluated.

Table I

Knee Injury Relationship to the
Short Leg Syndrome-200 Cases

Short Leg				Base Level				Long Leg	
Post op.		Post injury						Post op.	Post injury
R	L	R	L			R	L	R	L
61	69	11	22	4(Po.L.)		19	12	0	2

130 (65%) 33 (16.5%) 4(2%) 31 (15.5%) 2 (1%)

P.O. +
P. Inj. 163 (81.5%) + 4 (2%) + 33 (16.5%) = 200

DISCUSSION:

In the problem of knee injury it has to be recognized that there are known anatomical and mechanical causes: significant looseness of the ligaments of the knee during the teenage years (14-16) due to puberty changes (5), muscle strength imbalance of the legs (6), and the cleated heel of the football shoe (7).

Based on the evidence presented in this study it can be projected that asymmetries within the pelvis and legs (short leg syndrome) can also be considered as a factor related to knee injury. It was previously pointed out that there are certain anatomical anomalies (valgus knee and ankle pronation, etc.) as well as deficiencies in mechanical function (toeing outward movement) on the short leg side. These factors make the knee on that side more vulnerable to injury because the basic mechanisms of injury have been put into motion: inward rotation of the femur, outward rotation of the tibia, and the knee inside of the foot in weight bearing.

As to the correction of the toeing outward movement pattern: without correction of the lateral pelvis and leg asymmetry, it seems to be an impossible accomplishment despite the individual's concentrated effort. But with mechanical balancing of the pelvis and legs the ambulation deficiency is almost self-correcting; concentration does assist.

If the evidence presented within the scope of this study has any significance to the incidence of knee injury, then coaches, trainer, team and family physicians as well as pediatricians should become more concerned with this problem of lateral imbalance and its implications. Through preventive concepts as expressed by Rose (11) and corrective procedures such as use of the heel lift technique, as well as specific movement training, knee injuries as a consequence of skeletal asymmetry could be reduced.

REFERENCES

1. Beale, M.C., "A Review of the Short Leg Problem", J. Am. Osteo. Assoc., XLI:5, 1954.
2. Green, W.T., "Discrepancy in the Leg Length of the Lower Extremities". Am. Academy of Ortho. Surgeions Instructional Course Lectures VIII, (J.W. Edwards Co., Ann Arbor, Mich., 1951).
3. Klein, K.K. and J.C. Buckley, "Asymmetries of Growth in the Pelvis and Legs of Growing Children-Summation of a Three Year Study 1964-1967", Am. Corr. Therapy J., 22:2:53, 1968.
4. Klein, K.K. and J.C. Buckley, "Asymmetries of Growth in the Pelvis and Legs of Growing Children, A Clinical and Statistical study of 37 male subjects", J. Assoc. Phy. and Mental Rehab., 21:2:40. 1967.
5. Klein, K.K., The Knees, Growth, Development and Activity Influences, All American Productions and Publications, Greely, Colo., ch.3, 1967, 2nd. Edition, The Pemberton Press, Austin, Texas 1971.
6. Klein, K.K., The Knee in Athletics, Am. Assoc. Health, Physical Education and Recreation, Washington, D.C. ch. 2, 1963.
7. Klein, K.K. and F.J. Allman, Jr., The Knee in Sports Conditioning Injury Prevention and Rehabilitation. The Pemberton Press, Austin, Texas, ch. 3, 1969.
8. Pearson, W.M., "Early and High Incidence of Mechanical Faults", J. of Osteo., XLI:5, 1954.
9. Redler, I., "Clinical Significance of Minor Inequalities of Leg Length", New Orleans Med. and Surg. J., 104:8:308, 1952.
10. Strachan, W.F., "Lateral Imbalance and the Use of Lifts", J. Am. Osteo. Assoc., 41:190. Dec. 1941.
11. Rose, K.D., "Congenital Anamalies of the Low Back", Nat. Athletic Tr. Assoc., April 1962, p. 2 (Reprint from Medical Times, Oct. 1961).

Acromioclavicular and Glenohumeral Joint Injuries in Sport

Robert D. Grant, M.P.E., R.P.T.

The shoulder is the most frequently injured major joint of the upper extremity. It is quite vulnerable to injury in contact sports as well as sports requiring a throwing motion. The "sneaky" no contact injuries, usually less violent in nature, that occur during the swinging requirements in the racquet, paddle and stick sports are none the less frustrating and sometimes equally disturbing in terms of "time away" from competition. Swimmers injure their shoulders more seriously than any other part of their body due to the tremendous propelling efforts of the upper extremity required in their sport. All sports participants are subject to falls on the outstretched hand or on the point of the flexed elbow; which can cause an indirect insult to the shoulder. So it goes — the shoulder mechanism can break down, refuse to function smoothly and without pain from whatever cause. The harmonious synchrony of muscular action needed for smooth shoulder motion is no myth, it is an absolute necessity in throwing any object or making any movement of the shoulder in sports activity.

ANATOMICAL REVIEW

A background review of the anatomy of the shoulder is essential in evaluating injuries in this area. There are several components intricately related and these parts move upon each other as the arm moves. The joints are in direct contact in the momentary static state of a shoulder block in football, a handstand in gymnastics, or in a fall on the flexed elbow or the extended hand when the arm is straight.

The ball and socket glenohumeral (GH) joint is made up of the proximal rounded head of the humerus articulating with the shallow saucer like "socket," the glenoid fossa of the scapula. Immediately above the GH joint we find the acromioclavicular (AC) joint which is formed by the distal end of the clavicle joining the acromion process of the scapula. These two joints and their accompanying musculature form the contours of the shoulder (see figure 1).

GH JOINT

The GH joint is the most freely movable joint in the body. A loose articular capsule surrounds it. This capsule is reinforced by capsular ligaments blending into the top, the middle and at the bottom of the capsule. There is a ligament running across

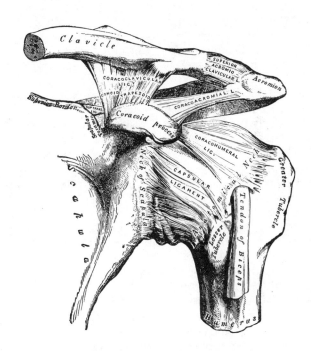

Figure 1. *The left shoulder and acromioclavicular joints, and the proper ligaments of the scapula. From Gray's Anatomy of the Human Body, 29th edition, edited by Charles M. Goss, Philadelphia: Lea and Febiger, 1973. Reproduced with permission of the publisher.*

the front of the joint near the top called the coracohumeral, this ligament attaches to a fairly long outward projection of bone coming off the front of the scapula near the GH joint called the coracoid process; the coracohumeral ligament attaches to the humerus at a rounded lesser projection of bone called the greater tubercle. It blends in with the capsule. Kent (1) states that the most important ligament of the GH joint is the coracohumeral. The bony arrangement, a rounded head fitting into a shallow socket, accompanied by a loose and lax capsule presents ample evidence to account for the extreme freedom of movement at the GH joint (2). Because of the loose fit and the shallow socket at the GH joint, mobility has been achieved at the sacrifice of stability (1).

AC JOINT

The AC joint joins the scapula to the clavicle. At this joint the clavicle acts as a shock absorber in the transmission of force to the center of the body (the sternum), from falls on the hand and from blows at the lateral aspect of the shoulder (3). This makes the clavicle subject to fracture in its middle portion. The AC joint is reinforced directly by the acromioclavicular ligaments surrounding the capsule, and indirectly by the coracoclavicular ligaments running from the coracoid process up to the clavicle. These ligaments help hold the clavicle down.

THE GH AND AC JOINTS COMPARED

When contusion is considered the GH joint receives some small degree of protection from the deltoid; the AC joint has no protection. In terms of stability the muscles help some in the GH joint and none at all at the AC joint. The rhythm and synchrony necessary at the GH joint for smooth action to occur is very important as the arm moves in any direction, for any reason. The constant normal relationship between the humeral head and the glenoid fossa during motion and at rest is maintained by a coordinated balance among all shoulder muscles involved (1). The muscles must work harmoniously to stabilize the shoulder joint in whatever degree.

When the shoulder muscles are not working in harmony, perhaps due to poor warm-up, they may strain rather easily. When shoulder muscle strength is overcome by an outside force such as in arm tackling or from a fall on the bent elbow or outstretched hand, the GH joint almost immediately becomes unstable and may subluxate or worse, dislocate. This injury is common at the GH joint from an indirect force and fairly common at the AC joint from a direct force.

MECHANICS AND MOVEMENT OF THE SHOULDER

The need for smoothness and rhythm in GH movement has been well established. Harmony, synchrony, scapulo-humeral rhythm are all necessary traits. Without these cooperative, flowing, smooth, efforts during GH motion, injury is likely to occur. The body moves in a continuum, so it is with the shoulder.

The wide variety of movement that takes place at the GH joint is possible because of the sphere like head of the humerus presenting a convex surface that rolls, glides, and rotates on the proportionally smaller concave surface of the glenoid fossa of the scapula. As the muscles move the arm in whatever direction desired it is here at the GH joint that the greatest movement occurs. A corresponding degree of pivot, glide, and rotation is occurring simultaneously at the AC and SC (sterno-clavicular) joints. *The whole unit is moving in harmony.* Since the GH joint is so freely movable and since a large "ball" is rolling on a much smaller "socket" an unstable state is visualized. Add on to this mechanical arrangement at the GH joint the loose capsular and meager reinforcing ligaments that allow great excursions of movement to occur and the stage is set for this joint to come apart rather easily. When excess stress is applied or the joint is forced beyond its mechanical limits there is very little in the form of check reins to keep the

joint totally congruent. The muscles move the GH joint but *do not* contribute appreciably to its stability.

SHOULDER JOINT INJURIES — RECOGNITION, ASSESSMENT, MANAGEMENT

The most important aspect of any acute injury situation is to be able to recognize what is going on. Recognition or suspicion of the problem leads to proper assessment at the scene. The first aid management is based on this assessment. When an athlete *stops functioning* because of an injury it is due to pain! In a game situation or even a spirited practice session when he/she stops due to pain there is no choice but to evaluate the cause and attend to the injured athlete.

The GH joint is very open to contusion in any sport where shoulder pads are *not* worn. Proper fitting of quality shoulder pads worn snug should automatically eliminate muscle contusion and bone "bruise" about the GH joint in the game of football. Theoretically, the same view applies to hockey and lacrosse. Indeed shoulder joint contusion per se should not be a problem in the contact sports mentioned; the area is vulnerable, but the pads do a good job warding off blows. This observation is not true of the AC joint in spite of good protective equipment. In the non-contact sports the GH and AC joints are not protected hence very open to contusion. In the baseball slide or collision, shoulder injury is very possible. In basketball where "bumping" makes the game a contact sport shoulder injury is also possible. In skiing the shoulder is vulnerable because of falls. Unplanned collisions or falls in any non-contact sport can lead to shoulder contusion or dislocation.

Contusion of musculature surrounding the GH joint is *not* a major problem for athletic trainers covering the contact sports at the college level; nor should it be so at the high school level. *Prevention is the answer!* (Good equipment placed on shoulders made strong and bulky during off-season weight programs). Not so at the AC joint! Inspite of good equipment, falls on the tip of the shoulder or the brunt of severe collisions taken at the AC joint (under the pads) do lead to contusion of this joint or worse, separation. It takes an *indirect force* to dislocate the GH joint; no amount of quality protective equipment or bulky strong muscles can prevent this unfortunate occurrence if severe stress forces are applied when the joint is at extremes of motion or is "jammed" in a fall. Some people have "looser" joints than others permitting easier dislocation when stressed. Even so, the GH joint is naturally unstable in everyone when compared to the other large joints of the body and is, consequently, rather easily dislocated.

Contusion and dislocation of the GH and AC joints is always a possibility in the non-contact sports. In the contact sports, severe contusion of the AC joint is a constant threat. Subluxation (partial dislocation) or dislocation of the GH and AC joints is also a constant possibility: in the AC from a direct blow and in the GH from indirect stress forces. In the writer's experience, sprain of the AC joint, in addition to contusion, is a distinct possibility. Mild to moderate sprain classification of the AC joint lies somewhere between an annoying contusion and actual separation (dislocation).

RULES FOR SHOULDER INJURY RECOGNITION AND MANAGEMENT: ON THE SCENE

1. DID YOU SEE THE INJURY OCCUR?

This is very important! Did the situation look violent to you? If you did not see the action, you must discern why he/she stopped functioning. Your index of suspicion will naturally rise and you will begin to speculate and go to check him/her.

2. WHAT DO YOU SEE?

— Is the athlete lying down, sitting/standing, or walking/jogging towards you? It is quite unusual to find an athlete lying down with a shoulder injury if that is all that is wrong — but, if this is the situation encountered your suspicion level should shoot up. The writer recalls a situation where a wrestler was slammed to the mat and knocked unconscious. This immediately became my first concern. He revived very quickly. Communication with him revealed a complaint of left shoulder pain. Before getting him up (he was on his stomach), an examination of the area revealed a separated AC joint. He was hospitalized over night for observation of the head injury from which he recovered in a short time. The AC separation "knocked out" his wrestling for the season.

If an athlete stops functioning and sits there either holding his/her arm with their other arm or, his/her posture reveals a guarded shoulder-arm mechanism, kneel down along side him/her and inquire softly as to where it hurts. On one occasion, while covering a baseball game "my" short stop put a tag on a sliding runner; there was a collision. As the dust cleared, "my" shortstop just sat there. Time was called, I went out to check him, kneeling down on one heel beside him. He stated rather calmly and disgustedly, "it's broke Bob, I heard it snap"; "where", I replied — he pointed to his left clavicle; examination confirmed my suspicion of fracture. The baseball uniform permitted easy access to the bone, it is just sub-dermal and with his non-involved hand he pointed to the injury — he *told* me what to expect. It was easy for me to palpate the bone and find tenderness to confirm what he "knew."

Frequently, an athlete stops play and is standing with a shoulder injury. He/she may look uncomfortable or be in real pain, patiently waiting for your assistance. As you approach him/her, what do you see? Shoulder "dropped"? or is his/her arm turned out?, or is the arm held across the torso?, pain on his/her face, (how much?) how well do you know him/her?, what do you see?

As an athlete walks/jogs towards you holding his arm with his non-involved hand supporting it in some manner, portraying pain you may be about to deal with an AC joint injury, a shoulder joint dislocation, a "nasty" contusion, or possibly a fracture. As he/she approaches you, observe closely. The problem may not necessarily be in the shoulder. There may be a dislocated elbow deformity visible about the time you hear, "its my elbow, my elbow." If he/she approaches you with the shoulder dropped, arm "dangling" at his/her side, suspect the neck "nerve pinch" injury. The fifth, sixth, seventh, and eighth cervical nerves contribute their fibers to form the brachial plexus which gives off the *major* nerve supply to the shoulder; a "rabbit" punch or similar type blow to the neck may produce a transcient shoulder paralysis and numbness. Women rarely sustain this type of injury, but it is fairly common in football.

3. WHAT DO YOU HEAR? WHAT DOES HE/SHE TELL YOU? (What is the history?) HOW DID IT HAPPEN?

— "Its broke Bob," — I believe them until proven otherwise.
"Its out Bob, I know it is." — I believe them until I investigate.
"I heard a snap!" (Tendon over tendon, tendon over ligament, or bone fracture.) You must be suspicious.
— Is he/she frightened, crying, loud, protesting? Calm him/her down!
— How well do you know him/her? You two are going to get better acquainted in the next few minutes that lie ahead.
— If you didn't see the injury occur, did he/she fall from a height off a gymnastics apparatus, trampoline? From others present, you hear: "He fell hard right on the tip of his shoulder, coach." "She landed on her outstretched hand." This is no time to discipline spotters if they were at fault; check the injury. It may be minor, moderate or —?

4. WHAT DO YOU (the coach or trainer) FEEL?

In the contact sports where the athlete is covered with protective equipment, "T"-shirt underneath, and jersey on top, whether lying or standing, DO NOT DISTURB THE SHOULDER COMPLEX! This is accomplished as follows:

Face the athlete, if he/she is lying on the ground, kneel down along side; if sitting, do the same thing; if he/she is standing in front you simply face them. Depending on which shoulder is involved you use *your same* hand and do the following: (example — athlete standing, left shoulder injury).

a) Peel clothing *out* of the pants with your left hand as you reassure him/her with your soft voice; your right hand can be placed on his/her left hip or low back, your legs can contact his/her's as you stand slightly around towards his/her left side. (Reverse for right side)

b) With your warmed left hand open palm and fingers flat against his/her stomach, "run" your left hand up his/her left side, then over his/her left upper chest allowing your fingers to reach the left SC joint. YOU ARE UNDER THE CLOTHING AND PADS WITH YOUR HAND ON THE ATHLETE'S SKIN — *YOU CANNOT SEE ANYTHING* EXCEPT HIS/HER FACE. EXAMINATION IN THIS MANNER PREVENTS ANY MOVEMENT OF THE JOINTS OF THE SHOULDER UNTIL YOU DETERMINE IF IT IS SAFE TO ASK FOR MOVEMENT IN ORDER TO FURTHER EVALUATE. DO NOT PERMIT ATHLETE TO MOVE HIS/HER SHOULDER COMPLEX UNTIL YOU SAY IT IS "OK!" YOUR MOUTH IS JUST INCHES AWAY FROM HIS/HER EAR SO QUESTIONS AND COMMANDS CAN BE GIVEN IN A SOFT REASSURING VOICE.

— What do you feel? How does this SC joint *compare with the opposite?* Feels "OK" to you? *If not, stop,* press gently and watch his/her face for reaction and interpret his/her answer to your statement/question — "I'm going to press gently, you tell me if it hurts?" — It may be painful to take a deep breath if the SC joint is injured.

— If you find pain or what you interpret is some degree of instability, *place* his/her open hand on his/her "belly" *palm in,* support the involved elbow *gently* in your left hand (do not push the elbow upward), put your right arm around their back at the waist, walk off together to the sideline. With the athlete sitting down, cut off the jersey and the pads at the laces, cut off the "T"-shirt, place the left arm in a sling and swath*and *send or take* to a physician with suitable covering placed over the shoulders.

— *SC joint feels "OK" to you — proceed* with the assessment. Allow your fingers to slowly travel from proximal to distal along the clavicle; it is practically right under the skin throughout its length. As your fingers follow the outline of the bone along its' "crankshaft" or lazy "S" path, you *feel* for disruption in the bone. If you feel a bump or indentation, what has he/she told you (heard a snap) or, after you inform them you will *very gently* apply *mild* pressure onto such a discovery, what is the reaction?; do they pull (flinch) away or inform you it hurts?, if so, that's it; *stop*; double check gently if you feel the need and carry out first aid *exactly* as described for a suspected SC joint injury. *No change, do it!*

The athlete may not have a fracture, but if you find/feel abnormality in the bony outline and he/she complained of pain, your choice is clear, carry out the first aid and seek the team physician or the family physician. Transport the same, everything the same!

This writer does not advise applying a figure of eight type of bandage over the padded axilla bilaterally, whereby the "X" of the figure eight crosses between the scapulae posteriorly. This procedure does not seem necessary when medical assistance is easily accessible. When out in the woods or some other distance from medical help, this method is justified.

— *Clavicle feels "OK" to you — proceed* with assessment. Allow your fingers to palpate the distal end of the clavicle as it joins the acromion to form the AC joint. Partial separation (subluxation) or complete dislocation is *not* unusual at this location.

As you allow your fingers to palpate the flattened distal end of the clavicle your fingers will drop down ever so *slightly* as you meet the acromion process at the AC joint. This is to be expected in a *normal* shoulder; so do not be alarmed at that finding. Dramatic sensation of a drop-off is a different story and is discussed thoroughly later.

If the joint is tender, suspect AC insult. Push down on the distal end of the clavicle. Possibly on pressure, the clavicle appears to ride down a little further than normal (some mobility is normal), but the usual relationship of the joint is not appreciably distorted.

— *Tenderness* and a hint of hypermobility. Remove him/her from play by walking off to the sideline. *Carefully* remove the clothing, taking uninvolved arm out of jersey and pads first, then slide the sleeve on involved side down arm easily (same with pads). When suspecting a slight AC sprain it is not necessary to cut off the pads, "T"-shirt and jersey as previously described, unless slight movement is too painful. Allow to shower, dress carefully and send or take him/her to the team physician, family physician, or consulting orthopedic surgeon. DO NOT TREAT OR IGNORE THIS INJURY. SEND TO A PHYSICIAN FOR EVALUATION. This injury can take as long as four to six weeks to heal satisfactorily. (6). The team physician may allow participation with the use of proper padding.(7).

— Partial separation (subluxation) of AC joint AC joint is *tender* and you illicit a movement by your pressure that leaves little doubt that some *hypermobility* of the joint is present.

This is a more serious injury, as there has been definite ligament tearing about the capsule and stretching of the coracoclavicular or suspensory ligament has occurred. "There will be pain, swelling and tenderness, with the pain increased by an attempt to separate the acromion and clavicle by pulling on the arm." (6). DO NOT ATTEMPT THIS TEST, THIS IS A DIAGNOSTIC TEST DONE BY A PHYSICIAN.

Your course is clear — when you illicit *some* hyper-tenderness and some hypermobility, handle *exactly* as the description given for a subluxation or dislocation of the SC joint. The athlete will return after seeing a physician with a bandage that holds the clavicle down.

— Dislocation of the AC joint

The AC joint is *very tender* and true laxity of the clavicle on the acromion is identified because you have no doubt about the hypermobility of the joint. It moves freely! This is more serious as there has been complete rupture of the Acromioclavicular ligaments *and* the AC joint capsule. There has been complete separation of the distal end of the clavicle, *but* the suspensory ligaments although stretched are still intact. DO NOT PULL ON THIS ARM!

Again your course is clear — handle *exactly* as for the description given for the SC joint injury.

When this injury occurs do not be surprised if the young athlete is referred to an orthopedic surgeon and a wire or pin is inserted through the acromion into the clavicle stabilizing the AC joint. This pin will stay in place for a minimum of six weeks. (3) Postoperatively the athlete will probably be wearing a sling and swath or similar form of immobilization. A more conservative approach is to use external fixation in the form of a restricting bandaging similar to that previously described. The clavicle must be held down firmly in proper alignment with the acromion process.

— Distal end of clavicle is found upward considerably away from the acromion

This finding represents a complete dislocation of the AC joint with rupture of the suspensory ligaments, the corcoid and the trapezoid; along with the previously described complete rupture of the AC joint capsule and acromioclavicular ligaments. The clavicle is perceived as being "loose" and in an upward position in relation to the acromion. It feels as if it is "sticking up" a half inch or more.

Your course is again clear — handle *exactly* the same as previously described for SC joint injury. Surprisingly the athlete may be "relatively" pain free as the complete ruptures "let the clavicle go." Some tension on the overlying skin will be experienced by the athlete. It is *very rare* when the distal clavicle pierces the skin in this type injury.

Most probably the young athlete will be operated on the day the injury occurs or the next day, when this injury is placed in the hands of an orthopedic surgeon. Open reduction with ligament repair and fixation of the AC joint is favored by many. (3, 6, 7). There is a possibility even this Grade III injury will be treated by closed reduction by some others. (7).

PREVENTION OF SHOULDER INJURIES

Before closing, let me outline some suggestions for the prevention of shoulder injuries.

1. There is no questioning the importance of properly fitting shoulder pads in contact sports. Pads that pinch the neck or fail to adequately protect the AC joint because of being too loose or too small leave the athlete vulnerable to shoulder injury. Pads must be snug as well as comfortable.

2. In sports such as football, ice hockey and lacrosse it is important to spend considerable practice time in coaching the proper use of the shoulder as either an offensive or defensive mechanism.

3. Off season weight training programs are highly recommended, providing they are properly supervised and for every strengthening exercise given a stretching exercise is taught.

4. In the throwing sports, e.g. javelin, shot put, discuss, football quarterbacks etc, good coaching is essential — throwing mechanics must be constantly analyzed, corrected and improved.

5. Following the baseball pitcher's performance, the arm should be stroked rather firmly with alcohol (but never massaged). As another method, you can give cold water whirlpools. Following either of these cryotherapy techniques, have the athlete, hang-stretch with both arms for 30–60 seconds for 2–3 sets.

6. Exercise programs designed by physicians, trainers, or therapists must be carried out and enforced by coaches as part of the rehabilitation process following an injury.

In summary, early recognition, prudent action by the coach or trainer and good medical management can help in reducing the incidence of shoulder injury in sport.

REFERENCES

1. Kent, BE: Functional anatomy of the shoulder complex: a review. *Phy Ther:* 51, pp 874, 871, 880.

2. Gray, H: *Anatomy of the Human Body 27th ed.* Edited by Goss CM Philadelphia, Lea & Febiger, 1959, pp 356.

3. Bateman, JE: *The Shoulder and The Neck.* Philadelphia, W. B. Saunders Company, 1972, pp 58, 348, 349, 348, 349, 389–390, 337.

4. Distefano, V: Functional anatomy and biomechanics of the shoulder joints. *Ath. Train.* 12: 142, 141.

5. Logan, GA and McKinney, WC: Kinesiology, William C. Brown Company, 1970, pp 18, 118.

6. O'Donoghue, DH: *Treatment of Injuries to Athletes,* 3rd ed. Philadelphia, W. B. Saunders Company, 1976, pp 164, 165, 162, 217, 65, 202, 203, 66, 66–67.

7. Hoyt, WA, Bailey, RW, Allman, FL, et al: Symposium on treatment of injuries to the shoulder girdle. *J Bone Joint Surg* 49–A: 753–792, 1967.

*swath — a bandage applied over the sling around the person's torso so as to hold the upper arm (brachium) firmly but gently at the person's side — applied *after* the sling, remember the elbow is flexed, palm is flat against the person's belly. (Practice this procedure, *it is not difficult,* and it is excellent first aid to use *before* team physician sees the athlete. (6).

Cryotherapy in Sports Medicine

Kenneth L. Knight, Ph.D., A.T.C.

PART I. RATIONALE

Ice or cold applications have been used extensively in Sports Medicine. Initially, ice was used only during the initial care phase of acute musculoskeletal injuries (along with compression and elevation) to control swelling. Now, however, ice is *also* being used widely during the rehabilitation phase. In fact, cold has replaced heat treatments in many athletic training rooms as the preferred form of therapy. What makes ice effective in both phases of injury care? Should the application of ice be the same during rehabilitation as during initial care? What is the most effective way of applying ice during each phase? Should ice be used instead of heat applications? To answer these questions we must investigate the pathological changes that accompany an acute musculoskeletal injury, the tissue's needs during injury and repair, and the physiological effects of both heat and cold. Only then can intelligent decisions be made concerning the proper use of ice during the various phases of injury care.

INJURY PATHOLOGY

Most types of musculoskeletal injuries/sprains, strains, and contusions result in the same pathological changes in the tissue. Trauma, whether due to a direct blow or to stretching and tearing, results in damage to both structural and associated tissues (muscles, tendons, and ligaments are structural tissues; nerves, capillaries, and blood vessels are associated tissues). As a consequence of the damaged capillaries and blood vessels there is internal hemorrhaging. After a period of time, depending on the severity of the injury, the damaged blood vessels seal up (clot). The blood that is outside the blood vessels and the tissue debris (damaged tissue cells) become organized into a mass known as a hematoma.

Neither swelling nor tissue damage are complete at this time, however. Edema causes additional swelling and more tissue dies as a result of hypoxic injury. Edema is the collection of blood fluids in the tissue spaces outside of the blood vessels. Because of the hemorrhaging and tissue debris there are increased amounts of "free" protein in the tissue spaces. The increased "free" protein causes increased tissue oncotic pressure which "pulls" water out of the blood vessels in an osmoticlike manner. Through this process edema formation can take place for up to 24 or 48 hours following the injury.

Hypoxic injury is secondary to the traumatic or primary injury. It results from the body's initial attempts to control the primary injury (5). The body responds almost instantly to an acute injury; in both the immediate vicinity of the trauma and on the fringes of the injury. In the immediate vicinity the body controls the hemorrhaging through the clotting mechanism. This is the same process that occurs with an external injury such as cutting an arm or a finger. On the periphery of the injury the body begins the inflammatory response, a series of events designed to rid the body of foreign or waste products: tissue debris, whole blood, and other elements of the hematoma.

The initial phase of the inflammatory response is a slowing down of blood flow. This allows the white cells in the blood stream to move to the walls of the blood vessel where they stick to both the blood vessel walls and to each other. Next, the permeability of the vessel increases and the white cells begin to work their way through the vessel wall into the tissue spaces. From here they move to the injury site to begin the process of cleaning up the area. Cleanup is performed by white cells known as macrophages which phagocytize (ingest and digest) elements of the hematoma. The digested particles can then be absorbed into the blood stream or into a lymphatic vessel to be carried away.

As a result of this decreased circulation, however, the delivery of oxygen to the area of the injury is also decreased. Tissue cells that escaped the trauma now suffer from lack of oxygen, and if severe enough, will undergo death from hypoxia. Remnants of cells that undergo this secondary hypoxic injury add to the remnants of the primary traumatic injury and the hemorrhaged blood to increase the size of the hematoma. Thus the total injury is greater than that caused directly by the trauma (6).

Pain and muscle spasm generally accompany musculoskeletal injuries to some degree. Pain is caused by damage to nerve fibers and/or by pressure on nerve fibers from the hematoma. Muscle spasm is a bodily mechanism intended to protect an injured area from further injury. The body attempts to splint or brace the area around the injured tissues. As muscle spasm develops it causes increased pressure on the nerve endings thus increasing pain. The body responds to the increased pain by increasing muscle spasm, which increases pain, etc. This is appropriately called the "pain-spasm-pain" cycle.

REPAIR AND HEALING

Repair of the injury site begins when enough of the hematoma has been removed to permit ingrowth of new tissue (i.e., fibrous connective tissue and new blood vessels). The formation of new tissues to replace those tissues that were damaged requires building materials and energy. Oxygen is essential to the production of that energy. Since both oxygen and the building materials are supplied by the blood, a great network of capillaries is developed. As the capillary network advances, fibrils of connective tissue are laid down haphazardly at first, then organized later so that they lie parallel to the direction of greatest stress. As they are organized the wound or injured area becomes stronger.

Heat treatments have been used extensively in Physical Therapy and Sports Medicine to aid rehabilitation. Locally applied heat causes an increase in local tissue temperature. In an attempt to prevent thermal damage (cooking the tissues) the body increases blood flow to the area. The increased blood flow carries the heat away, but at the same time it carries away increased amounts of tissue debris and delivers increased amounts of oxygen and nutrients to the injury site. Thus heat treatments promote healing by speeding up the body's natural repair processes. The only problem with using heat is that if used too soon it will increase secondary hypoxic injury and swelling (10).

PHYSIOLOGICAL EFFECT OF COLD APPLICATIONS

The physiological effect of ice has been a popular topic recently in both Sports Medicine and Coaching Journals. Many excellent reviews of the subject have been written (9). Authors have written that cold causes: an anesthetic effect, decreased muscle spasm, increased relaxation, interruption of the pain-spasm-pain cycle, decreased metabolism, decreased circulation, and increased circulation. These various effects can be summarized into five basic effects.

1. Decreased pain
2. Decreased muscle spasm
3. Decreased metabolism
4. Decreased circulation
5. Increased circulation

Circulatory Effects. The circulatory effects of ice have received the greatest attention in the Sports Medicine literature, however this literature is very confusing. One is lead to believe that if ice is applied during the immediate care phase it controls swelling by decreasing circulation, but if applied during the rehabilitation phase it promotes healing by increasing circulation. Will cold decrease circulation one day and then increase circulation the next day, just because the trainer's reason for applying it has changed? Reason would say this is absurd, yet many intelligent people are unknowingly advocating just such reasoning.

A number of respected trainers have attributed the success of cryokinetics to cold induced vasodilitation, a process whereby cold increases circu-

lation (12). Cold induced vasodil[...] shown to occur, but in special situatio[...] in the face, fingertips, around the brea[...] genital areas; areas that are prone to fros[...] — indeed, it appears to be a protective mechanism to guard against frostbite (8). Thus far, no one has demonstrated an increase in blood flow as a result of therapeutic cold applications. Knight and Londeree (7) have shown, however, that hydrocollator colpaks (chilled to 17°C) applied to the ankle cause a decrease in ankle blood flow. Blood flow progressively decreased during the 25 minutes that the cold packs were applied (one on top and one under the ankle). Blood flow continued to decrease for 20 minutes after the cold packs were removed.

Decreased Pain and Spasm. Although the circulatory effects of cold have received the greatest attention in Sports Medicine, the other effects of cold may prove to be more important. Cold applications are very effective in decreasing pain and muscular spasm, which lead to earlier mobilization and use of an injured body part (Fig. 1).

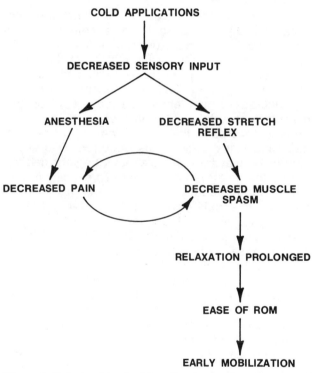

Figure 1. *Relationship of cold applications to Pain, Spasm, and Mobilization.*

As illustrated in Figure 1, local application of cold causes a decrease in sensory nerve input, or in other words, a decrease in impulses from the sensory nerves in the area of the cold application. This results in both a relative local anesthesia and in a decreased stretch reflex. The local anesthesia causes a decreased pain sensation and the decreased stretch reflex results in decreased muscle spasm. Decreased pain allows muscle spasm to decrease and the decreased muscle spasm allows pain to decrease; thus the pain-spasm-pain cycle is broken. The decreased muscle spasm prolongs relaxation of the muscle which allows easier range mobilization and use of

[...]he physiological aspect of [...]scussed least in the Sports [...] its effect on cellular metabo[...] [...]e cellular energy needs thereby [...]e requirements for oxygen. In a [...]d tissues undergo a partial hibernatio[...] [...]ows down or stops many of the function[...] [...]e individual cells within the cooled tissue. As t[...]e function of the cell decreases their energy requirements are lessened and thus the tissue needs less oxygen. This especially is important during the immediate care phase of sports injury care (6).

IMMEDIATE CARE OF INJURIES

Ice, compression and elevation are used almost universally for immediate care of sports injuries; to control swelling and decrease the magnitude of the hematoma. Generally it has been reported that ice controls swelling by decreasing circulation, however, this idea needs to be examined more closely.

The previous discussion of an acute musculoskeletal injury pointed out that a hematoma was composed of material from four sources: cellular debris from primary traumatic injury, cellular debris from secondary hypoxic injury, whole blood from hemorrhaging, and fluid from edema formation. Will decreased circulation have any effect on primary traumatic injury? No. In fact, nothing can be done to decrease the magnitude of the primary traumatic injury once it has occurred. Decreased circulation may have some effect on hemorrhaging, but by the time the injury has been examined, and ice applied (usually 3-5 minutes), the clotting mechanism should have sealed the ruptured blood vessels and stopped the hemorrhaging.

Decreased circulation will not decrease the magnitude of secondary hypoxic injury, but ice will. Decreased circulation (caused by the damaged vasculature and inflammatory reaction) and the resultant lack of oxygen is the cause of the secondary hypoxic injury. Ice, however, decreases the metabolism of the cells so they don't need the oxygen that isn't there. The cells in the injured area that escaped destruction by the trauma are "put into hibernation" by the cold applications. This allows the cells to survive the period of hypoxia brought on by vascular collapse. The result is less damaged tissue which means a smaller area to be repaired, and also a smaller hematoma to be removed, which allows repair to begin sooner (Fig. 2). The result is less damaged tissue, a smaller hematoma to be removed, and a smaller area to be repaired.

Edema can be controlled or decreased by increasing the tissue pressure outside the blood vessel and by decreasing the hydrostatic pressure within the blood vessel. This is accomplished by compression and elevation. An elastic wrap or elastic tape provides compression to the body part which in turn increases the pressure outside of the

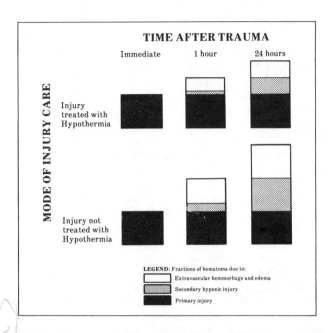

Figure 2. *Development of a hematoma following an acute musculoskeletal injury. In contrast with the lower model (no ice application), the upper model illustrates the effect that immediate ice application has on each fraction of the hematoma. Relative size of the fractions of the hematoma is not implied by this model. (Reprinted by permission from Knight KL: The Effects of Hypothermia on Inflmation and Swelling. Athletic Training 11:70-10, 1976.)*

blood vessel. Elevation decreases the hydrostatic pressure inside of the vessel. Both of these factors tend to decrease edema. In addition to compression and elevation, the decreased tissue debris (resulting from controlling secondary hypoxic injury) decreases tissue oncotic pressure which also helps to control edema.

The use of ice, compression, and elevation for initial care of sports injuries is indicated. The beneficial effects of ice appear to result from decreased tissue metabolism rather than decreased circulation. Ice also is beneficial at this stage in decreasing pain and muscle spasm, which usually accompany sports injury.

USES OF ICE FOR RECONDITIONING

Ice is becoming increasingly popular as a therapeutic modality. In 1964, Grant (3) and Haden (4) introduced a procedure of ice application followed by exercise which they called cryokinetics. As a physician-physical therapist team, they had developed the procedure to treat assorted musculoskeletal injuries at Brooke Army Hospital. Their clinical successes were quite dramatic and the procedure was soon adopted by athletic trainers. The procedure was very effective in treating athletic injuries, allowing athletes to return to competition much sooner than when treated with conventional heat therapies (5). For instance, injuries that required 1–2 weeks of treatment with heat modalities often responded after only 2–4 days of cryokinetics treatment, although not all treatments were this dramatic.

Three theories have been postulated to explain the clinical success of cryokinetics. Grant (3) felt that exercise and restoration of normal function in the injured area was the key to the success of cryokinetics; ice was simply an adjunct measure utilized to relieve pain and allow early motion. Behnke (1) proposed the cold induced vasodilitation theory. After an initial period of vasoconstriction cold would cause an increase in blood flow that was 3–4 times normal blood flow. Edwards (2) introduced the reflex vasodilitation theory. According to this theory, for up to 60 minutes after removal of the cold packs, blood flow would increase to levels greater than heat pack application.

The cold induced vasodilitation theory has had the greatest acceptance in sports medicine, however, as mentioned above, Knight and Londeree (7) found that there was no cold induced vasodilitation during 25 minutes of cold pack application to the ankle; nor was there a reflex vasodilitation during the 20 minutes following cold pack application. In the same study cryokinetics was compared to a heat pack treatment and found to result in a significantly greater increase in blood flow. During the cryokinetic treatment blood flow decreased during the initial 13-minute cold pack application but increased greatly during and after exercise (walking on a treadmill). Grant's (3) theory appears to be the most viable. Exercise and active motion rehabilitate an injured area; ice acts only to decrease pain and allow active motion.

SUMMARY

Ice is effective in both phases of acute injury care: for immediate care and during rehabilitation. Locally, ice causes decreased circulation, decreased muscle spasm, decreased pain, and decreased metabolism. The effect of decreasing metabolism is most important during immediate care. Tissue cells in the area of the injury, that escaped damage by trauma, are able to withstand secondary hypoxic injury if their metabolism is decreased. This decreases the total amount of damage and minimizes the effects of the injury. Decreasing pain and muscle spasm are important during rehabilitation. The ice induced anesthesia allows pain-free active exercise which in turn increases blood flow to the injury site. The increased blood flow carries away the hematoma and delivers oxygen and nutrients to be used in rebuilding the injured tissue.

PART II. TECHNIQUES & PROCEDURES

Proper use of cryotherapy during both immediate care and rehabilitation can make a difference of up to three weeks in an athlete's recovery from sports injury. Cryotherapy means literally cold therapy, so any therapeutic use of cold would be considered cryotherapy. In this article three specific cryotherapeutic techniques are discussed: immediate care, cryokinetics, and cryostretch. The rationale upon which each of these techniques is based was presented in a previous article.

IMMEDIATE CARE

An acute musculoskeletal injury should be treated with ice, compression, and elevation within five minutes after the injury occurs. During the initial five minutes the injury should be elevated and the

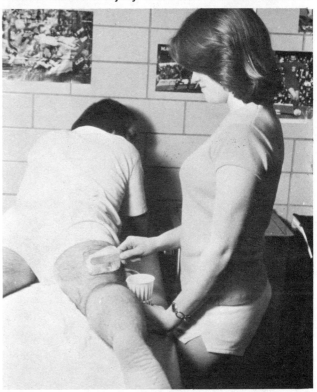

Figure 3. *Trainer applying ice massage.*

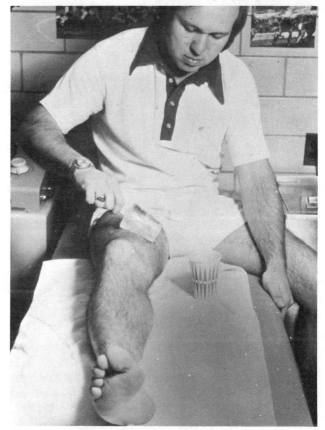

Figure 4. *Athlete giving ice massage to self.*

55

Figure 5. *Ice immersion technique.*

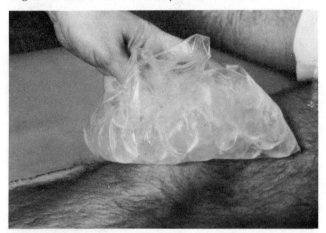

Figure 6. *Application of ice bag.*

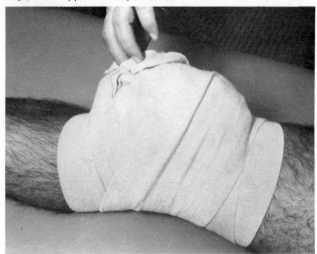

Figure 7. *Application of compression wrap over ice bag.*

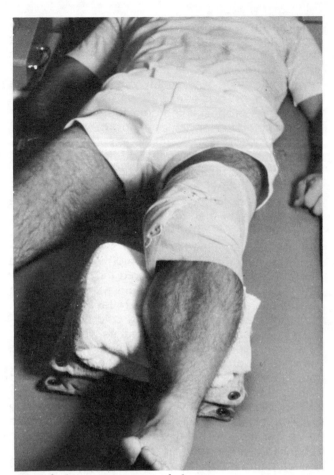

Figure 8. *Ice, compression, and elevation.*

athlete moved from the playing field, court, rink, etc. Ice and compression should be applied before moving the athlete to an infirmary, hospital, training room, or doctor's office. The sooner the ice is applied, the more effective it will be in retarding secondary hypoxic injury.

The most convenient form of ice application is an ice bag, made from cubed or crushed ice in a plastic bag, secured with a piece of wire "twisty." One-gallon plastic food "baggies" seem to be an ideal size. Plastic bags are relatively inexpensive and

can be reused numerous times.

Other forms of cold application for immediate care include ice packs, ice caps, ethyl chloride spray, and chemical "cold" packs. Ice packs are formed by wrapping crushed or cubed ice in a towel. It is used the same as an ice bag, but becomes very messy when the ice begins to melt and drip. An ice cap is a molded rubber bag with a plastic cap that will screw off and on. There is no difference in usage between an ice cap and an ice bag, except the caps cost a lot more. If an athlete fails to return an ice bag you haven't lost much, but most training supplies budgets would be hard pressed to replace many ice caps. Ethyl chloride spray evaporates quickly after being sprayed on the body, thus cooling the body part. It was quite popular in the 1950's and 60's; however, there is a danger of frostbite if too much is sprayed on, and the cooling effect does not last nearly long enough. Chemical "cold" packs are convenient to use, but are relatively expensive. In addition they are neither as cold nor as long lasting as ice bags. Of the many forms of cold application, ice bags appear to be the most convenient and least expensive.

As mentioned earlier, ice should be applied as soon as possible after the injury. This necessitates having ice bags available at the field or gym. The time taken to transport an injured athlete from the field to a training room could make a difference in the recovery time of one or two days. One- or two-gallon plastic double-walled water coolers are excellent for storing ice bags on the field or court. Ice bags can be made up and put into the cooler before practice. Even on the hottest day the cooler will keep the ice bags from melting during practice. Small styrofoam chests are not as sturdy as plastic water coolers, but they are as effective as the coolers in keeping the ice bags from melting.

Initially the ice bag should be applied for 30 minutes and then removed. After 1½ hours it should be reapplied for an additional 30 minutes. Throughout the evening the ice should be on for ½ an hour and off for 1½ hours. Ice need not be applied overnight. Unfortunately, the ice would melt within an hour or so and if the bag breaks, it would spill over the bed. A good night's sleep is more important than the extra ice application. The following day the injury should be reevaluated and a reconditioning program started.

CRYOKINETICS IN RECONDITIONING

The goal of reconditioning is full functional use of the injured part. Since normal motion is usually limited, or even impossible, for several days following injury, cryokinetics is an extremely valuable treatment modality. During cryokinetics (which means ice and motion), ice is used to partially anesthetize or numb the injured area so that active motion is possible.

Ice can be applied to the injured area in a number of ways. For foot, ankle, hand, and forearm injuries, ice immersion is the preferred form of application. A five-gallon bucket or a deep plastic dish pan is filled with cold tap water and crushed or cubed ice. The athlete then immerses her/his injured part into the ice water, which should be deep enough that the injured body part is at least one inch below the water level. For larger body parts ice is applied with an ice pack, ice bag, or by ice massage.

Ice massage utilizes a large cube of ice; made by freezing water in 6– 8–ounce paper cup. A "popsicle" can be made by placing a tongue depressor in the cup, so that after the water freezes the ice cube has a handle. If the tongue depressor is not used, a towel should be wrapped around the ice cube so that the applicator's fingers are protected during application. During application the ice cube is gently rubbed over the affected area with even rhythmical strokes. A towel placed under the affected area will soak up the water from the melting ice cube and decrease the mess of ice massage.

Ice application lasts for approximately 10–15 minutes, however, the sensations felt by the athlete determine the length of treatment. The first sensation felt by the athlete will be appreciation of the cold or pain. For many this pain will be very intense during their first session. The athlete should be told beforehand that it will be painful and the trainer-therapist should remain with them during the first session to "talk them through it." The first treatment is almost always the worst. After the first application of ice the body adapts to the ice and succeeding applications are usually not as painful.

TABLE 1
SUMMARY OF CRYOKINETIC PROGRAM

1. Make sure the injury has been evaluated by a physician or trainer.
2. Apply ice to the injured areas by:
   a. Immersion in ice water
   b. Massage with ice cubes (made in 6–8 oz. paper cups)
   c. Ice bag (ice in plastic bag)
   d. Ice packs (ice folded in a towel)
3. The ice application lasts through four sensations (approximately 10–15 minutes):
   a. Appreciation of cold-pain
   b. Warming
   c. Ache or throbbing
   d. Relative skin anesthesia-numbness
4. Exercise the area (as explained below) as long as it remains numb (approximately 3 minutes).
5. Reapply the ice until numbness is again reached (approximately 3–5 minutes).
6. Exercise . . . ice . . . exercise . . . ice
7. The injured area should be exercised, with numbness in between, at least 5 times during each treatment.
8. Exercising, not the ice, causes rehabilitation. The ice numbs the area and makes it possible to exercise pain free.
9. Principles of cryokinetic exercising:
   a. All exercising should be active — performed by the patient.
   b. Exercise must be graded; that is begin with range of motion exercises and progress through increasing levels of difficulty. Full sport activity is the final level of activity.
   c. Go through a complete range of motion (or as much as is possible) during all exercise.
   d. Let pain be your guide. Never use an exercise or motion that causes pain. If a particular exercise does cause pain return to the former activity level.
10. A complete cryokinetic session consists of:
    a. 10–15 minutes ice application for initial numbness
    b. Five exercise bouts with numbness in between
    c. Each exercise bout consists of active exercises during the numbness (about 3 minutes).

This adaption appears to be physiological, as a person who has adapted to the cold in one foot will experience extreme pain during the initial session with their other foot.

Ice immersion seems to be more painful than ice massage, but should be used for the hand and foot nonetheless. It has been suggested that wearing a sock will lessen the pain but we have not found that to be the case. Some place a plastic bag around the foot and ankle so that the water does not come into direct contact with the skin. Others feel that if the athlete places both feet in the ice water it will lessen the pain. None of these methods will decrease the pain enough to make much difference. The important thing is to talk to the athlete during her/his initial ice application session. Explain the technique; let the athlete know what is going on; explain how the pain will help rehabilitate their injury and that the next time ice is applied pain will be almost negligible. Talking to the athlete about anything will help take her/his mind off the pain, but also by informing the athlete of the technique also will make the pain easier to endure.

The pain experience will last for 6–8 minutes (in the average case). The athlete will then feel a warming sensation. This may be the absence of pain, but most will report that if feels like the treated part is getting warm. This sensation lasts only a minute or so and is then replaced with a slight throbbing or tingling sensation. Finally, the athlete feels a numbness. For some this is not a definite sensation; it is just an absence of any other sensation. This numbness is not a total anesthesia as would be caused by an injection of xylocain. Tactile sensation still exists and if the athlete is overzealous in her/his exercise she/he will feel pain before further injury occurs.

With numbness the athlete is ready to begin exercising. The type of exercise program used will depend on the type of injury, severity of injury, and the sport of the athlete. All exercise should be performed pain-free and should progress as fast as possible from active range of motion to full participation in the athlete's sport. For some grade I or mild injuries the program is completed after two days. For more serious injuries it often takes three to four weeks. Continual progressive exercise and pain are the keys. As long as activity is pain-free, the athete should be encouraged to increase her/his level of activity. If an activity is painful the athlete should drop back to a lower level of activity.

As an example, for a sprained ankle, after the ankle is numbed the athlete should take the ankle out of the water and move it through a full range of motion (or as much as possible). Plantar and dorsiflexion, inversion-eversion, and circumduction should be performed. After 2–3 minutes the numbness will begin to wear off. At that point exercise should be discontinued, and the ankle renumbed by placing it back into the ice bucket. The second numbness will occur within three to five minutes, and as explained above, the pain will not be nearly as great as during the initial session. The athlete should exercise for the duration of the second numbness (approximately three minutes). She/he alternates numbing and exercising for a total of four to six exercise bouts.

With most ankle sprains the athlete will be able to stand on the ankle and perform weight bearing range of motion exercises during the second exercise bout. If possible the athlete should also begin walking during the second or third exercise bout. Walking must be done pain-free and without a limp. Succeeding levels of activity are: Walking briskly,

TABLE 2
SUMMARY OF CRYOSTRETCH PROGRAM
1. Make sure the injury has been evaluated by a physician or trainer.
2. Apply ice to the injured areas by:
   a. Immersion in ice water
   b. Massage with ice cubes (made in 6–8 oz. paper cups)
   c. Ice bag (ice in plastic bag)
   d. Ice packs (ice folded in a towel)
3. The ice application lasts through four sensations (approximately 10 minutes):
   a. Appreciation of cold-pain
   b. Warming
   c. Ache or throbbing
   d. Relative skin anesthesia-numbness
4. Exercise the area as explained in #9 below.
5. Reapply the ice until numbness is again reached (approximately 3–5 minutes).
6. Exercise . . . ice . . . exercise . . . ice
7. The injured area should be exercised, with numbness in between 3 times during each treatment.
8. Exercising, not the ice, causes rehabilitation. The ice numbs the area and makes it possible to exercise pain free.
9. Cryostretch exercise
   a. Both passive and active exercise will be used.
   b. Trainer passively stretches the muscle by moving the affected limb until the athlete begins to feel tightness and/or pain.
   c. Trainer holds the limb in that position for 20 seconds.
   d. Athlete actively contracts the affected muscle for 5 seconds. Begin slowly and build up to a maximal contraction. Trainer provides resistance so that the limb does not move.
   e. Athlete relaxes the contraction. Trainer moves the limb until the athlete feels tightness and/or pain. (Range of motion should be greater than in step b.) Hold for 10 seconds.
   f. Contract-relax-move limb and hold — contract-relax-move limb and hold, i.e., repeat steps c, d & e twice.
   g. Return limb to anatomical position and rest for 20 seconds.
   h. Repeat steps b-g.
   i. Apply ice for 3–5 minutes.
10. A complete cryostretch session consists of:
    a. 10–15-minute ice application for initial numbness
    b. Three bouts of exercise with numbness in between.
    c. Each exercise bout consists of two 65-second repetitions of static stretch — static contraction with 20-second rest in between.

straight ahead jogging, jogging in a lazy "S" pattern, running a lazy "S," five- to ten-yard sprints, sharp "S" running, planting and cutting, team drills at ¾ speed, team drills at full speed. Progression through these exercises should proceed as fast as possible, providing it's done pain-free. The main points of cryokinetics are summarized in Table I.

As the injury heals the numbness will not be needed to allow active motion and the ice applications can be discontinued. After complete function has returned the athlete should be placed on a weight program to strengthen the injured body part, and thus help prevent reinjury. Even though an athlete may "feel fine" and be able to perform well, she/he is susceptible to reinjury until the body part is stronger than prior to the injury.

Most joint injuries (i.e., sprains and strains) respond very well to cryokinetics. With injuries where there is muscle spasm (for instance, accompanying most muscle pulls) the exercises should be aimed at relieving the spasm. Cryostretching utilizes both cold applications and stretching exercises to relieve muscular spasm.

CRYOSTRETCH FOR RELIEF OF MUSCLE SPASM

Ice massage or ice bags generally are used for cryostretch. A whirlpool filled with water and ice can be used, but this cools the whole limb. Since only the injured muscle group needs to be cooled, the immersion method cools a great deal more tissue than is necessary. The length of application is the same as with cryokinetics, i.e., until numbness is achieved.

Whereas only active exercises are used for cryokinetics, both active and passive exercises are used during cryostretching. Exercises consist of a combination of static stretching (passive) and the contract-relax technique of proprioceptive neuromuscular facilitation (active).

The exercise begins with a 20-second static stretch and is followed by alternating 3-second static contractions and 12-second static stretches; three of each. The muscle is then allowed to rest for 20 seconds and the above procedure is repeated. As an example, consider a contused or pulled hamstring that results in a spasmed hamstring. With the athlete on his back the trainer passively flexes the hip (keeping the knee extended) until the athlete begins to feel tightness or pain. The limb is held at this point for 20 seconds, during which the fibers within the muscle will relax and lengthen a little. With the limb held in the same position, the athlete next contracts the hamstrings for three seconds. The contraction must begin slowly and build up to a maximal contraction. The trainer must provide enough resistance that there is

no movement. After the athlete relaxes her/his hamstring from this static contraction the trainer moves the limb (flexes the hip) until the athlete begins to feel tightness or pain. The static stretch is held for 12 seconds after the contraction. Three-second hamstring contractions are performed a second and third time with 12-second static stretches following each one. After each contraction the muscle should relax to a greater degree than it was prior to the contraction. By "taking up the slack" after each contraction the muscle will also relax a little after each static stretch. Following the third 12-second static contraction the trainer passively extends the hip, or returns the leg to rest on the table. The muscle is allowed to rest for 20–30 seconds and then the complete exercise routine is repeated. Each cryostretch exercise bout consists of two repetitions of the 65-second static stretch-static contraction routine. A treatment session consists of three exercise bouts with numbness in between (Table 2).

SUMMARY

In an athlete, "lost time" due to injury can be decreased considerably through the proper use of cryotherapy. Within five minutes after an injury an ice bag should be applied to the injury site and secured with an elastic bandage. The ice application should last for about 30 minutes and should be repeated every two hours.

Cryokinetics and cryostretch are two reconditioning techniques which utilize cold applications. During cryokinetics cold numbs the injured area so that active motion is possible. The active motion leads to injury healing. During cryostretch both ice and static stretching are utilized to decrease muscle spasm.

REFERENCES

1. Behnke, R. Cryotherapy and vasodilitation. *Athl Training* 8:106, 133-137, 1973.
2. Edwards, A.G. Increasing circulation — with cold. *J Nat Athl Trainers Assoc* 6(1):15-16, 1971.
3. Grant, A.E. Massage with ice (cryokinetics) in the treatment of painful conditions of the musculoskeletal system. *Arch Phys Med Rehab* 45:233-238, 1964.
4. Hayden, C. Cryokinetics in an early treatment program. *J Am Phys Ther Assoc* 44:990-993, 1964.
5. Juvenal, J.P. Cryokinetics, a new concept in the treatment of injuries. *Sch Coach* 35 (May): 40-42, 1966.
6. Knight, K.L. The effects of hypothermia on inflammation and swelling. *Athl Training* 11:7-10, 1976.
7. Knight, K.L., Londeree, B.R. Comparison of blood flow in normal subjects during therapeutic applications of heat, cold, and exercise. *Med Sci Sports* 9:62, 1977.
8. Fox, R.H., Whyatt, H.T. Cold-induced vasodilitation in various areas of the body surface of man. *J Physiol* 162:289-297, 1962.
9. Olson, J.E., Stravino, V.D. A review of cryotherapy. *Phys Ther* 52:840-853, 1972.
10. Stillwell, G.K. General principles of thermotherapy. in Licht S (ed): *Therapeutic Heat and Cold* 2nd ed. New Haven, Conn: E. Licht. 1965, p. 232-239.

Therapeutic Exercise for Injury Prevention and Injury Care

Dennis Aten, M.S., R.P.T., A.T.C.

Although therapeutic exercise is only one area in injury prevention, it is felt that it is probably the most neglected area of health care. It is our purpose here to discuss this area generally and give a few specifics regarding the prevention and care of some of the more common injuries.

Although many coaches develop off-season weight and conditioning programs, these programs are usually designed primarily for skill improvement. There is nothing wrong with this; however, it is suggested that this also should include strength and flexibility workouts on injury areas most common to the particular sport. Football coaches usually attempt to develop strong legs, back and shoulders in their players. For knee injury prevention, however, a more specific approach is necessary. Not only should strength be developed in all the muscles crossing the knee joint, but it is es-

sential that specific muscles and specific ranges of motion be emphasized. For instance, in one study at Eastern Illinois University most college football players could extend their knee against more than 75 pounds of resistance; however, many of them could not achieve complete extension with 20 pounds resistance. This range of motion factor is critical in knee injury prevention. To insure that individuals exercise specific areas of their own vulnerability, pre-season testing becomes an important part of an injury prevention program. Therefore, it is essential that quadriceps strength programs include the final 5-15 degrees of motion in knee extension. Eastern Illinois University routinely tests ankle strength, vastus medialis strength (the quadriceps muscle mostly involved with the last 10-15 degrees of knee extension), general hamstring strength, and hamstring flexibility.

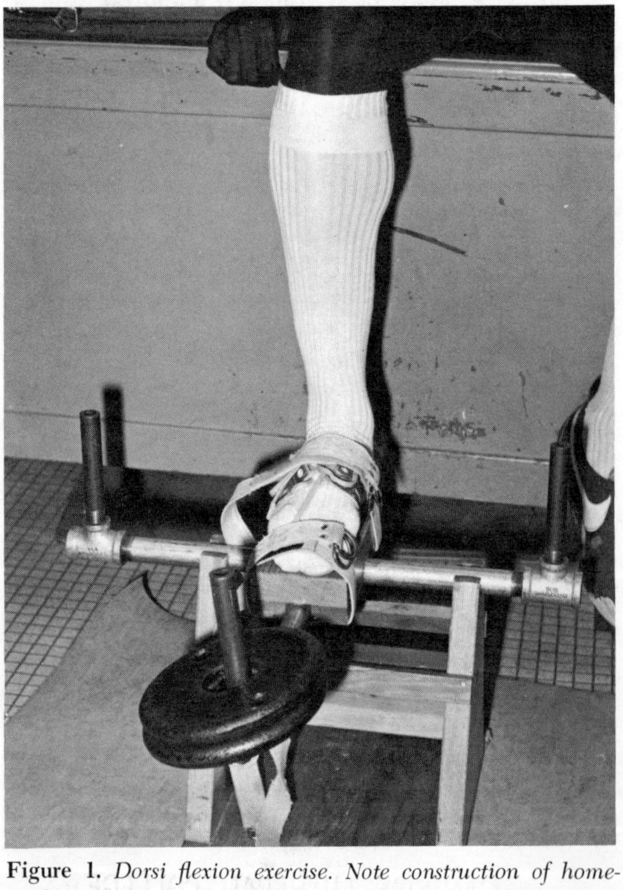

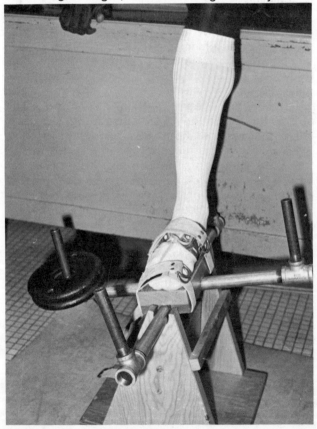

Figure 1. *Dorsi flexion exercise. Note construction of homemade apparatus.*

Figure 2. *Eversion exercise. Note construction of homemade apparatus.*

The ankle strength is tested on a homemade version of an elgin ankle exerciser. (Fig. 1 & 2) Dorsiflexion (bringing the back of the foot upward, toward the knee) and eversion (turning the sole of the foot outward) are the two ranges of motion most critical. Arbitrarily it is recommended that an athlete be able to evert at least 15 pounds and dorsiflex at least 20 pounds when tested. Any athlete testing less should be put on an exercise program.

Strength testing for the vastus medialis can be done with any of the various weight resistance methods used for knee extension. (Fig. 3, 4, 5, & 6)

Figure 4. *Knee extension.*

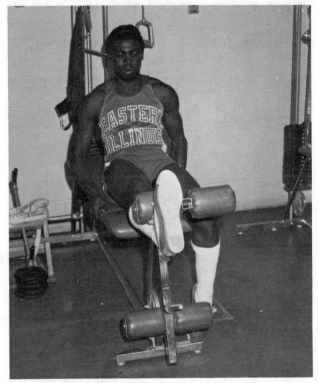

Figure 3. *Knee extension.*

Leg press apparatus should not be used because it also utilizes hip extension and does not isolate knee extension. This author also prefers weight resistance rather than the isokinetic machines. It is difficult to test or resist, at maximum levels, complete knee extension on these machines. Arbitrary standards require that his/her athlete be able to lift 1/3 of his/her body weight ten times through complete extension. Complete extension is always emphasized.

Hamstring strength can usually be tested using the same resistance apparatus that was used in knee extension. (Fig. 7 & 8) This knee flexion exercise usually requires at least ten repetitions of 1/6 of body weight for a minimum test.

Hamstring flexibility is tested in a general manner that does not isolate the hamstring muscles. Unfortunately, back extensor muscles are also involved in this test. This presents no problem if we are merely concerned with the function of bending and touching one's toes. It does pose a problem in dealing with potential or actual ham-

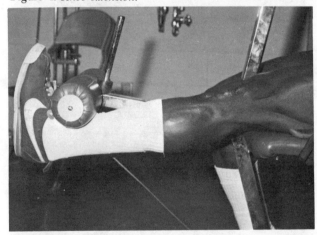

Figure 5. *Knee locked in extension.*

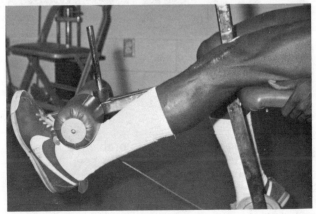

Figure 6. *Knee not locked in extension — If the athlete cannot extend the knee more than this, resistance should be lowered until athlete can extend the knee as in Figure 5.*

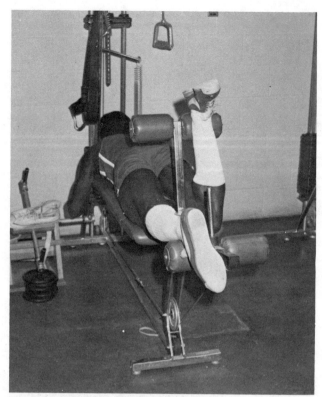

Figure 7. *Knee flexion.*

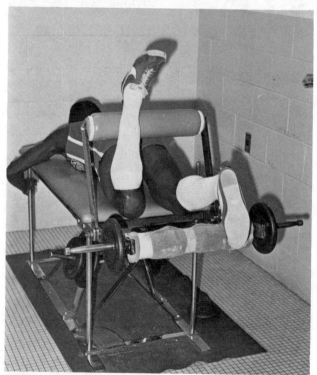

Figure 8. *Knee flexion.*

string injuries. To diminish this problem it is important to emphasize that the athlete keep his back straight when testing or exercising. Eastern Illinois University tests their athletes' hamstring flexibility utilizing a homemade wooden box with a yardstick nailed across the top. (Fig. 9 & 10) The athlete sits on a table with knees straight and soles of feet (shoes off) flat against the box. He then reaches

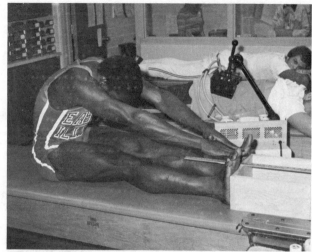

Figure 9. *Hamstring flexibility test.*

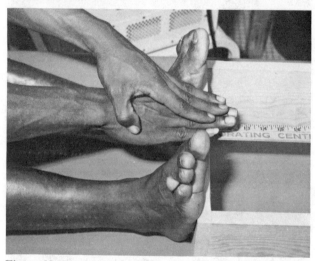

Figure 10. *Hamstring flexibility test. Note the yardstick measurement.*

forward to touch the yardstick with both hands. The yardstick reading where it is touched is an index of that athlete's flexibility. Our "flexibility boxes" are constructed with the 10″ mark on the yardstick placed on the edge of the box where the feet will touch. Arbitrarily we use 12 inches as a minimum test.

Hopefully, with more universal testing, there will eventually be more objective data on which to determine minimal test standards.

When testing is completed, athletes are given therapeutic exercises to meet their needs. There are basically three reasons that we insist that athletes complete our exercise programs.

1) The athlete could not meet our minimal standards on the pre-test.
2) The athlete has a history of an injury to the area with subsequent problems.
3) The athlete has a current injury to a given area.

Since we are dealing with injury or commonly injured areas, there are several principles that should be closely followed relating to all these exercise programs. It may not be necessary to follow these principles in general conditioning programs, but it is felt that they are essential when dealing with injury. These principles should not be considered the final word in therapeutic exercise. This is just one author's attempt to organize some concepts in athletic therapeutic exercise.

Strength Therapeutic Exercise Principles

1) *Isolate the muscle*

In exercise that attempts to strengthen for injury prevention, it is necessary that the precise muscle in question be exercised. Gross motor movements are not adequate. Oftentimes, an athlete will use an uninjured or stronger muscle to substitute for an injured or weaker muscle. This must be prevented by proper positioning and supervision.

2) *Keep Resistance Under Control*

Although maximum efforts should be emphasized, it is important that the resistance should be kept at levels where the athlete has complete control during all phases of the exercise.

3) *Do Not Allow Momentum to Substitute for Muscular Work*

There are two major problems when momentum is introduced to therapeutic exercise. Athletes get a false sense of achievement when momentum is allowed to assist in the movement of a resistance. A greater problem lies in potential aggravation of an injury site. When momentum accelerates movement, there is often a jerking or recoiling effect felt at the terminal range of motion. This can aggravate joint linings and retard healing.

4) *Exercise Should Be Pain Free*

This probably is the most important principle. Any time pain occurs, especially in the injury area, there are potential hazards of healing regression and inflammatory buildup. Therapeutic exercise can usually be started as soon after injury as they can be done pain free.

5) *Require Complete Range of Motion*

If the exercise is attempting to strengthen muscles to assist in stabilizing a joint, then full range of motion must be attained. If the exercise is attempting to strengthen a defect in the muscle, complete range of motion of that particular muscle must be attained.

6) *Overload Level*

To gain strength, maximum resistances must be used. Consideration of some of the other principles may require more time than usual to be able to reach overload levels.

7) *Gradualism*

Progress in these exercises should not be expected overnight. It takes a long time to develop strength. It should also be noted that reaching minimum standards is not a sign to stop the exercise. Excellence is never attained using minimal standards.

There are no magic numbers involved in therapeutic exercise for repetition or resistance. Utilizing some aspect of DeLorme's theory is most widely accepted. This program utilizes three sets of ten repetitions. The first set uses 1/2 of the maximum resistance that can be handled by a specific athlete. The second set uses 3/4 of maximum. The third set uses the maximum resistance that the athlete can handle ten times. The first two sets are used to accomplish warm-up.

Another variation is the DAPRRE (daily adjustable progressive resistive reconditioning exercise) program devised by Knight at New York State University at Brockport. This program recognizes that a person can regain strength which has been lost during immobilization or inactivity much more quickly than they developed the strength originally. The key to the DAPRRE program is that there is an objective means of increasing resistance as the athlete becomes stronger. The first two sets are for warm-up and muscle reeducation. They consist of 5 repetitions each at 1/2 and 3/4 of the working weight. On the third set the athlete is instructed to do as many full pain-free repetitions as possible with the full working weight. The working weight is then adjusted for the next day according to the number of repetitions achieved during the third set. (i.e., if less than 5 are performed the working weight is decreased for the next day; if more than 7 repetitions are performed, then the working weight is increased.)

Flexibility Therapeutic Exercise Principles

1) *Isolate the Muscle*

As in strength programs, it must be ascertained that the muscle intended is the one being placed on a stretch.

2) *Allow No Ballistics Motion*

Bouncing motions may be fine for warm-up on healthy muscles but have no place in rehabilitation or flexibility programs. Bouncing may cause further damage to weakened soft tissue areas. It also causes a stretch reflex which retards the development of flexibility.

3) *Stretch to Tolerance*

A static stretch for flexibility should only be done to the extent that it is not painful to the athlete. These exercises are not designed to be torture. The athlete should feel a definite stretch which may be somewhat uncomfortable, but should never go to extremes of pain.

4) *Allow the Stretched Muscle to Relax*

When stretching muscle, it is most effective if that muscle can be in a relaxed state. This can usually be attained if the antagonistic (opposite) muscle is contracting. Positioning is also important. The muscle to be stretched should never be positioned in a way that requires it to stabilize the body.

5) *Practice Gradualism*

Flexibility takes a long time to develop. Fifteen minutes of "stretching" prior to practice does not condition an athlete's flexibility for practice any more than lifting weights prior to practice makes an athlete strong for practice. Good flexibility programs should be year around. The efforts today will probably not show their effects until next season.

Warm-Up Vs. Flexibility

A brief statement should be made regarding the relative aspects of flexibility and warm-up. With the recent emphasis on flexibility, some coaches have gone to a flexibility program in lieu of warm-up. This is not totally wise. Warm-up exercises should increase body temperature and heart rate. They should prepare an athlete physiologically for physical activity. Flexibility exercises are designed to permanently elongate soft tissue to allow a greater range of motion to be available to the athlete.

Warm-up activities may temporarily increase flexibility but will not progressively develop a more flexible state. Flexibility and warm-up exercises can be done during a prepractice period, but it is important to recognize each area and be sure that both are adequately included.

Five Specific Exercises

In line with the foregoing principles, the following are descriptions of some of the more common therapeutic exercises used in the athletic program at Eastern Illinois University.

1) *The Towel Exercise* (Fig. 11)

This exercise is designed to strengthen muscles in the arch to help protect the foot and arch area from various stress problems. Along with lower leg exercises this exercise is also a helpful adjunct in the prevention and care of "shin splints."

To accomplish the exercise the athlete should sit down with a towel spread out at his feet. With bare feet the athlete utilizes his toes to dig into the towel. The towel is brought steadily under the foot. Other foot muscles can be worked by moving the towel from side to side or by pushing the towel away. Newspaper can be substituted for the towel. Resistance can be increased by placing small weights on the towel. It is recommended that athletes work intensely at this exercise for 3-5 minutes daily.

2) *Elgin Ankle Exerciser* (Fig. 1 & 2)

The foot is strapped securely in place and weights are placed on the desired arm of the apparatus. The athlete is required to raise the weight using foot and ankle movement only. Supervision is necessary to rule out hip and knee movements. Eversion and dorsi-

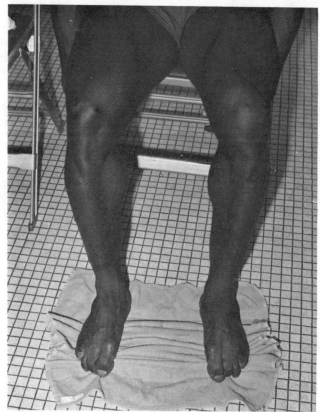

Figure 11. *Towel exercise to strengthen the arch.*

flexion are emphasized in most situations. Inversion can be used for medial leg and ankle problems. Plantar flexion can be obtained more efficiently by doing resisted toe raises.

3) *Ankle Rolls* (Fig. 12, 13, & 14)

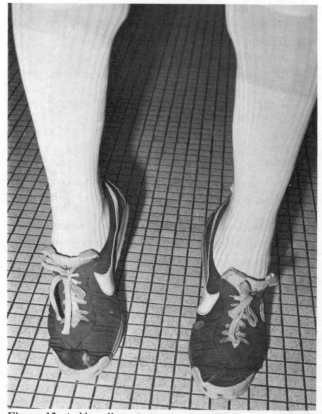

Figure 12. *Ankle rolls — Step 1. Raise on the toes.*

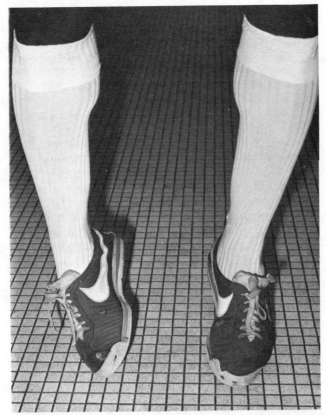

Figure 13. *Ankle rolls — Step 2. Roll slowly to the outside.*

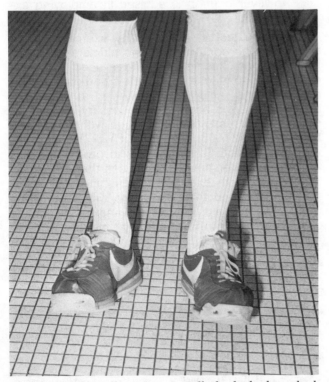

Figure 14. *Ankle rolls — Step 3. Roll slowly back on heels and raise toes as high as possible.*

This exercise is considered the best all around exercise for the ankle and lower leg by this author. Its advantages include no special equipment needed, a broad range of muscles are developed in the area, it is easy to do, and is involved in a kinesthetic experi-

ence. Although there is no research to support the kinesthetic theory, it is believed that high repetition through all the extremes of motion in the ankle will help develop the "position sense." It is felt that many young athletes who chronically sprain their ankles often do so not because of weakness, but because they are unaware of the foot's actual alignment when it makes contact with the ground to support the body weight. The big disadvantage is that it is difficult to measure progress. Measurement of progress is a good motivation device.

4) *Knee Extension* (Fig. 3, 4, 5, & 6)

Knee extension exercises may be done on many different types of machines. Any resistance form requiring work from the quadriceps mechanism will achieve most of the rehab goals. My personal preference is machines using a cable and pulley where the resistance is lifted directly against gravity through the entire range of motion of the exercise. Weighted boots and lever systems with weights attached at the distal portion of the lever are also good; however, the resistance varies throughout the arc of exercise. Nautilus has attempted to counteract various mechanical advantages produced by lever systems but their product is expensive. The many isokinetic machines are also valuable; however, they have two disadvantages. Attempted speed of movement increases the resistance. In knee extension the movement will slow down as terminal extension nears. This means that the resistance is least where strength gain is most essential to protect the knee. Also, isokinetic machines provide resistance in only one direction, when the knee is extending (called concentric contraction). Work must also be done eccentrically to let the weight down slowly when using weighted resistances.

Instructions to athletes doing knee extension exercises should include the following: 1) Sit on the table or machine with both knees flexed at 90°. 2) Extend the knee against the resistance slowly until the knee is "locked" in terminal extension. 3) This contraction should be held for several seconds. There are many methods advising specific amounts of time to hold the contraction. It is not clear at this time if there is any advantage in any particular method. I usually require only 2 or 3 seconds. 4) Let the weight back down slowly. 5) It is all right to lean back or firmly grasp the table during these lifts. This does not allow the athlete to use other muscles to extend the knee. It stabilizes the body so that the resistance does not lift the body off the table. It also decreases the resistance of tight hamstrings. If the athlete has to lean back excessively using light weights resistances, hamstring flexibility should definitely be evaluated.

If there is pain in the joint area or around the patella during exercise the activity should be altered. "Quad setting" or isometric type exercises can be substituted. If the pain occurs only during a certain phase of extension, that part of the exercise can be eliminated. Manual resistance can also be utilized.

Remember that it is most important to "lock" the knee into full extension. It is only during the terminal 10°-20° that the vastus medialis (that portion of the quadriceps most involved in knee stability) is working to full capacity. This can readily be seen by palpating the area during forceful knee extension. (The vastus medialis is the large defined muscle mass just medial and proximal to the kneecap.)

5) *Hamstring Flexibility* (Fig. 15)

Figure 15. *Hamstring flexibility exercise.*

As in all exercises there are many ways to achieve flexibility. If the exercise can meet the general principles it will probably achieve your goals; however, there is a specific exercise for hamstring flexibility that this author recommends more than any other. It requires that the athlete place one foot on a hip high table or other support. (This is often done using the buddy system where the partner cups his hands at hip level and the exerciser's heel rests in the cupped hands.) The toes of the opposite foot must be pointed the same direction as the elevated leg. When the toes turn outward the exercise tends to stretch the adductors more and the hamstrings less. The athlete should then reach forward using the same hand as the elevated leg. A "rule of thumb" goal is to be able to touch the toes with the wrist while the knee is straight. This goal varies as arm and leg length vary. Remember gradualism. It will probably take months (sometimes years) for many athletes to reach this goal. In this exercise the pelvis is prevented from upward rotation which would remove stretch from the hamstrings. Bending down trying to touch the head to the knee utilizes back flexibility and is not recommended for hamstring flexibility exercises.

Usually athletes are instructed to do this exercise ten times with either leg, three to five times per day. At least one set should be supervised. The length of time recommended to hold each stretch varies. At Eastern Illinois only a 3-second hold is required. In principle, however, the longer that soft tissue is held in an elongated position the better the chance to retain that flexibility. Therefore, longer periods of stretch might be recommended; however caution is advised in employing extremes.

These are just a few of many exercises. They should not be construed as the ultimate nor used in a cookbook fashion. Exercises need to be individualized to meet each athlete's particular needs and problems. Also, do not give an athlete more exercises than is absolutely necessary. These exercises are usually boring enough without making them a program consuming much of the athlete's time. The athlete is more likely to give quality effort in a few well chosen exercises than he would in many random exercises given him from some "list." It is hoped that this article will not only introduce some helpful exercises and testing methods, but promote further study in this area.

REFERENCES

American Medical Association (Ed.). *Handbook of Physical Medicine and Rehabilitation.* Philadelphia: The Blakiston Company. 1950. pp. 381-451.
Arnhein, Daniel D. and Klafs, Carl E. *Modern Principles of Athletic Training.* 4th ed. St. Louis: The C. V. Mosby Company. pp. 255-267.
Johnson, Perry B., *et al. Sport, Exercise, and You.* New York: Holt, Rinehart, and Winston. 1975.
Katch, Frank I. and McArdle, William D. *Nutrition, Weight Control, and Exercise.* Boston: Houghton Mifflin Company. 1977. pp. 233-279.
Krusen, Frank H. (Ed.). *Handbook of Physical Medicine and Rehabilitation.* Philadelphia: W. B. Saunders. 1965. pp. 365-406.
Licht, Sidney (Ed.). *Rehabilitation and Medicine.* Baltimore: Waverly Press, Inc. 1968. pp. 18-20.
Licht, Sidney (Ed.). *Therapeutic Exercise.* Baltimore: Waverly Press, Inc. 1958.

The Lateral Step-Up

Joseph Godfrey, M.D.
Ed Abramowski, M.S., A.T.C.
'Bud' Tice, M.S., A.T.C.
Bob Reese, A.T.C.

The lateral step-up is a relatively simple exercise to perform, but very difficult to explain without pictures. We are currently working on a booklet and a movie which will explain it more effectively.

To perform the lateral step-up the weak ("bad") leg's foot is placed on a block and need not be removed until the exercise is completed (see figure 1). The "good" foot is placed parallel to the foot on the block, resting on the floor, with the toe of the "good" foot approximately at the instep of the "bad" foot. This rehabilitative exercise should be started with the feet close together (4" to 6"). As the athlete progresses, the feet can be placed further apart to a maximum of 12" to 14". The athlete lifts his body with the "bad" leg, holds 5 seconds, and lets himself down slowly and deliberately. A point to remember for doing it properly is to lift off the "good" heel and to land on the same heel. This way the athlete will not cheat by pushing off with the stronger leg and insure a greater range of motion of the injured extremity.

The lateral step-up develops the muscular strength of the entire quadriceps femoris group, the hip abductors and adductors, the stabilizers of the trunk, pelvis, thigh and hip, the posterior tibialis, the peroneals and other muscles important for balance, agility, and the stability of the hip, knee and ankle joints. Therefore, in addition to knee rehabilitation, we also use the step-up for hip and ankle strengthening and rehabilitation.

The step-up is initiated for rehabilitation after 90° of knee flexion has been achieved. It begins with use of a 4" to 6" block, keeping the "good" leg and foot close to the block (see figure 1). As the leg gets stronger the "good" leg should be gradually moved away from the block until a distance of 10" to 12" is attained. At this point the height of the block should be increased until it is at least 10" high (see figures 2-4). We have found that a 15" metal milk carton is more than adequate for even the largest of our athletes.

Another point that we feel is very important is to do the step-up for a set amount of time and not for a set number of repetitions. When starting rehabilitation, the exercises are done 6 to 8 times per day and are gradually increased until they are done for a 5-minute session. These 5-minute ses-

sions should be increased to 8 to 10 times per day, using a 10-second cycle for each step-up (2 seconds up, hold 5 seconds, 2 seconds down, and rest 1 second).

One of the great advantages of this exercise is that it can be done practically anywhere; at home, on stairways between classes, or in the dorm. If no stairs are available, a concrete block or milk carton is all the equipment that is needed. An unstable elevation should not be used.

An important point that we stress to our athletes is that running in any form (jogging, striding, or sprinting) is the very last thing to do and then only when the quadriceps girth of the injured leg is 90% that of the original size. Just like riding a bike or driving a car, you never forget how to run. This helps to keep the athlete from developing chondromalacia, chronic synovitis, and other problems that would complicate rehabilitation.

Although we have had some of our athletes com-

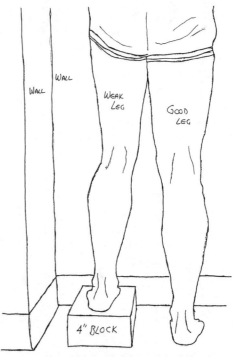

Figure 1. *Posterior view of the starting position for the initial phase of rehabilitation using the lateral step-up.*

pletely rehabilitate their knees without lifting any weights, this does not mean that we disdain their use. On the contrary, any rehabilitative weight routine that is employed can be used in conjunction with the step-up. It just should not be overdone. Remember that the athlete is already lifting his body weight through a range of motion, both "positively" (concentric) and "negatively" (eccentric) for almost an hour a day.

Our results with the step-up have convinced us to incorporate it into our general weight training and conditioning regimen. The athletes do three or four sets per day on each leg, sometimes using a weighted vest (10-20 pounds) for increasing the work load.

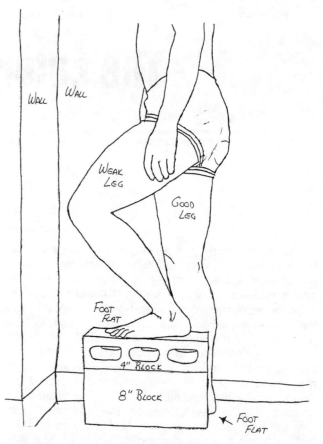

Figure 3. *Side view of figure 2.*

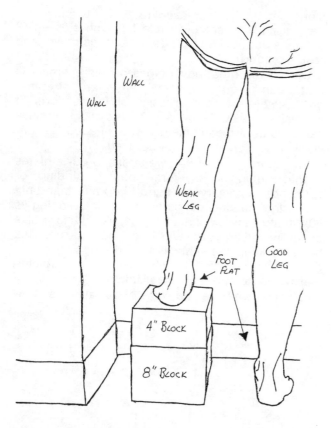

Fig. 2. *Posterior view of a later phase of rehabilitation using a higher "step".*

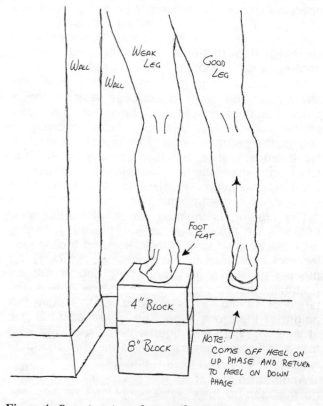

Figure 4. *Posterior view of a complete step-up.*

Gymnastics Injuries: Recognition and Management

Charles J. Redmond, M.S., A.T.C.

With the increased media exposure from the Munich and Montreal Olympics, gymnastics, men's and women's, has grown in popularity both as a spectator activity as well as a recreation and competitive activity. As a result of this increased participation, injury incidence has increased. The injuries include the standard musculoskeletal injuries (sprains, strains, etc.), as well as injuries specific to gymnastics. Some are a result of equipment and others due to the mechanisms of the sport. This paper will attempt to identify both the standard injuries as well as those common to gymnastics. By examining the major body areas individually some insight into: Prevention, Recognition and Management will be provided.

Figure 1. *Hand injuries are as serious to gymnastic performance as are ankle and knee injuries to a runner's performance.*

HAND INJURIES:
BLISTERS AND CALLUSES

A problem seen in most gymnasts at one time or another is the torn blister or callus on the hand or fingers. Although this is not what most would consider an acute problem; to the high bar, side horse, uneven parallel and parallel bar performers it can be as disabling as an ankle or knee injury. Common by-products of intense training on many pieces of equipment are the callus formations found on hands and fingers. If a blister, callus or skin tears the result is a very painful open wound. After a tear occurs, it should be treated as a significant problem and cleansed thoroughly. Previous

to the next work-out, dead skin should be trimmed and the area covered with an astringent (skin-toughener) to assist in further formation of callus. Any sign of infection should be treated appropriately.

Prevention of "tears" includes the following:
1. Gymnasts with chronic problems may find immersion in cold water during and/or after workouts helpful in minimizing primary or secondary blister and callus formation.
2. Wearing protective hand guards or taping the hands and fingers as needed.
3. Rubbing vaseline or skin lotion into tender areas after washing and drying the hands.
4. Trimming dead skin.
5. Keeping the apparatus clean and free of caked chalk.
6. When "hot spots" develop limit workout on certain pieces of equipment.

TENDONITIS AND FOREARM SPLINTS

Activities such as vaulting, floor exercise, and side horse, where repeated stress is placed on the wrists and forearms, may lead to one or two problems which have similar characteristics: 1) "tendonitis" of the musculature crossing the dorsal aspect of the wrist moving up the forearm toward the elbow and 2) "forearm splints" — an irritation of the interosseous membrane between the radius and ulna. The signs and symptoms include varying degrees of discomfort and pain both on active movement and palpation. The athlete may also experience weakness in wrist and hand movements.

Both of the conditions seem to be associated with early season participation. This would indicate a lack of preseason conditioning. It is felt by many that problems such as these are a result of "poor muscular endurance." Accordingly, conditioning on the apparatus during the early season should insist on gradually intensified and individualized training.

When a problem does develop there seems to be no guaranteed management. Success has been shown using some or all of the following:
1. Extended rest until most active movements are pain free.
2. The use of cryotherapy and/or thermotherapy may supplement the period of inactivity.
3. Gradual return to the apparatus, emphasizing

flexibility and progressive intensification of the work-out using pain as an indicator of when to let up.

4. Development of good muscular endurance.
5. Ice or cold application after the workout may assist in controlling further inflammation in tendons and associated injuries.
6. Some, suggest strapping the forearms with tape may allow limited participation. Our experiences indicate, as with "shin splints," this may ease some of the discomfort but does not deal directly with the problem. A conservative approach encouraging a period of rest and gradual retraining is likely to show the most consistent results.

SHOULDER INJURIES: TENDONITIS AND BURSITIS

The shoulder is prone to the same type of tendon injuries as the wrist and as we will see in the foot and leg. Ring and high bar performance are particularly susceptible because of the repetitive stresses put on the shoulder complex. Inflammation of any of the tendons and bursae of the shoulder is possible. These conditions are manifested by varying levels of discomfort, marked limitation of motion, weakness, and lack of endurance.

Ideas on prevention and management include:

1. Gradual individualized preseason training including flexibility, strength, and muscular endurance.
2. If stiffness develops: ice applications and limited participation on associated pieces of equipment.
3. Extended rest supplemented with cryotherapy and thermotherapy and rehabilitation as necessary.

FOOT, ANKLE AND LEG INJURIES: STRESS FRACTURES

A significant injury often overlooked by the most experienced athletic injury care specialist is the "stress or fatigue fracture." A stress fracture is the result of a series of sub-maximal stresses, any one stress being unlikely to cause a fracture. The gymnast will develop stress fractures of the metatarsals (march fracture), tibia and lumbar vertebrae (to be discussed later). The vaulters are particularly susceptible to lower extremity stress fractures because of the repeated approaches and take-offs from the vaulting board.

Pain over the metatarsals and along the tibia which persists despite rest and traditional care should make the coach suspicious of a stress fracture. The athlete then should be referred to the appropriate specialist for definitive diagnosis and care. Stress fractures will heal very well with period of rest and appropriate rehabilitation.

TENDONITIS AND ARCH INJURIES

Injuries to the tendons and arches of the gym-

nast's feet occur in vaulting, floor exercise, and a result of hard and repetitive dismounts. Anatomically the foot with its numerous bones, tendons, nerves and series of arches is a very complex area. It is the opinion of the author that it is the most difficult body area to deal with consistently. Most instances of tendonitis and arch strains result from repetitious actions where muscular endurance was not sufficient. Occasionally on some of the softer mats a tendon(s) may be strained. As with other tendon and related problems they are characterized by pain on active motion (with or without resistance), point tenderness, fever, and weakness. Management includes:

1. Examining the arches of both feet for possible problems.
2. A period of rest avoiding painful activities supplemented with cryotherapy or thermotherapy.
3. Proper reconditioning.
4. Appropriate strapping has proved useful as a supplement to rehabilitation.
5. Remember problems to the lower extremity will not respond as quickly as similar injuries to the upper extremity because of the weight bearing factor.

ANKLE

The common problem here is the traditional inversion sprain where the ligaments on the lateral side of the ankle are injured. This type of sprain is usually associated with dismounts into hard or soft mats. It is difficult to distinguish a sprain from a fracture so be conservative and when in doubt, get it X-rayed. During the interim ice, compression and elevation are important to control the swelling.

LEG

The structure of the leg, like the arm, is susceptible to repetitive activities such as those involved in vault approaches, the actual take off, and the landing following the various aerial moves in floor exercise, balance beam and other events. Typical injuries include tendonitis of the anterior group of muscles, injury to the achilles tendon, "true shin splints" (irritation of the membrane between the tibia and fibula), and tibial stress fractures. Prevention and management include:

1. Proper individualized conditioning.
2. Recognition of the problem developing pain, fever, weakness, lack of endurance.
3. Rest, cryotherapy, and/or thermotherapy with gradual reconditioning.
4. Although strapping may allow some temporary relief it is too often used as a replacement for proper management, rest and rehabilitation. This may result in the development of a chronic problem.

LOW BACK

Dismounts and landing from the various aerial

stunts can be quite stressful to the low back. Most of the problems will be simple spasm from a single stress or fatigue. Spasms will respond well to a short period of rest, thermotherapy, flexibility training and controlled workouts.

Spasm, however, may be a symptom of more serious problems, nerve injury, disc injury, or stress fractures of a lumbar vertebrae. Anytime one or more of the following are present referral to the appropriate specialist is indicated:

1. Pain and disability persisting despite a period of extended rest.
2. Point tenderness along the spine.
3. Pain radiating down one or both thighs.
4. Weakness and limited range of motion.

The back is a complex area and even with ideal care may be a long-term problem. Be sure proper management is provided as soon as the problem surfaces.

THE YOUNG GYMNAST

Because of the need for years of intense practice to reach high levels of skill many pre-adolescent and adolescent athletes are being directed toward gymnastics. In many instances they are rapidly progressing to skills and stunts attempted by older athletes only a few years ago. The implication here is whether the young athlete's body (particularly the bones) can withstand the stresses.

The primary areas of consideration are the epiphyses or growth centers of these young athletes. The growth centers of the young athlete are particularly susceptible to stress; the complication being permanent damage to the growth centers. Accordingly, the coach should be highly suspicious of the young athlete complaining of pain around the growth centers at the ends of bones. The tibia, elbow, and low back are potential problem areas. Pain is not always an expected by-product of intense training. Be suspicious and conservative.

SUMMARY

At this point it seems clear that gymnastics is a risk activity. As a result of the equipment involved and the nature of the various skills, injuries, some potentially acute, are a regular occurrence. Those individual's coaches and/or trainers, responsible for the gymnasts health should be prepared to deal with these injuries.

1. They must understand the nature of the activity and its skills.
2. They must identify the risk skills and control them.
3. They must be prepared to respond in a conservative, consistent, and systematic manner when evaluating and managing suspected injuries.
4. They must have appropriate and immediate follow-up (emergency transportation) available.

   (Note) the success of a quality athletic injury care program depends on the availability of competent and interested physicians in order that the coach may refer the injured athlete for definitive diagnosis and management.
5. The use of tape should not replace proper management and rehabilitation but supplement it.
6. Despite all the suggested management methods, *rest* and a *conservative* approach is likely to provide the most consistent long-term results.

REFERENCES

Klafs, Carl E. and Arnheim, Daniel D. *Modern Principles of Athletic Training.* The C.V. Mosby Company, 1977.
O'Donoghue, Don H., M.D. *Treatment of Injuries to Athletes.* W.B. Saunders Company, 1970.
Redmond, Charles J. *Laboratory Manual Prevention and Care of Athletic Injuries.* Springfield College, 1977.

Hockey Injuries: Prevention and Care

Michael Rielly, M.S., A.T.C.

Ice hockey is a game in which a highly organized group of plastic and foam padded athletes equipped with wooden or fiberglass sticks pass a six-ounce hard rubber disc at tremendous speeds upon a frozen surface. This game, where body position and movement are maintained through contact of a pair of sharpened steel blades has developed into one of the fastest and most interesting sports of modern times. A recent survey of International Ice Hockey Federation member nations has shown that two million individuals registered with their National Federation are currently participating in organized hockey.

Regardless of the sport or safety precautions taken, the potential for injury is ever present. In an effort to minimize the occurrence of injuries in hockey, numerous preventive avenues have been explored with major emphasis being directed toward the development of superior protective equipment. The primary function of equipment is protection; however a major consideration in equipment selection is weight and allowance for full ranges of limb movement. The manner in which quality equipment is manufactured today satisfies these requisites. Irrespective of the brand of equipment that is selected, proper fitting is paramount to ensure maximum protection. Equipment should always be selected to suit the needs of specific playing positions.

Helmet

Although a variety of helmet styles are currently available, the protective features should remain standard. Depending upon need and preference, the helmet may be of an adjustable or non-adjustable design. If adjustable, it should provide the same degree of protection at any size setting. The shell should be constructed of a rigid, high impact material and feature a suspension system or layers of impact-absorbing and sizing foam. The shell should include a series of portholes for ventilation. The helmet must fit snugly upon the head and be secured with a chin strap. Naturally, there should be no sharp edges present along the shell. A helmet that hinders vision or hearing should not be utilized. It is recommended that helmets be certified and approved by complying with the safety standards of a recognized association.

In the event that facial protection is desired or mandated, a variety of masks are available (Fig. 1). Except for one style of mask for a goalkeeper, face masks are attached to the helmet and have been designed for specific playing positions. Like the helmet, a mask should not interfere with normal vision. The face mask must be hinged to the helmet in such a manner that it may be adjusted to allow for the wearing of eyeglasses, yet be stable enough to prevent the mask from being driven onto the face. Proper face mask attachment will enable the transfer of forces on the mask to the helmet. A wire mask should have an attached foam chin cup for additional protection and support.

Figure 1. *Protection of the head and face:*
- *A. Extraoral mouth guard with chin cup.*
- *B. Intraoral self-moulding mouth guard.*
- *C. Extraoral mouth guard.*
- *D. Suspension helmet.*
- *E. Helmet with full cage.*
- *F. Foam lined helmet.*
- *G. Full cage with lexan shield.*
- *H. Helmet with lexan eye shield.*
- *I. Helmet with lexan shield, half cage, and padded chin cup.*

In cases where a face mask is not worn, a mouth guard should be employed to protect the mouth, lips and teeth (Fig. 1). In most organized league competition, this piece of equipment is mandatory. Mouth guards are found in three styles — intraoral, extraoral and combined intra-extraoral. The intraoral mouth guards may be custom-made and fitted by a dentist or purchased and moulded to fit the individual. A simple "self-moulding" mouth guard is not as satisfactory as a custom-made dental appliance (4). The material should be constructed of tough, resilient dental vinyl or a similar compound. Extraoral mouth guards must be attached to the helmet with adjustable straps and be constructed of a high impact material cushioned on the inner side. A properly fitted mouth guard should not interfere with normal respiration.

Shoulder Pad

Much of the strategy in hockey involves participants checking or playing the body off the puck. This type of play frequently results in substantial forces being directed to the surrounding bones and musculature of the shoulder. As the game has become increasingly specialized, the demand for varying degrees of shoulder and chest protection has subsequently increased (Fig. 2).

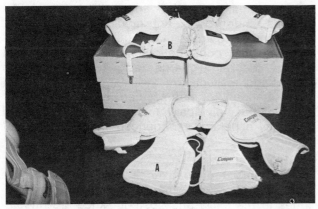

Figure 2. *Shoulder pads:*
   A. Defense pad with extended chest protection.
   B. Forward pad.

A major consideration when selecting shoulder pads is usually weight, when in reality, emphasis should be directed toward suiting the demands of the playing position. The pads should fit snugly upon the shoulders and cover the deltoid muscle. A foam wrap-around pad will extend from the deltoid cap for the purpose of protecting the biceps in a manner that permits a non-restrictive full range of motion. A loosely fitted pair of shoulder pads will move excessively during activity, thus eliminating the function for which they were designed and predisposing the athlete to injury.

The degree of chest protection will be determined by nature of the playing position. Female hockey participants should utilize the specially designed shoulder pad that has breast shields incorporated into the protective structure of the chest area.

Elbow

The elbow is a structure that is extremely vulnerable to injury, therefore must be protected. The entire olecranon is subcutaneous, as are the medial and lateral epicondyles and the supracondylar ridges (4). Direct blows to the medial aspect

occur less frequently due to its protected position.

Regardless of style, elbow pads should be constructed of a lightweight material with a design that permits complete freedom of movement (Fig. 3). The pads must feature protection for the sensitive lateral condyle, radial head and relatively insensitive olecranon process (4). An elongated forearm or slash pad will provide additional protection. Properly fitted elbow pads should be snug and extend from the bottom of the biceps guard of the shoulder pad to the top of the glove cuff with no overlap.

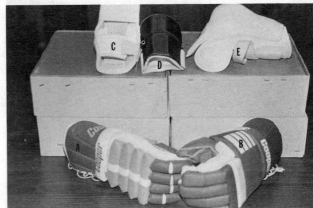

Figure 3. *Arm and hand protection:*
   A. Glove with a padded, hinged back roll.
   B. Glove with non-hinged, wrap around padding.
   C. Foam padded elbow pad.
   D. Vinyl elbow pad with felt padding.
   E. Elbow pad with moulded cap for lateral protection and extended slash pad.

Hand

The hand's location at the end of the extremity and its function expose it to a variety of traumatic episodes (4). The importance of providing adequate protection to the hand is paramount for an injury to this region would most certainly limit performance.

A hockey glove must be well padded to protect the vulnerable dorsum of the hand and fingers, yet allow wrist and finger flexion. The index finger should be padded laterally because of its predisposition to injury during play. Requisites for quality gloves include moulded thumbs and cuffs (Fig. 3).

Thigh—Hip—Pelvis

Protection for the lumbosacral spine, kidneys, pelvis and anterior thigh is provided through integration of moulded polyethylene in the hockey pants (Fig. 4). Each moulded part should be encased in foam for comfort and shock absorption. A pair of pants should fit loose enough to provide unimpaired movement of the hips and waist, but should not be allowed to hang low, leaving the flank and iliac crest exposed to injury. Hockey pants should be fitted approximately six sizes larger than dress pants, however, sizing is proportionate to a player's somatotype. Measure the player's waist; if of slim or medium build, order pants six inches

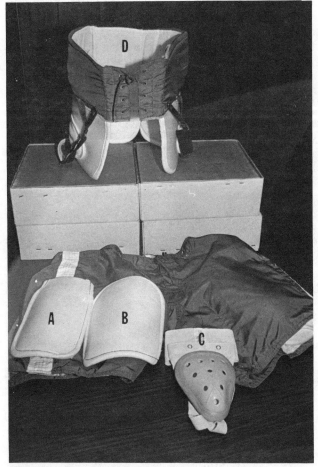

Figure 4. *Upper and lower pant:*
  A. Lateral thigh slash pad.
  B. Anterior thigh guard.
  C. Athletic supporter with protective cup.
  D. Upper portion of pant. Hip — pelvis — spine pads.

larger than the waist. If the player is heavy in the thighs, buttocks, and hips, order pants eight inches larger than the waist (7).

Groin

A necessary piece of equipment that should be mandatory for hockey participants is the athletic supporter with cup, designed to protect the male genitalia (Fig. 4). The moulded cup is inserted into the pouch of the cup protectors. An athletic supporter must be selected according to waist size in order to provide maximum support and protection. Moulded polyethylene foam padded pelvic protectors are available for female participants. This vital piece of equipment is likewise selected according to waist size.

Knee — Shin

The knee, probably the most vulnerable joint of the body from the standpoint of athletic injury, and the tibia, are two subcutaneous regions predisposed and exceedingly sensitive to trauma (4). Due to the absence of muscular or adipose tissue at the tibia, forces are not absorbed and dissipated, thus the periosteum receives full force of any impact delivered to the shin. Although lying within

the quadriceps tendon and surrounded by bursae, the patella similarly lacks muscular and adipose protection. Forces directed upon the patella result in a myriad of disabling injuries.

The shin guard, protective equipment designed for the knee and shin, is constructed of high impact polyethylene with an attached flexible kneecap. It is heavily padded with foam and flared with energy absorbing material to protect the gastrocnemius, suprapatellar region, and the medial and lateral aspects of the knee. The bottom of the shin guard should be adequately padded to protect the instep from chafing. Proper fitting of the shin guard is crucial. The length of the guard should coincide with measurements taken from the center of the patella to the instep.

Foot — Ankle

The skate is probably the most individualized piece of equipment selected for hockey competition. The ultimate goal during this selection process is to obtain a comfortable lightweight skate that provides maximum foot and ankle support. An achilles tendon guard and moulded protective toe are essential features that should be incorporated into the boot construction. Moulded high impact energy absorbing guards designed to protect the instep and malleoli are available for players and recommended for defensemen. It is advised that the feet be individually measured for length and width by a person experienced with the fitting of skates.

Neck

A properly equipped hockey player will not be protected at the neck, axilla or posterior knee. Injuries to the axilla and posterior knee are uncommon, while the incidence of serious injury to the neck occurs at a higher rate. Flexible steel wire reinforced throat collars are currently available for protection against skate cuts, puck blows, and glancing sticks.

The outfitting of players with properly fitting equipment merely augments a single segment of the injury prevention process. The glancing stick or flying puck that strikes an athlete in a vulnerable position, or a stiff body check on an unsuspecting player adds another dimension to injury production termed the mechanism. It is the mechanism that must be thoroughly understood for each injury before treatment may be initiated.

Recently, a classification of injuries based upon etiology has been presented for an effective approach to identify the mode of production and indicate the most effective means for management. Williams (5), has stated that a majority of true sporting injuries are of the intrinsic or self-inflicted variety; however those injuries common to ice hockey are generally of the extrinsic category.

Common sense dictates that prevention, a four facet concept, is the ultimate treatment for an injury. Its constructs are:

1. Physical examination.
2. High level of fitness obtained by developing

the required physiological parameters.
3. Skill acquisition and development.
4. Equipment fitting and selection.

Upon development of these requirements, the preventative process nears completion, although the possibility of injury remains.

From the sport of hockey come a variety of unique injuries of which the contusion and laceration appear to occur most frequently.

Contusion

Damage to a muscle, whether of intrinsic or extrinsic origin, will result in tearing and disruption of muscle fibers, connective tissue and blood vessels. When extrinsic force is applied to a muscle, subcutaneous and deep connective tissues are damaged and become the site of bleeding and hematoma formation (Fig. 5). It has been reported

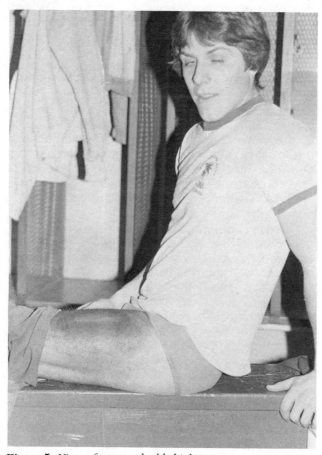

Figure 5. *View of one-week-old thigh contusion.*

that intramuscular hematomas are more commonly produced by intrinsic tears and interstitial hematomas by external trauma (5). Hemorrhage from the site of injury will cease as intramuscular tension builds to compress the bleeding parts. Supplemental ice application will result in vasoconstriction. This will help control bleeding and edema formation.

While the anterior thigh is well protected by the hockey pants, a violent force directed upon or to the lateral margins of the thigh guard might produce a deep contusion or "charley horse." Even if complete rupture of the rectus femoris does not

occur, muscle damage tends to be quite extensive with marked intramuscular bleeding. A possible complication of the hematoma is myositis ossificans, where calcium deposits are laid down within the hematoma, later to be converted into a species of cancellous bone (5). Treatment, rehabilitation and recovery time will depend largely upon the extent of injury.

An injury that manifests itself when players are fitted with pants that are too loose and hang low or when a stick slides over the top of the hip pad is the contused iliac crest or hip pointer. This has been reported to be one of the most handicapping injuries in sport and is one that is difficult to manage (3). Usually the injury is confined to the soft tissues of the hip and abdomen; however the possibility of fracture should not be eliminated. In severe cases, medical referral should be arranged. O'Donoghue (4) has expressed certainty that the majority of hip pointers are undertreated rather than overtreated, since they are considered to be simple contusions when they are actually muscular avulsions.

Although adequately protected, a violent external force to the region of the low back might result in a kidney contusion (Fig. 6). An athlete displaying the signs of shock, rigidity of the back muscles, or hematoma must be referred to a physician for further evaluation.

Figure 6. *Contusion producing mechanism. Player receiving a blow to the low back.*

Possibly the most frowned upon violation in hockey is employment of a technique termed "butt ending," where the butt end of a stick is thrust into the abdomen of an opponent (Fig. 7). The end result of this maneuver could range from a simple abdominal contusion to a rupture of an internal organ that might present a life-threatening situation. The spleen, the greatest single collection of lymphoid tissue in the body, is located at the upper left quadrant of the abdomen (2). When ruptured, the immediate danger lies within the organ's ability to splint itself through hematoma formation. Slight movements might dislodge the hematoma and cause profuse hemorrhaging. Injury sustained to the left abdominal region should be recognized promptly so treatment of this potential medical emergency will not be delayed.

Figure 7. *Abdominal injury resulting from a "Butt End."*

Contusions to the abdomen might also result in a temporary paralysis of the diaphragm, more commonly referred to as "having the wind knocked out." The blow produces a neurogenic shock due to stimulation of the solar plexus (5). This condition has the potential of being serious, however anxiety and inability to resume normal breathing rhythm are usually the greatest problems. Where symptoms persist, serious injury must be kept in mind. Special attention must be given the athlete who appears to have recovered, then experiences severe abdominal pain. This may be attributed to a delayed hemorrhage or intestinal damage (5). If the athlete becomes cyanotic, artificial respiration might be necessary.

Laceration

The laceration, a frequently occurring athletic injury (3), is probably the most common injury eminating from ice hockey. A crushing or tearing force, rather than a direct cut, is generally the mode of production, therefore the laceration will often be accompanied by a contusion (Fig. 8). Since blood vessels are torn or mashed, this wound will not bleed freely (1). The degree of damage may range from a fissure-like wound with little external evidence of injury to extensive tissue tear-

Figure 8. *Laceration producing mechanism.*

ing with considerable separation of skin. The lack of bleeding, coupled with possible contamination, provide the necessary ingredients for infection.

The face, with subcutaneous bone, is often unprotected and subject to contusion and laceration. When cut, a rich blood supply at this region results in a period of profuse bleeding. Each laceration should be carefully examined with the skin margins separated sufficiently to explore the depths of the wound. It is important with lacerations of the forehead and scalp to determine whether underlying muscle or bone has been damaged (5). Due to the presence of an areolar space at the forehead, extensive swelling is likely to follow a blow to this area (4).

The eye is often the recipient of forces in hockey that produce trauma. Injury to the eye is usually dramatic, giving rise to pain and immediate loss of effective vision (4). The immediate swelling that takes place following injury may hinder the routine field examination. The importance of specialist referral cannot be overemphasized when injury has occurred to the eye or around the orbit. In cases where there is absolute certainty that no underlying ocular complication exists, immediate first aid procedures should begin. The most important measure during the early stages of injury treatment is ice application; however if the athlete has an intraocular injury, the ice pack or any other device increasing pressure upon the eye should not be applied (4).

The eyelids are likewise vulnerable to injury and are frequently incised or lacerated during hockey participation. Wound management should remain standard except when damage is suspected to the lacrimal apparatus. An athlete with a laceration extending through these structures should be immediately referred to a specialist for evaluation and treatment.

Fracture

As with most of the soft tissue of the body, bones are subject to injury from the compression or crushing trauma of an external force. The resulting damage may range from a contusion to a variety of fractures. Those areas vulnerable in hockey are the bones of the face and skull, calcaneous, fifth metatarsal and malleoli.

The normal function and position of the palmar aspect of the hand during play does not require much protective padding. Infrequently, the execution of a "slap shot" forces the stick into the metacarpal phalangeal joint of the thumb, producing a painful contusion or chip fracture. Injury to this area should not be taken lightly.

The catching or glove hand of a goalie is the object of tremendous forces that often result in severe contusion. The incidence of fracture is low, however an athlete may experience paresthesia of varying intensity for a considerable duration.

Unless the player is wearing a protective face mask, fractures of the face are possible from a variety of mechanisms. As a result of initial trauma, many fractures will be accompanied by an open wound. The rapid onset of edema may mask bone deformity and the fracture itself. Routine evaluation of violently produced facial injury should warrant x-ray examination.

Nasal fractures, the most common fractures of the face, appear frequently as a separation of the frontal processes of the maxilla, a separation of the lateral cartilages, or a combination (4) (Fig. 9).

Figure 9. *Fracture producing mechanism. Face being driven into the glass with force directed to the nose.*

Hemorrhage will be profuse following a blow due to the immense blood supply of the nasal mucosa. Although bleeding is usually easy to control, nasal packing may become necessary. Dry sterile gauze is an excellent method, however removal of this pack often results in the reinitiation of hemorrhage. Vaseline gauze appears to be most effective as a packing material. It is important not to pack the internal nares and leave enough material visible to facilitate easy removal. The likelihood of serious infection is ever present, thus a nasal pack should not be left in place for prolonged periods of time (4).

The unprotected mandible is a structure that is predisposed to fracture from a direct blow (Fig. 10). What initially looks to be a contusion is usually the first indicator that calls attention to the actual injury. All contusions involving the mandible should

Figure 10. *High stick forcefully applied to the face.*

undergo careful examination that includes palpation, observation of tooth aposition, and range of motion. A more detailed evaluation must be conducted by a physician if uncertainty exists as to the severity of the injury.

The degree of protection at the foot and ankle depends upon the quality of skate construction and presence of supplemental padding. A puck traveling at a high rate of speed is usually responsible for the contusions and fractures at this region. Due to anatomical location and position during play, the fifth metatarsal, lateral malleolus and calcaneus become extremely vulnerable to injury. Initial evaluation will be limited as the boot will serve as a splint and allow movement to continue. Upon cessation of activity, the rapid onset of edema and pain will most likely render a complete field examination impossible. The athlete must be referred to a physician for evaluation and positive diagnosis.

An uncommon but possible injury resulting from hockey is the malleolar or bi-malleolar ankle fracture. The mechanism is typical (3), however the boot again acts as a splint and may allow the athlete to continue play. Immediately following skate removal, weight bearing and movement become difficult as the obvious fracture signs appear.

Sprain

A joint may be injured when subjected to a variety of mechanisms that create stress to the bone and stabilizing structures. The outcome is motion that forces structures beyond normal limitations. More common than overuse of an unconditioned joint or faulty technique, external force is generally responsible for a sprain. The amount of force is variable and may occur in one or a combination of directions. Treatment of joint sprains has been covered in another section of this text.

The manner in which body checks are applied on the ice or along the boards precipitates the acromioclavicular sprain. The force is directed to the tip of the shoulder and pushes the acromion process downward. Strength development, a state of readiness, and proper technique for absorbing the check should aid in preventing the separated shoulder.

Although play is conducted upon a frozen surface, a high degree of friction is maintained through contact of the sharpened skate blades, thus a knee sprain resulting from hockey will resemble the classic mechanism for athletic injury. The foot is fixed to the ice surface as the thigh rotates internally. The knee shall be forced inward toward the opposite leg and stress received on the medial ligaments. This mechanism may take place with or without external force. The rotational sprain on a flexed weight bearing knee may result from a sudden change of direction on the ice that parallels the "cut back" motion of a runner.

Strain

The rigors of ice hockey demand maximum development of the total fitness components as the nature of the sport places considerable stress upon the musculature of the abdomen, back and legs. While the exact causative factors underlying muscle strains are unknown, overuse, sudden over stretching, postural deficiency and improper technique have been suggested (3, 5, 6). Most frequently the strain is restricted to a few muscle fibers and supportive tissues.

Prevention of the acute or chronic muscle strain is possible and should be included in the pre-season conditioning and daily warm-up routines. Those techniques for injury prevention and treatment involve the basic principles of flexibility (8), and have been discussed in another portion of the text (Appendices A and B).

While the incidence of athletic injury can only be anticipated, various measures may be undertaken to reduce the possibility of occurrence. Proper equipment fitting, coupled with an attempt to reduce those potentially serious mechanisms that predispose an athlete to injury are simply two steps in the involved process of conducting a sound and safety conscious athletic program.

REFERENCES

Books

1. Erven, Lawrence, *Handbook of Emergency Care and Rescue*, London: Glencoe Press, 1976.
2. Gray, Henry, *Anatomy of the Human Body*, C.M. Goss, Ed., Philadelphia: Lea and Febiger, 1966.
3. Klafs, Carl and Arnheim, Daniel, *Modern Principles of Athletic Training*, St Louis: C.V. Mosby Co., 1977.
4. O'Donoghue, Don, *Treatment of Injuries to Athletes*, Philadelphia: W.B. Saunders Co., 1976.
5. Williams, J. and Speryn, P., *Sports Medicine*, Baltimore: Williams and Wilkins Co., 1976.

Periodicals

6. Burkett, L.N., "Cause and Prevention of Hamstring Pulls," *The Athletic Journal*, 51: February, 1971.
7. *Cooper International Hockey Catalog*, 1978.
8. Holland, George, "The Physiology of Flexibility, a Review of the Literature," *Kinesiology Review*, 36: 49-62, 1968.
9. *United States Hockey and Arena Biz*, 6: 7-12, January, 1978.

Common Injuries in Women's Volleyball

Marge Albohm, M.S., A.T.C.

The sport of volleyball has gained national prominence as a high level athletic competitive activity over recent years. With increased participation by women athletes at all levels of competition comes an increase in injury incidence and an increased concern for the safety and well-being of female athletes participating in the sport. Injuries in athletics cannot totally be prevented, but with a thorough understanding of the types of injuries that commonly occur and the proper athletic first aid techniques that should be utilized, injuries can be minimized and athletes may quickly and safely return to activity without fear of injury recurrence. It is the obligation of athletic personnel to familiarize themselves with these techniques and to therefore create a safer athletic environment for all participants.

To effectively deal with any injury it is necessary to understand the principles behind proper immediate first aid of athletic injuries. Regardless of the location or extent of injury, immediate first aid should consist of *pressure, ice* and *elevation.* This important treatment serves to prevent swelling in an injured area by providing compression, decreasing circulation and combating the effect of gravity. Swelling is the primary limiting factor in returning an athlete to activity and everything must be done to minimize this result of injury.

Only *pressure, ice* and *elevation* should be utilized in the management of a new injury and there is no other acceptable treatment. When the swelling has been controlled and there is no further chance for internal bleeding to occur heat treatments may be utilized. If initiated too early, heat will cause further swelling by its physiological effect of increasing circulation. Heat, however, is valuable in assisting the healing of injury once the swelling is controlled.

COMMON INJURIES

The fingers are commonly injured in volleyball due to the large amount of ball handling skills that are required. These injuries are many times regarded as being insignificant but they can be extremely disabling and present permanent disability to the athlete if not handled properly.

FINGER INJURIES

I. **Prevention**
    A. Maintain good strength and flexibility
        1. grip and spread exercises
        2. ball squeezing
        3. fingertip push-ups (wall or floor)

II. **Injury Evaluation**
    A. Visual inspection
        1. obvious deformity may indicate dislocation and/or fracture — refer to physician immediately
    B. Manual inspection
        1. palpate area, feeling for abnormality or point tenderness (the presence of point tenderness can be an indication of fracture)

III. **Immediate First Aid**
    A. Apply pressure—reduce swelling.
        1. cover finger snugly with elastic tape
    B. Apply ice
        1. place finger in ice bag or ice slush for twenty-minute intervals over a period of twenty-four to forty-eight hours or until swelling is controlled

IV. **Treatment**
    If a fracture is ruled out the following treatment procedures can be utilized.
    A. Continue ice until swelling is controlled
        1. ice bag
        2. ice slush
    B. Heat (only when swelling is controlled)
        1. warm water soaks — 20 minutes — twice daily. Have athlete begin to move finger as much as possible.
        2. paraffin bath — hot wax treatment — 15-20 minutes, twice daily.
    C. Tape support
        When normal movement in the finger is regained the athlete may return to activity with tape support.
        1. tape fingers together
        2. tape finger separately with spiral pattern — refer to Appendix D

V. **Rehabilitation**
    Injury presents muscle atrophy and weakness. The injured area must be rehabilitated to prevent injury recurrence.

A. Exercises
 1. grip and spread fingers
 2. ball squeezing
 3. push-ups (wall or floor)

Various contusions (bruises) are commonly seen in volleyball due to the dive and roll techniques utilized. These contusions most frequently occur to the elbow, knee and hip areas. They can be extremely painful and may limit the athlete from activity for several days. Simple preventive methods can be employed to prevent these problems.

Many contusions are a result of improper execution of skill technique. Therefore, it is extremely important to instruct athletes in the proper movement techniques. While learning the various skills protective padding should be utilized to prevent injury. Manufactured pads can be used as well as separate vinyl foam padding specifically cut and fit for the individual.

CONTUSIONS

I. **Prevention**
 A. Pad areas most vulnerable to injury
  1. elbow pads
  2. knee pads
  3. hip pads to cover interior aspect of iliac crest

II. **Immediate First Aid**
 A. Cover area with wet elastic wrap — compression
 B. Apply ice — reduce swelling
  1. ice bag — 20 minutes
  2. ice massage — use ice cup (frozen water in 8 oz. paper cup and apply in small, circular motion for 15 to 20 minutes)
 C. Elevate — combat gravity

III. **Treatment**
 A. Continue ice treatment
 B. Heat (when swelling is controlled)
  1. moist heat packs — 20 minutes, twice daily
 C. Pad area for protection when returning to activity
  1. manufactured pads
  2. vinyl foam padding taped to area

III. **Treatment**
 A. Continue ice treatment
 B. Heat (when swelling is controlled)
  1. moist heat packs — 20 minutes, twice daily
 C. Pad area for protection when returning to activity
  1. manufactured pads
  2. vinyl foam padding taped to area

Shin splints are a very common problem in women's volleyball and can be caused by a number of factors. Shin splints are characterized by a dull ache or pain arising on the anterior aspect of the lower leg. The exact cause of shin splints is not well defined but the musculature of the lower leg is definitely involved and becomes irritated and inflamed with continued activity.

Shin splints are often related to a weakness in the arches of the feet. The arches are subject to a great deal of stress in volleyball, due to the great amount of jumping activities involved in the sport. Care must be taken to insure proper support for the arches through quality footwear. Shin splints may become extremely disabling if left unattended and total rest may be the only possible course of treatment.

SHIN SPLINTS

I. **Prevention**
 A. Maintain good strength and flexibility in the lower leg
  1. gastrocnemius stretches
  2. toe raises
  3. avoid running on hard surfaces
  4. isometric exercises at the ankle joint involving dorsiflexion, plantar flexion, inversion and eversion.
 B. Support arches of feet
  1. quality footwear with good arch supports and good shock absorbing material in soles
  2. arch pads for inner longitudinal arch
  3. x-arch taping pattern (see Appendix D)

II. **Treatment**
 A. Warm whirlpool treatments — to increase circulation — 20 minutes, 104°, once daily
 B. Massage with ice cup — apply ice in small circular motions — 15 minutes, before and after practice
 C. Ice packs — apply for 15 to 20 minutes, before and after practice
 D. Limit activity

Severe knee injuries, affecting the ligaments and menisci, are not often experienced in women's volleyball due to the lack of physical contact. However, several chronic conditions of the knee are often seen. These include chondromalacia, an irritation of the underside of the kneecap (patella) and "jumper's knee" a condition affecting the patellar ligament (tendon).

Chondromalacia is characterized by a grating and grinding sensation in the region of the patella. It is a condition that commonly affects women more than men due to the anatomical structure of the female pelvic girdle. The female pelvis is wider than the male's. The femur (upper leg bone), therefore, is positioned at a more acute angle than that of a male. This creates a different "line of pull" of the quadriceps musculature and tends to displace the patella laterally. This slight lateral displacement may cause the under-surface of the kneecap to become irritated.

Chondromalacia can become extremely acute and disabling, and may progress to the point where total rest must be prescribed.

CHONDROMALACIA

I. Prevention
   A. Strengthen thigh musculature
      1. specifically strengthen vastus medialis muscle to maintain proper patellar alignment.

II. Treatment
   A. Ice packs — 20–25 minutes, before and after practice
   B. Aspirin — 2 tablets — 4 times daily to aid in reducing inflammation
   C. Limit activity — especially extreme flexion and extension

"Jumper's knee" is characterized by pain and point tenderness in the area directly below the kneecap. The condition involves the patellar ligament which attaches to the lower portion of the patella and extends to the tibial tuberosity. Excessive jumping activities will put extreme stress on this ligament and may cause irritation and inflammation.

"JUMPER'S KNEE"

I. Prevention
   A. Strengthen thigh musculature
   B. Stress proper jumping mechanics

II. Treatment
   A. Ice packs — 20–25 minutes, after activity
   B. Warm whirlpool — 20 minutes, 104°, once daily
   C. Moist heat packs — 20 minutes, twice daily
   D. Limit jumping activities

Ankle sprains are common in all sports and women's volleyball is no exception. Fortunately, the ankle sprain experienced in volleyball are usually mild to moderate in severity and the athlete is able to return relatively quickly to the activity.

ANKLE SPRAINS

I. Prevention
   A. Condition lower leg musculature
      1. gastrocnemius stretches
      2. toe raises
      3. isometric exercises at the ankle joint involving dorsiflexion, plantarflexion, inversion, and eversion.

II. Injury Evaluation
   A. Inspect both lateral and medial aspects
      1. note deformity
      2. limitation of movement
      3. point tenderness
   B. Pain above ankle bones (malleoli) suspect fracture — refer to physician immediately.
   C. Pain below, in front of, or behind ankle bones (malleoli) may indicate ligamentous damage

III. Immediate First Aid
   A. Apply pressure — limit swelling
      1. cover area snugly with wet elastic wrap
   B. Apply ice — constrict blood vessels
      1. place ice packs on lateral and medial sides
   C. Elevate — combat gravity
      1. raise ankle above hip level
   D. Continue treatment for 25-minute intervals for 48 to 72 hours or until *swelling is controlled*

IV. Treatment — (swelling controlled)
   A. Warm whirlpool — 15 minutes, 104°, twice daily — promote range of motion
   B. Use compression wrap or taping when weight bearing

V. Rehabilitation
   A. Regain full range of motion
   B. Strengthen area
      1. gastrocnemius stretches
      2. toe raises
      3. dorsiflexion, plantarflexion, inversion, eversion with resistance

VI. Return to Activity
   A. Use supportive taping
   B. Run figure eight patterns and circles of decreasing size. If there is no limp and no apparent movement impairment the athlete may resume normal activity.

Soccer Injuries

Marc Gruder, M.A., A.T.C.

Why didn't you have a championship season this year? Was it because a few key players were injured or that some of your starters could not participate at one hundred percent? Perhaps this article will aid your team in achieving their goals by telling you the way that the Cornell Soccer team, 1977 Ivy League Champions, manage some common soccer injuries.

As soccer grows in popularity, the need for research pertaining to athletic injuries is also in demand. There has been little research to date on soccer injuries in America and much of the foreign research has conflicting reports. Due to the nature of the sport there are injuries that are more prevalent in soccer than other athletic activities. These injuries and their management will be discussed in this article.

Preseason

The preseason practice period plays an important role in developing a conditioning base for the rest of the year. It can also be the beginning of lost days of practice due to injury, if not conducted properly. No matter how hard your athletes have been working in the off season, they will push themselves a little bit harder when the coach is there. Trying to do too much, too soon, can only lead to problems that can cost valuable practice time.

The biggest fear I have during preseason is the potential for heat illness. These heat related problems include, heat cramps, heat exhaustion and heat stroke. Death can result from ignoring the symptoms of heat illness. Table 1 outlines the symptoms and recommended treatment for each.

TABLE 1

WARNING SIGNS AND TREATMENT OF HEAT ILLNESS

Illness	Symptoms	First-Aid
Heat Cramps	Painful spasms in voluntary muscles. Pupils dialate with each spasm, possible heavy sweating, skin cold and clammy.	Firm pressure on cramping muscles. Warm wet towels, three or four doses of salty water at 15 minute intervals.
Heat Exhaustion	Profuse sweating, weakness, disorientation, skin cold and pale, clammy with sweat, thready pulse. Temperature normal or subnormal. Possible vomiting.	Move to cooler enviroment. Bed rest, salty water. Medical help for severe cases.
Heat Stroke	Weak, disorientation, excessive sweating; sweating stops just before heat stroke. Temperature rises sharply, pulse is bounding delirium or coma common	Heat stroke is a severe medical emergency. Get medical help immediately. Move to cooler enviroment, reduce body temperature with ice bath or sponging.

Most of these heat related problems can be avoided. An unlimited supply of water should always be available for the athletes. Modified practices on days when the heat and humidity are high will also help. It has been recommended that on days when the temperature and humidity are high and especially before the athlete has had time to acclimate to the conditions, that for every one hour of practice there should be fifteen minutes of rest. This rest period does not have to be one of inactivity but may be utilized for chalk talk or demonstrations.

A proper stretching program throughout the entire season will help reduce the frequency of muscle strains. This is especially important in the preseason when many of the muscles will be stressed to a greater degree than they have been in the past few months of the off season. A slow static stretch, held between 5-10 seconds, is the preferred method. "Bouncing" when stretching should be avoided due to a reflex contraction of muscle upon sudden stretch of a muscle.

Common Injuries

Soccer being a game of kicking and running puts a great amount of stress on the lower extremities. Naves[1] reported that seventy percent of all injuries occur to the lower extremities and that the ankle was the joint most frequently injured. Most ankle sprains occur from forceful inversion of a plantar flexed foot.

The position that the legs are put in when stretching for a ball and tackling are optimum for injury. The knee is very vulnerable in these positions. The most frequent injuries to the knee are sprains of the collateral ligaments, mainly the medial, sprains of the anterior cruciate ligament and tears of the meniscus cartilage.[2]

Contusions are a common soccer injury. The shin, calf and quadriceps are frequent problem areas. Ossification in the quadriceps area must be considered when a contusion of the thigh is accompanied by swelling or there are repeated blows to the same area.

Fractures are not of a high incidence but they do occur. The areas that are most common are the shaft of the tibia or fibula or both. Fractures of the metatarsals, especially the fifth can be produced from kicking or being stepped on. A fracture of the base of the fifth metatarsal can often occur by the pull of the peroneus brevis tendon.[3]

Goal keepers, due to the nature of their position,

often have injuries that are not common among other participants. Sprained fingers are often encountered from stopping shots or being stepped on. Shoulder separations and dislocations can occur due to their diving technique. I have found a high incidence of concussions among goalies when they dive attempting to take the ball off an opposing player's foot and when coming out to play a crossed ball.

Management of Injuries

The proper immediate care of an injured athlete can reduce the time it takes for him to return to play. Rather than attempting to continue participation with an injury, immediate first aid should be administered. The recommended first aid for most injuries is ice, compression and elevation. This includes muscle strains and ligamentous sprains. Frostbite is a possibility when ice is applied directly to the skin so it is recommended that either two layers of wet towel or a layer of wet elastic bandage be placed between the skin and the ice. The ice will help reduce localized swelling and can be used for its anesthetic effect. Cold treatments should continue from twenty-four to seventy-two hours after an injury, depending on the severity of the injury and the amount of swelling. This judgement must be made on an individual case basis.

Once the swelling is controlled it is important to ascertain that the athlete has a full range of motion. Cold treatments combined with exercise will help achieve this. The ice is applied to the injured body part and then that part is taken through the range to the best of the athlete's ability. This should be done without causing pain. If it is a musculotendonous injury have the athlete stretch. If it is a ligamentous or joint injury have the athlete move the joint through its normal range. I have many of our players with sprained ankles trace the alphabet with their foot making sure they go through the full range. This method of ice combined with exercise will help increase the drainage of the body part and will facilitate the healing process. This treatment can be started soon after the injury occurs as long as it is pain free.

The loss of strength and conditioning are always a problem when an injured athlete is out of competition for a period of time. We try to reduce this loss with weight lifting with the non-injured parts of the body and with a rehabilitative running program if possible. The key factor in this running program is that the athlete must be able to do these exercises without pain.

The first step is to have the athlete jog. Once he can do this he may go from a slow start, to a sprint in the middle, to a slow stop. Next is a fast start, to a sprint, to a slow stop. Once all of these can be done the athlete may do straight ahead wind sprints. If all of the above can be accomplished without pain, the athlete can start working on planting and cutting. The athlete will do some zigzag running and large figure eight running. To begin, place two pylons fifteen yards apart for figure eight running. They can be brought in closer as the athlete progresses. No matter which level the athlete is at in this program it is important that he work hard to keep himself in shape. He should be well fatigued not only for conditioning but to determine if the injury can withstand the stress of competition. Oftentimes an athlete will feel as if he can play but the injured body part can not withstand the combined effect of endurance and the stress of competition.

Contusions amount to a large number of the injuries treated. An inexpensive method of managing this type of injury is ice massage. Paper cups are filled three-quarters of the way and then placed in a freezer. The athlete then peels back the paper and gently rubs the affected area until it becomes numb. I have found this especially effective in areas that are not covered by muscle mass (e.g., the tibia). The bruised area can then be covered by either a commercial shin guard or a foam doughnut can be placed on the back of the shin guard. To protect a contusion of the quadriceps, a football thigh pad held in place by either an elastic bandage or elastic tape works well.

Standard first aid procedures of immobilization and splinting should be used for all fractures. Any dislocation should also be treated as a fracture. The procedures for immobilization vary with each body part and will not be discussed in this article. It is recommended that any coach responsible for the first aid treatment of his athletes be certified in standard first aid and cardiopulmonary resuscitation.

Summary

No matter how knowledgeable a person may be in the area of sports-medicine there will be a percentage of athletes that are injured. There is no way to completely control this but there are ways of reducing the frequency of injuries from the norm. The coach plays an important role in keeping this number of injuries to a minimum. The modification of practice sessions to daily conditions is a contributing factor in the reduction of injuries. The weather, field conditions and the athlete's condition are all factors that must be considered. A coach that fatigues his players day after day will eventually wear down the athlete's resistance, leaving him more susceptible to injury. On the other hand, a coach that takes stress factors into consideration and modifies his practices accordingly will probably field a healthier team. The coach who is aware of the potential for injury can greatly reduce the risks by becoming more knowledgeable in the area of prevention and management of these injuries.

REFERENCES

1. Pardon, ET, "Lower extremities are site of most soccer injuries," *Phys Sportsmed,* June 1977, p. 45.
2. Ibid.
3. Ibid.

Prevention and Care of Wrestling Injuries

Jeff Fair, M.S., A.T.C., C.C.T.

Wrestling is a sport in which injuries play a major role. The injury rate (number of injuries per number of athletes) is just below that of football with the noncontact sports such as basketball, baseball, track, swimming, etc., far behind. Because of the high incidence of injury and the possibility of severe injury, wrestling deserves considerable attention from the athletic trainer and the team physician.

Figure 1. *Injuries to the head and neck are frequent in wrestlers.* Photo courtesy of the Ithaca Journal, Ithaca, New York

Injury prevention should be the primary goal of the coach and sports medicine personnel. Having well conditioned athletes who possess strength, endurance and flexibility is the best insurance running and flexibility exercises are a necessity for a well conditioned wrestler.

Like most high school and college athletics wrestling has become a year-round sport. Off season is an excellent opportunity for the athlete to accelerate his weight work while continuing his flexibility exercises. The wrestler must constantly watch his weight so that a drastic weight loss will not be required just before the start of the season.

WEIGHT CONTROL

Weight control should be discussed often with the team, and last minute large weight losses by dehydration should be discouraged. Common sense, proper diet, self-discipline and good planning will lead to a successful weight control program. The psychological problems of losing weight can be more of a problem to the athlete than actually losing the weight itself. In order to reduce the anxiety of weight loss some method of checking body fat needs to be used to reassure and set reasonable goals for the wrestler. Periodic checks of the wrestler's subcutaneous fat should be taken by the team physician or athletic trainer. This information needs to be interpreted and given to the coach and athlete. Skin fold measurements using Lange skin fold calipers can be used to measure the athlete's subcutaneous fat. Six skin fold measurements are usually taken in different areas and are added together. The total measurement should be ideally within the 25 mm to 35 mm range. By calculating his body fat the wrestler's potential weight class can be determined. Thus, the wrestler could begin the season at a higher weight class, gradually reduce his subcutaneous fat during the season and conceivably safely drop a weight class for important tournaments at the end of the season. Dehydration will not affect the subcutaneous fat reading because the majority of fluid in the body is stored in the muscles. Perhaps the best physical activity to reduce subcutaneous fat quantities is distance running. Dehydration tends to reduce muscle size and hampers chemical reactions within the muscle itself. Athletes who are dehydrated seem to fatigue more quickly and have more muscle spasms and cramps.

INFECTIONS

Infections such as impetigo and boils can spread through a team in a short period of time leaving the athletes unable to wrestle. Most problems of infections can be prevented with good hygiene on the part of the individual wrestlers and proper care of the wrestling area. Wrestling mats should be swept and mopped with a strong disinfectant that will kill both staphylococci and streptococci bacteria daily.

Boils are usually caused by staphylococci which produce a pustule. As the pustule enlarges, the area becomes reddened, tender and painful. The area should be treated with hot packs and oral antibiotics prescribed by the team physician.

Eruptions of small vessels that form into pustules and later form yellow crustations are characteristic of impetigo. The infected area should be washed several times each day using a medicated soap to remove all crustations. After the area has dried an ointment prescribed by the team physician should be applied.

INJURIES

As in any other contact sport wrestlers are vulnerable to the full spectrum of injuries. Because of the involvement of the head and neck in wrestling, injuries to this area are frequent. Black eyes, fractured noses, mild concussions and cuts over the eye, cheekbone and chin are frequent. These injuries do require a doctor's examination, especially concussions. Any wrestler with a possible concussion must not be allowed to participate any further until he has been examined by a physician.

Officials and coaches need to strongly discourage illegal butting (hitting with the head) during matches and practice. By doing this, concussions, fractures of the nose and cuts of the face and head can be reduced.

Wrestlers are very aware of the fact that during a match they are allowed an injury time of three minutes. At the end of three minutes a decision has to be made as to whether the athlete can continue the match or forfeit. This decision should be made by the attending physician. The use of direct pressure over small cuts on the face and head usually stops bleeding in a few minutes and, depending on the cut's size and location, the athlete may be able to continue wrestling. Possible fractured noses are a different matter. In most cases the athlete should not be allowed to continue the match.

Neck injuries in wrestling are the most frightening injury in the sport. Slams, unusual positions and bridging sometimes result in neck injuries. These injuries should be handled carefully by the attending medical staff and, if there is any question as to the extent of the injury, the athlete should be transferred to the hospital using a back and neck board for x-rays and neurological examination. Every wrestler should possess strong neck muscles. The muscles surrounding the wrestler's neck are his best protection against a severe neck injury. Resistive exercises to strengthen the neck muscles are a necessary part of any wrestling weight program. Bridging should be discouraged by the coach as a neck exercise, because the exercise itself can injure the neck by forcing it into hyperextension.

Common shoulder injuries found in wrestling are the rotator cuff injuries, usually caused by forcing the joint into extremes in its range of motion. This area is hard to treat because of the depth of the injury. Rest and short wave diathermy seem to help this condition.

Other injuries common to the shoulder girdle are sternoclavicular separation and acromioclavicular separation. These injuries usually occur when an athlete falls on his shoulder or falls on his side forcing the clavicle to separate at either or both ends. These conditions are slow healing and should be treated with ice massage for the first two or three days, and then contrast treatments with ultrasound. Both of these areas need to be taped when the wrestler returns to practice for support and protection.

Costochondral separations occur frequently in wrestling when the athlete's trunk is forced into flexion usually causing the separation of ribs 10-11-12 from the cartilage connection to the sternum or the cartilage between the ribs themselves. This is a very painful condition that requires time and rest to heal. Pain medication may be needed so that the athlete can sleep. In some cases, ice massage can help relieve some of the soreness. Taping over the injured ribs may help when the wrestler returns to practice, but rest and time are the two important factors in treatment.

Cauliflower ear is much less prevalent in today's wrestlers because of the requirement that headgear be worn in matches. Coaches should be reminded of the importance of wearing the headgear for practice. Even with the headgear occasionally a wrestler will develop cauliflower ear. The area will need to be drained by the team physician and a collodion cast should be applied to the ear after the fluid is removed. The collodion cast should be worn for three to four days to control swelling.

Knee injuries are all too common in wrestling. The mechanism of knee injuries in wrestling usually occur primarily in two ways. The first is a twisting mechanism caused when the wrestler makes a quick move to the right or left and the sole of the shoe sticks to the surface of the mat. This usually results in cartilage damage. The second mechanism is the spraining of the ligaments on the medial or lateral side of the knee caused by twisting, turning and general predicaments the wrestlers seem to get their legs into. Having a shoe that has **less affinity for the mat and keeping the mat clean can help reduce some of the cartilage injuries** caused by the first mechanism mentioned. To avoid the second mechanism of injury the wrestler should possess good flexibility and well-developed muscles adjacent to the joints. Also, well trained officials who know and understand the rules should stop the match when knees or any other joints become endangered.

A conservative approach is recommended for treating knee injuries. Knee sprains may need to be placed in a cast or splinted with a velcro splint for a length of time dependent upon the severity of the injury. During this time the athlete should receive treatments of ice massage, non-resistive range of motion exercises, and straight leg lifts. After the sprain has had adequate time to heal, the quadriceps, hamstrings, adductors, abductors and gastrocnemius should be rehabilitated to their pre-injury strength before returning to practice or competition. In cartilage injuries the wrestler may need to rest and ice massage his knee for several days until all swelling, soreness, or fluid in the joint has subsided. If the condition continues the cartilage may need to be removed surgically. When taping a wrestler's knee it is important to remember that wrestling requires a full range of motion at the knee joint. This can be accomplished by using primarily elastic tape for support. During the time of inactivity caused by the knee injury (or any other injury) the athlete should be given exercises to maintain his conditioning and weight.

Ankle injuries in wrestling are usually not severe, but they hamper the athlete's mobility on the mat. These sprains are usually the inversion type and should be treated with ice, compression and elevation. Treatment should continue with ice for 24-48 hours or until swelling has started to diminish, at which time contrast treatments can be started. In taping a wrestler's ankle it is important to remember that he needs more range of motion than a football or basketball player. The ankle should be taped so that the wrestler has protection from inversion but is still able to plantarflex and dorsiflex the ankle.

Wrestling is an exciting and enjoyable sport that can be hampered by untimely injuries. A well qualified coaching staff and good medical care are essential for any successful wrestling program. Prevention of injuries is the key and can be obtained by having well conditioned and flexible athletes. With proper planning and hard work, success can be within the reach of the well prepared wrestler.

REFERENCES

1. American College of Sports Medicine, Positions Stand on Weight Loss in Wrestlers. *Medicine and Science in Sports.* 8:XI-XIV, 1976.
2. Mathews, Donald K., D.P.Ed. *Measurement in Physical Education.* W. B. Saunders Company, Philadelphia, 1973.
3. Zambraski, Edward J., Ph.D. "Wrestling and Research," *Toward an Understanding of Human Performance.* Mouvement Publications, Ithaca, New York, 1977.
4. O'Donoghue, Don H., M.D. *Treatment of Injuries to Athletes.* W. B. Saunders Company, Philadelphia, 1970.
5. Cooper, Donald L., M.D. and Fair, Jeff, ATC. "Treating 'Cauliflower' Ear." *The Physician and Sports Medicine.* Vol. 4, No. 7, 1976.
6. Umbach, Arnold W. and Johnson, Warren R. *Wrestling.* Wm. C. Brown Company, Dubuque, Iowa, 1966.

Prevention of Overuse Injuries in the Distance Runner

Donald Maron, D.P.M.

In recent years there has been a new and exciting trend in the practice of sports medicine. Physicians, trainers and coaches alike have found that it is possible to predict and sometimes prevent certain systematic injuries in sport. In other words, they are trying to "prevent injuries before they happen."

The practice of *preventive sports medicine* is of special significance to the distance runner. We have found that these superb biological machines, capable of magnificent physiological feats of endurance, are subject to predictable types of maladies which we might collectively classify as "overuse" or "stress" injuries. The prevention of these overuse injuries should be a major goal of all those concerned with the training of the distance runner.

Most sports activities involve walking and/or running, and since these means of locomotion are dependent upon the use of the lower extremity, it is only logical that the podiatrist is a key physician in the diagnosis and treatment of sports medicine problems. In discussing the "runner," Dr. Steven Subtonick explained "that a sports medicine podiatrist must act as a doctor as well as a counselor and at times even as a coach. The decisions made can be heartbreaking for the runner, parent and coach, but above all must protect the patient (the athlete)" (6).

Let's begin our discussion of the role of the sports podiatrist and his/her relationship with the distance runner through a brief analysis of the biomechanics of human locomotion.

BIOMECHANICS OF HUMAN LOCOMOTION

Locomotion is the transportation of the body from one point to another. Human locomotion has been compared to a wheel rolling over the ground with our legs serving as spokes. The spoke that touches the ground constitutes the *stance phase* and the spoke that moves about the axle is the *swing phase* of walking. Man attempts to keep his center of gravity moving in a straight horizontal line during locomotion. Man's *center of gravity* is located just forward to the lower back, midway between the hip joints.

Man's walking and running patterns have been systematically analyzed in three dimensional views by the use of high speed cameras, mirrors, electronography and other scientific tests (2). In order to understand running, it is first necessary to examine the normal walking cycle (see Figure 1).

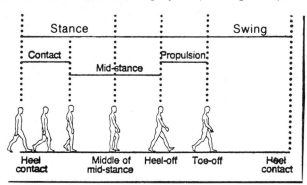

Figure 1. *The walking cycle.*

Walking is inititated by inclining the body, thus placing it ahead of its center of gravity. To regain balance, one leg must be brought forward ahead of the shifting center of gravity. The leg that remains weight bearing is the "stance" leg and *must always* be in contact with the ground. The leg that moves to regain balance is the "swing" leg, as it returns the body to the center of gravity, resulting in forward movement. Walking, therefore, can be divided into:

1. *Stance phase* in which the leg is weight bearing and
2. *Swing phase* in which the leg is moved to another point of contact.

The *stance phase* occupies about 60–65% of the walking cycle. It begins as a heel strikes the ground and ends following the "swing" phase of the opposite limb.

In the *swing phase* the foot is in contact with the ground and the lower leg is internally rotating. The first 15–25% of the stance phase occurs as the heel and then the foot make contact with the ground, while the limb is still internally rotating. The foot *cannot* internally rotate due to reactive forces of the contacting surface which prevents this type of motion. Subotnick (6) states: "the foot is dependent upon the subtalar joint, a universal type joint, which allows for internal transverse plane rotation of the leg to be manifested in the foot" (see Figures 3–6). Following heel contact the foot becomes a loose adapter to the ground and then becomes a rigid lever for toe off (push off). Most

Figure 2. *Phases in running. This figure is based on the work of Slocum, D.B. and James, S., "Biomechanics of Running," Journal of American Medical Association, 205:721–729, 1968. The support phase is found in numbers 2–8 while the recovery period may be illustrated by numbers 9–10, 1–2. In the support phase, note foot strike in 5, mid support in 6, and take-off in 7–8. In the recovery period, note forward swing in 9, follow through in 10 and foot descent in 1–2.*

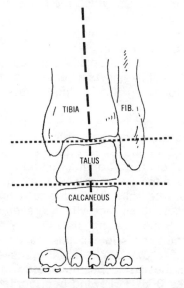

Figure 3. *The normal foot and leg. From: Podiatric Sports Medicine by S. Subotnick, Futura Publishing Company, Mount Kisco, N.Y. Reproduced with permission of the publisher.*

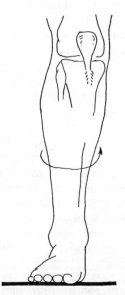

Figure 4. *Prolonged pronation of the foot in the athlete. From: Podiatric Sports Medicine by S. Subotnick, Mount Kisco, N.Y. Reproduced with permission of the publisher.*

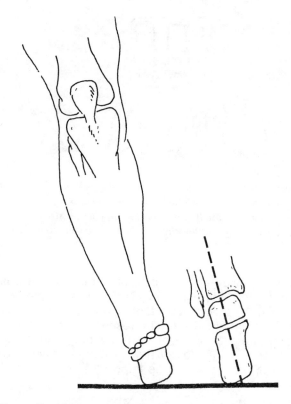

Figure 5. *Tibial varum. Note heel contact from: Podiatric Sports Medicine by S. Subotnick, Futura Publishing Company, Mount Kiscom N.Y. Reproduced with permission of the publisher.*

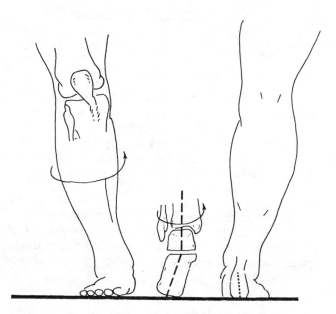

Figure 6. *Compensation for tibial torsion with lateral patellar subluxations. Note the internal rotation of the lower limb proximal to the subtalar joint, as the foot is fixed in the stance phase. From: Podiatric Sports Medicine by S. Subotnick, Futura Publishing Company, Mount Kisco, N.Y. Reproduced with permission of the publisher.*

injuries are due to a malpositioning of the subtalar joint at heel contact, resulting in excessive stresses on the muscles, ligaments and joints proximal to the foot.

Running is a form of locomotion in which the body is alternately supported by each lower extremity with an intervening air-borne period when neither of the lower extremities are in contact with ground. This differs from normal walking where there is always one foot on the ground.

Slocum & James (4) have broken down the support and recovery phases into periods. In the support phase, the three periods are *foot strike, mid-support* and *take off.* Foot strike begins when the foot first touches the running surface and continues for the brief moment during which the foot becomes firmly fixed. Mid-support starts once the foot is fixed and sustains until the heel begins to rise and continues until the toes leave the running surface.

The recovery period is divided into a period of *follow-through, forward-swing and foot-descent.* Follow-through begins when the trailing foot leaves the ground and continues until the foot stops its rearward motion. Forward-swing begins with the beginning of forward motion of the foot and terminates when the foot reaches its most forward position. Foot-descent begins after the recovery foot reaches its most forward position, reverses direction and descends toward the running surface in a rearward direction and terminates with foot strike. At the instant the foot touches the running surface the thigh swings rearward with the knee moderately flexed. The foot makes contact with the running surface initially in a supinated position and proceeds into pronation until the forefoot is securely fixed to the running surface (as you read this why not try to simulate these motions with your own foot). As the foot moves slightly in between stance phase and heel rise (push off), it is subjected to constantly changing stresses. The body then moves forward over the ankle until the knee becomes almost straight (extension); tension is built up in the gastroc muscles in preparation for heel to forefoot contact.

In review, the phases of running are similar to those of the walking cycle in that the contact foot goes through the same motion. The speed and the distance of the run will result in slight alterations in the kinematics of running. In the support phase, *sprinters* usually have a tendency to stay on the ball of the foot. The heel may sag towards the running surface during mid-support. *Middle distance runners* frequently contact the ground on the ball of the foot initially and the heel may (some do, some don't) momentarily strike the running surface. In the *long-distance runners,* the foot strike is usually with the heel and forefoot simultaneously contacting the running surface ("flatfooted").

EXAMINATION OF THE RUNNER

It is of great importance that the team physician, coach and trainer work together with the common goal of preventing injuries before they occur. A proper, thorough physical and podiatric examination is of special importance for the runner. The following examination is given to all of my runners (patients) in order to ascertain if there is either a foot/leg problem or improper construction of the runner's shoes. The examination is aimed at *prevention* of future injuries!

PODIATRIC SPORTS EXAMINATION:

1. Name: Age:
2. How many years have they been running?
3. Type of Training   Miles per week
4. Distance   Average time
5. Has the runner ever experienced:

Toe Cramps	Yes ( ) No ( )	Right ( )	Left ( )
Arch Cramps	Yes ( ) No ( )	Right ( )	Left ( )
Knee Pains	Yes ( ) No ( )	Right ( )	Left ( )
Leg Cramps	Yes ( ) No ( )	Right ( )	Left ( )
Lower Back Aches	Yes ( )		No ( )
Weak Ankles	Yes ( ) No ( )	Right ( )	Left ( )
Shin Splints	Yes ( ) No ( )	Right ( )	Left ( )
Stress Fractures	Yes ( ) No ( )	Right ( )	Left ( )
Groin Pains	Yes ( ) No ( )	Right ( )	Left ( )
Hip Pains	Yes ( ) No ( )	Right ( )	Left ( )

6. Have you had to wear any corrective shoes or devices?
   Yes ( ) No ( )

The runner is then examined clinically by a simple test for subtalar malposition. The runner is asked to stand on one leg as I look for excessive motion (uneven or even) of the foot. As you read this stand up and try to balance on one foot; do you notice any "rocking" motion?

If there is a subtalar malposition, then a complete podiatric examination is given, including a study of the runner's normal walking and running gaits, length of both legs, dorsiflexion and plantar flexion of both feet in relationship to the lower leg, and girth of calf and thighs. Then I proceed to measure the subtalar joint for either excessive inversion or eversion. I might add that this is a complex clinical examination involving the precise measurement of possible abnormal range of motion occurring at the subtalar joint. A complete description of this procedure is beyond the scope of this paper; however, the reader is referred to the book by Sgarlato (3) for further information.

When there is no subtalar instability I will check the training and racing shoes for the following:

1. Rigidity of the sole — if the sole is not flexible the runner may have to use undo pressure (10 lbs. or more) in flexing the sole, which may result in shin splints, tendonitis of the tendon achilles and possible knee pains.

2. The counter of the shoe (cup around the heel) should always be in neutral position when observing the shoe from the back (see Figure 7).

The most important tools for the runner are his/her feet. Close behind are the running shoes. I am often asked to give the factors to be weighed in evaluating a running shoe. The running shoe

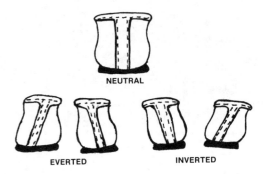

Figure 7. *Shoe construction in three positions. When the counter is in an inverted or everted position (because of poor shoe construction), this will cause the foot upon heel strike to contact the running surface in an abnormal position and can cause injuries.*

should provide (1) support cushioning of the ball, (2) firm arch support and (3) flexibility of the sole for easy push off. The foot should be measured while the athlete is standing (especially for females) in the late afternoon or early evening, since feet swell during the day. When selecting shoes (see Figure 8), there are three important areas to consider.

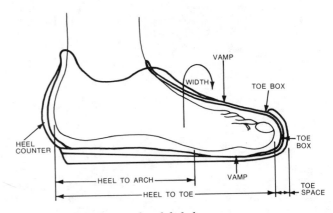

Figure 8. *The running shoe labeled.*

1. The heel counter should fit snugly around the heel yet not be so stiff as to cause irritations. A loose fitting counter can cause blisters on the heel or possible tendon irritations from excessive motion.

2. The vamp should be wide enough to accommodate the forefoot without being too loose, otherwise it can cause blisters, especially on the ball of the foot. Too tight a vamp, however, will cause corns, toe deformities and muscle cramping.

3. The toe box should allow free movement of the toes without pressure. A cramped toe box can cause blood blisters, as well as ingrown and bleeding toenails.

I have found the lacing of shoes to be another important factor in the prevention of injuries. The Maron lacing technique (see Figure 9) was developed in cooperation with a shoe manufacturer in order to better support the ankle and foot. For a comparison, have the athlete lace one shoe normally and the other with my technique and see if he/she notes a difference.

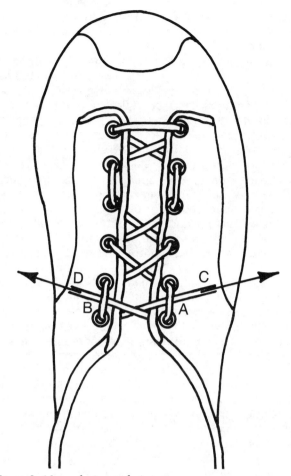

Figure 9. *Maron lacing techniques.*
1. *Lift up lace A, pull lace C under lace A*
2. *Lift up lace B, pull lace D under lace B*
3. *Pull tight in direction of arrows*
4. *Tie in usual manner.*

FLEXIBILITY AND STRENGTH NEEDS OF THE RUNNER

The mechanics of running develop the particular anatomical structures involved in a differential fashion. Gravity muscles in the runner are the hamstrings, gastrocnemius-soleus groups and ilio-psoas. The anti-gravity muscles of significance in the running athlete are the quadriceps and lower anterior chamber (shin area) groups. We have found that the runner's legs adapt in a predictable fashion to the stress of over 300 foot strikes per minute, _____ hours per day, _____ days per week, _____ weeks per year.

In my experience, the distance runner is often characterized by unusually *weak* (1) abdominal, (2) quadriceps and (3) lower leg anterior muscle groups. At the same time, the runner is often very strong (tight) in (1) the hamstrings and (2) the gastrocs group. Thus, the runner's exercise program should be geared to strengthen the former muscle groups while stretching the latter.

The coach or trainer who truly wants to prevent overuse injuries in his/her distance runners *must demand* that they participate in fifteen minutes of continuous muscle strengthening and stretching exercises both before and after each "run." You

are referred to Appendix B and to the paper by Aten in the present volume for a description of exercises for each of these muscle groups.

INJURIES TO RUNNERS

In a recent survey of our local high school and college runners we found the following injuries and their incidence.

1. Knee pains — 60%
2. Lower back aches — 58%
3. Tendonitis of tendo-achilles — 42%
4. Runner's cramps — 41%
5. Shin splints — 40%
6. Weak ankles (ankle sprains) — 30%
7. Toe cramps — 26%
8. Arch pains — 20%
9. Heel pains — 16%
10. Blisters — 25%
11. Stress fractures (leg and/or foot) — 8%
12. Blood blisters — 10%
13. Loss of toenails — 7%
14. Corns and/or callouses — 4%

These injuries which we might collectively classify as "overuse injuries" were not isolated; most athletes had experienced a combination of two or more. The sad fact is that many of these injuries could have been prevented!

Of all the injuries which occur to runners, the most common are problems associated with the knee. The so called "runner's knee" can denote any number of conditions; the most common in my experience being the muscular-tendonous inflammation of the medial aspect of the knee. This condition may be caused by an *excessively pronated foot* at heel contact and or mid-support and push off phase.

Another common knee problem is chondromalacia. Some knee injuries can spell misery for the runner, chondromalacia can spell "doom." For the sake of simplicity I define chondromalacia as a condition in which the posterior aspect of an abnormally positioned patella becomes damaged.

RUNNER'S KNEE

The causes of runner's knee are quite varied; however, four of these deserve special attention: direct trauma, weak quadriceps, foot structured abnormalities, and overuse.

DIRECT TRAUMA

Direct trauma is actually self-explanatory. It commonly involves a physical blow being applied to the knee as in the football player who gets "clipped" from behind. With the thousands of participants in recent national and international marathons, direct blows to the knee, stemming from crowding and pushing, are not infrequent.

WEAK QUADRICEPS

Weak quadriceps muscles (particularly the vastus medialis) are sometimes offered as a cause for knee problems. A weakened condition may allow the patella more freedom of lateral motion, especially when combined with the strain of distance running. Since the distance runner's quadriceps are trained for endurance activities, rather than activities requiring great thigh strength, a weakened condition may combine with one of the following causes to disable the runner.

FOOT ABNORMALITIES

The human foot consists of 26 bones bound together by ligaments, propelled by muscles and equipped with nerves and blood vessels. A marvel of biological engineering, the foot is a highly complex bioengineered organ of balance and propulsion. The foot is continuously subjected to stress and is particularly vulnerable to injury in a sport such as distance running.

Dr. George Sheehan and other leading sports physicians and podiatrists theorize that foot abnormalities add to stress placed upon the knee, causing displacement of the patella and increased friction between the patella and the femoral condyles. One such abnormality is prevalent in running related injuries, the Morton's toe (a congenitally shorter first toe). In an individual with Morton's toe, the foot adapts by either (1) bearing most of the weight on the second metatarsal, thereby causing a stress fracture or (2) by pronating the foot (rolling over to the inside of the foot) and opening a Pandora's box of overuse injuries.

Pronating the foot may also cause the quadriceps to pull the kneecap to a position that is more directly over the lateral femoral condyle than is normal. Several foot abnormalities are too complex for the present discussion. The "local runner's physician" should always be contacted.

OVERUSE

A distance runner puts varying degrees of strain on the quadriceps tendon and the patellar region over long periods of time. The effects of this strain day after day may cause a disturbance of rhythm of the patellar function. Differences in running speed, length of stride, direction of stride and variations in the running surface may all cause the patella to be displaced slightly and abruptly. This displacement, combined with repetitive action of running, could cause some wearing of the patellar articular cartilage.

Distance runners are subject to overuse problems almost constantly. Constant repetition of the knee action in running, when combined with slight patellar displacement, will cause *patellar malacia* to develop. If the displacement is caused or worsened by structural abnormalities of the foot, the condition is likely to be more severe, and more difficult to treat.

SHIN SPLINTS

In my recent survey of local high school track teams, I found that next to the knee, shin splints were the next most serious problem among runners. The term "shin splint" is a category which covers several associated injuries. When asked the common question, "What are shin splints?", I reply that they involve an inflammation of the tissues surrounding the shin bone (tibia) in the lower leg. The true medical definition is that it is a musculotendenous inflammation occurring either in the anterior (front) or the posterior (back) aspect of the

lower leg. It is depressing to find that these injuries which often repeat themselves are commonly left untreated.

The major culprit in shin splints is muscular imbalance. The muscles which pull (dorsiflex) the foot are weak. The opposing muscles in the calf are short and tight, and don't let the foot flex to its normal 10 degrees. Shin splints occur almost exclusively among runners with short calf muscles. Pain is usually of the middle one-third or lower one-third of the tibial crest (shin).

The causes of shin splint problems are related to climate, track, running on hard surfaces, conditioning procedures, poor biomechanics of running, pre-existing foot and arch problems, running over uneven terrain (as in cross-country training) and over-exertion without proper conditioning. Therefore, the problem of shin splints is not limited to any one sport. Pain is usually precipitated when the untrained or unconditioned athlete over-exerts, changes to a hard playing surface or changes his/her footwear. The stress of over-exertion or over-loading with constant work increases the tightness and strength of the gastrocnemius muscle group which is used in the push-off phase of gait. The anterior tibial muscle group only has to maintain ankle stability during the stance phase and produce dorsiflexion during the swing phase, thus creating an antagonistic muscle. Poor footwear for workouts and "street use" contributes to the problem also.

Uphill running, as in cross-country running, creates the problem of a tight gastrocnemius muscle group too. This problem is again compounded with the forward body lean for balance, increasing lower leg stress.

It is necessary to x-ray the lower extremity to eliminate the possibility of stress fractures which may be masked with the same symptoms as shin splints. The runner who trains while experiencing shin splints will sometimes develop an incomplete fracture of the long bones of the lower leg (stress fracture). This condition will incapacitate the runner for at least six weeks. We have discussed stress fracture problems in national class teenage female distance runners in an earlier paper (1).

A shin splint condition in the anterior muscle group is best treated by (1) dorsiflexor exercises with the use of a weighted shoe or weights placed on the toes in order to strengthen this muscle group (2) cessation of running for a week or (3) cryotherapy techniques as described by Knight in the present volume.

THE ORTHOTIC

In recent years, sports podiatrists have been able to achieve success in treating runners, most frequently, by use of what might be described as the "magic wedge," the *orthotic*. This angular-shaped plastic, leather, or foam rubber insert fits inside the shoe and, in effect, tells the foot (in a form of biofeedback) "where to go." The orthotic permits the foot, despite any deformity, to land flat, thus avoiding the twisting motion as the leg struggles to balance the weight of the body. This twisting motion is the main cause of most leg problems.

Biomechanical orthotic devices create near normal function by maintaining the angular anatomical relationships between the forefoot, rearfoot, leg and the horizontal plane (the ground you walk on). This is done by the inherent contours in the neutral position module or shell and by the acrylic posts on the front, rear or both ends, which cause the device to move into specific positions at certain times during the gait cycle. Thus, the jarring effect created by conventional arch supports is eliminated. The end result is the reduction of abnormal motion without total restriction of normal motion, and a decrease or elimination of foot symptoms, excrescences (corns, calluses, etc.) and leg and back fatigue resulting from using the wrong muscles at the wrong time.

Through the use of orthotics the foot is guided, both in space and upon contact, to a neutral position at the middle of midstance (remember your biomechanics of running) when weightbearing is at its maximum. On contact, the foot should land directly beneath the body such that the various stresses to the joints are evenly distributed. Improper gait will result in an imbalanced running form. Steindler (5) refers to the "kinetic chain" in which the various joints proximal to the foot work together as a balanced whole to achieve efficient movement. With the foot placed in proper balance (neutral position), no joint of the kinetic chain should be abnormally stressed and thus most of the knee/patella problems are solved.

Orthotics, once unheard of among runners, have now become so prevalent among people with previous leg problems that they have almost become fashionable, faddish or trendy. Rather than consider them a form of weakness, runners brag about their orthotics. People without them yearn to own a pair, as though they were a new set of headers for their Corvette. I have people coming into my office now who demand that I give them orthotics, even though they don't need them.

To summarize, the orthotics are not actually a foot support. The orthotic does not support the foot; it merely allows the foot to get into the proper position such that the muscles can "do the job" in aligning the joints, and the bony architecture of the foot can do its job in actually supporting the body weight.

REFERENCES

1. Brush, F., Burke, E. J. and Maron, D. Strenuous training of teenage female distance runners: an apparent dilemma. A paper presented at the AAHPER national convention, Seattle, Washington, 1977.
2. Ducroquet, R. *Walking and Running*, Philadelphia: J.B. Lippincott Co., 1965.
3. Sgarlato, T. E. *A compendum of podiatric biomechanics.* San Francisco: California College of Podiatric Medicine, 1971.
4. Slocum, D. B. and James, S. Biomechanics of running. *JAMA* 205: 721–729, 1968.
5. Steindler, A. *Kinesiology of the human body,* Springfield, Illinois: Charles C. Thomas, 1964.
6. Subotnick, S. *Podiatric sports medicine,* Mount Kisco, N.Y.: Futura Publishing Company, 1975.

Toward An Elimination of a Life Threatening Situation In Football

John Sciera, M.S., A.T.C., L.P.T.

In this author's opinion, football is one of the outstanding games invented by the mind of man. Names and events associated with the game are legendary. Twentieth century America has been greatly enriched by such heroes as: Jim Thorpe, Tad Jones, the Four Horsemen, Knute Rockne and George Gipp, Red Grange, Vince Lombardi, O. J. Simpson, Tony Dorsett, Joe Namath, Jim Brown, Roger Staubach and Brian Piccolo. Further evidence for football's effect on the American scene include: the raccoon coat, the Thanksgiving Day game, the Rose Bowl, Super Bowl Sunday, and the marching band. Football is a game of emotions. It is fear and it is courage. It is tragedy and it is comedy. Football has grace, strength, anger, joy, sadness and hope.

This great game should continue but something has been introduced that may very well give football's opponents legitimate ammunition in influencing administrators and school boards to consider its elimination, and perhaps rightfully so. The problem is not with the lack of participation or interest but rather with the increasing number of youngsters who have suffered life threatening or permanently disabling injuries (1).

A trainer or coach shudders at the thought of a serious head or neck injury in one of his athletes. This is a problem of such severe magnitude that it overshadows ankle, knee or shoulder problems. Consequently, we should be primarily interested in the prevention of these types of injuries. Thus, the purpose of this paper will be to reflect on the athletic trainer's responsibility in these matters.

CERVICAL DISLOCATION
CERVICAL FRACTURE
CERVICAL SPRAIN
CERVICAL STRAIN
BRACHIAL PLEXUS

PNEUMO THORAX
CARDIAC ARREST
HEMO THORAX
FRACTURE

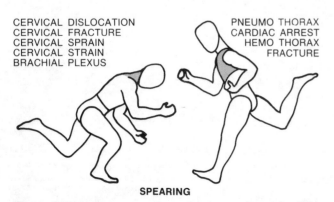

SPEARING

Figure 1. *Spearing can result in damage to the neck of the spearer and to the chest area of the player being speared.*

The wary trainer or coach must be prepared for the possibility of the serious head and neck injury. Necessary equipment may include: bolt cutters for cutting the face mask, the spinal board, and the tracheotomy kit for the physician to use, if necessary. Trained personnel must also be aware of the signs and symptoms of a concussion or a serious cervical injury. While we should be prepared for the possible emergency, we all hope that it will never occur to one of our athletes.

Our main emphasis should without question be in the area of prevention. To quote a worn-out cliche, "an ounce of prevention is worth a pound of cure." Every text on athletic training is in agreement on the importance of this area of emphasis for those involved with sports medicine. First, we encourage the athlete to develop strong and powerful neck musculature. We check to see if the helmet fits properly. We apply the foam cervical roll to protect the neck and recently we have seen teams with straps attached from shoulder pads to the helmet to check hyperflexion of the neck.

Even with all the protective equipment and preventive measures, the primary problem is the common practice of utilizing the helmet as a weapon. One argument against the technique may be made from a kinesiological viewpoint. Is the neck musculature strong enough to withstand the forces to which it is subjected? The neck, according to tests we have done with a tensiometer, can pull in forward flexion approximately 45 to 65 pounds of pressure. A back who weighs 200 pounds and runs a 10-second 100-yard dash is coming through with a force of approximately 750 foot pounds. If the head becomes the initial point of contact, there could result an unacceptable force to be absorbed by the head and neck.

Kinesiologists and anatomists note that the neck is a very hypermobile structure. Phylogeny apparently has sacrificed strength for mobility. The cervical vertebrae and their ligamentous and muscular structures are not sufficiently developed to stand the abuse which football sometimes creates. In contrast, the shoulder girdle is able to lift approximately 300–400 pounds. Apparently, the shoulder is constructed to take this abuse better than the head and neck. Throughout history and across cultures one can see the shoulder being used to carry heavy objects. As an illustration of the relative strength of the shoulder girdle we can imagine a

Figure 2. *Butt-blocking, consisting of driving the face mask, frontal area on top of the helmet directly into an opponent. Not only is this dangerous to the blocker and the man being blocked, but it is also a personal foul! Taken from the 1977 High School Football Rules — Simplified and Illustrated, published by the National Federation of High School Associations, Elgin, Illinois, 60120. Reprinted with permission of the National Federation of State High School Associations.*

Figure 3. *The use of the shoulder in blocking is recommended. In executing this block, it is important that the blocker hold his head in an upright position, tucked in between his shoulders and make contact with his shoulder. Taken from the 1977 High School Football Rules — Simplified and Illustrated, published by the National Federation of State High School Associations, Elgin, Illinois, 60120. Reprinted with the permission of the National Federation of State High School Associations.*

Figure 4. *Face tackling, consisting of driving the face mask, frontal area on top of the helmet directly into the runner. Not only is this dangerous to the tackler and the man being tackled but it is also a personal foul! Taken from the 1977 High School Football Rules—Simplified and Illustrated, published by the National Federation of State High School Associations, Elgin, Illinois, 60120. Reprinted with permission of the National Federation of State High School Associations.*

Spearing is a disqualifying personal foul. Spearing is deliberately and maliciously driving the helmet into the player who is down or who is held so he's going down or who is held so his forward progress is stopped or who is obviously out of the play.

When a runner contacts the ground with anything other than a foot or hand, the ball is dead immediately. It is spearing and a disqualifying personal foul for a defensive player to drive his helmet into a runner who is sliding along the ground.

Figure 5. *Spearing, driving the helmet into a player who is down. This is a disqualifying personal foul.*

man sitting on another man's shoulder. The person doing the lifting would probably have little problem in "shrugging" the weight a distance of from four to six inches. In contrast, if the same man attempted to lift the other's body weight while perched on his forehead, he would find it impossible. Thus, the greater strength found in the shoulder girdle provides evidence for the encouragement of its use in blocking and tackling.

Medical authorities are uniform in their condemnation of using the head as a "weapon." Dr. Carl Blyth in the "Forty-Sixth Annual Survey of Football Fatalities" advises coaches to drill the athlete in proper execution in the fundamentals of football techniques, particularly blocking and tackling. He also admonishes that the player be taught to respect the helmet as a protective device and that the helmet should not be used as a "weapon."

Dr. Schneider in his recent text *Head and Neck Injuries in Football,* makes the following positive statement: "The head and neck can never be protected completely to withstand a direct impact force, no matter how good the equipment may be. The teaching of the head butting technique is one of the most serious errors being perpetuated throughout the country." (2) This statement by a leading neurosurgeon is in substantial agreement with other sports medicine specialists in the U.S.A. (3,4,5,6,7)

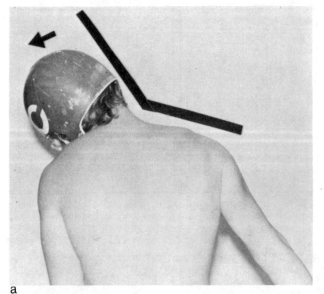

a

b

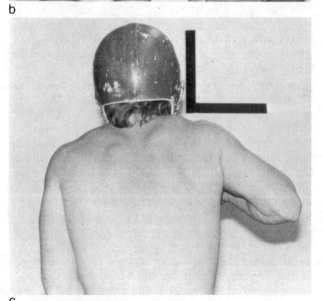

c

Every trainer knows the significance of the separated shoulder, the glenohumeral dislocation or fracture of the surgical neck of the humerus. For all of their pain and discomfort to the athlete, these injuries cannot compare in severity to the fractured or dislocated cervical vertebrae with the possible consequent damage to the spinal cord. Similarly, the subdural or epidural hematoma are far more serious than any of the shoulder injuries mentioned. We have all seen ball players who have had serious shoulder injuries and have seen them return to contact sports. However, once a serious head or neck injury is even suspected, the athlete is usually disqualified from play.

In summary, how can athletic trainers be influential in changing the technique of tackling and blocking with the head? First, we should try as tactfully as possible to persuade the coach that this technique places his young athlete's very life in danger and furthermore the shoulder tackle is effective and sensible from a kinesiological viewpoint. Secondly, as professionals interested in the welfare of our young athletes, trainers and coaches should collectively oppose the practice of using the head as the initial point of contact in blocking and tackling.*

*Editor's note: Primarily through Mr. Sciera's efforts, the Eastern Athletic Trainer's Association developed an official statement in 1975 opposing the use of the head as the initial point of contact for blocking and tackling in football. Soon after, the National Athletic Trainer's Association officially endorsed this statement as well.

REFERENCES

1. Blyth, C. S. and Arnold D. C., "The Forty-Sixth Annual Survey of Football Fatalities 1931-1977," The American Football Coaches Association, The National Collegiate Athletic Association and The National Federation of State High School Athletic Association, Feb. 1977.
2. Schneider, R., Head and Neck Injuries in Football, Williams & Wilkins Company, Baltimore, MD, 21202, 1973.
3. Reid, S. E., Epstein, H. M., and M. W. Louis, "Brain Trauma Inside a Football Helmet," The Physician and Sports Medicine, August 1974.
4. Hughes, J. R., and Wilms, J. H., Adams, C. L., and L. W. Combs, "Football Helmet Evaluation Based on Players' EEGS," Physician and Sports Medicine, May 1977.
5. Sciera, J. L., "Spear Tackling, The Most Dangerous Game," Scholastic Coach, May 1965.
6. Robinson, R. I., "NCAA Football Head and Neck Injuries in Eastern Colleges," July 1, 1973.
7. Schneider, R. C., Reifel, E., Crisler, H. O., and A. B. Oosterbaan, "Serious and Fatal Football Injuries Involving the Head and Spinal Cord," J.A.M.A., August 12, 1961.

Figure 6. (a) The neck in a weak position for blocking and tackling (b) this tackler is vulnerable to injury (c) the athlete should be taught to contract the large neck muscles for proper tackling and blocking.

An Analysis of Physical Fitness

Edmund J. Burke, Ph.D.

As an individual concerned with the prevention and care of athletic injuries you must be an effective communicator of information. You will be continually called upon to pass information from the physician to the coach and athlete and vice versa. In the normal course of activities you will undoubtedly find yourself in discussions related to the concept of physical fitness and related areas. Too often words such as "being in shape," "getting fit," wind, strength, flexibility, etc., are "tossed around" in a manner which is either confusing or downright meaningless to the coach or athlete. Clearly, one of the important aspects of professionalism is the ability to understand a topic and communicate a knowledge of that topic in meaningful, concise terms.

Commonly, I hear individuals use the term physical fitness as if to indicate that it can be objectively assessed in some easy manner. Unfortunately, an abundance of research (6, 19, 25) seems to be telling us that physical fitness is a broad construct consisting of several abilities. In earlier papers, I have attempted to examine the physiological basis, the training and the measurement of these abilities which we call the components of physical fitness (7, 10). It is my view that physical fitness contains six major abilities or components: aerobic power, anaerobic power, strength, local muscle endurance, flexibility and body composition. These components have differential impor-

tance to performance based upon the sport involved (10). Of particular importance to the athletic trainer, each is trained differently and each is measured differently. Thus, the purpose of this paper is to reflect on each of these components of physical fitness with the goal of making the implications as clear as possible for all those concerned with the prevention and care of athletic injuries.

AEROBIC POWER

Aerobic power refers to the ability of the individual to use oxygen during prolonged and strenuous exercise. Although the term aerobic power is preferred, the ability is sometimes referred to as cardiovascular endurance, cardio-respiratory endurance, circulo-respiratory endurance, wind, stamina or "being in shape." Since aerobic metabolism is the most efficient way of transferring the energy in our food to ATP and consequently to the muscle for work, this is truly an important ability for the athlete to improve upon.

For those interested in the prevention and care of athletic injuries the implications of improved aerobic power are several: (1) there should be a lower incidence of fatigue related injuries (2) the effects of dehydration may be less serious (3) improved aerobic power is often accompanied by decreased fat accumulations and improved performance on the field (4) rehabilitation following immobilization may be more effective with an im-

Physical Fitness Component	AEROBIC POWER		ANAEROBIC POWER		STRENGTH			LOCAL MUSCLE ENDURANCE		FLEXIBILITY	BODY COMPOSITION				
Subcomponent	O₂ Transport System	Muscle	Speed	Repeated Exercises at high intensity	Isotonic	Isometric	Power	Isotonic	Isometric		Height	Lean Weight vs. Fat Weight	Weight	Body Type	Fluids vs. Solids
Optimal Development	General development by exercise such as: long running, swimming, etc. Interval training	Specific to sport, play the sport	High resistance weight training Isokinetics. Flexibility	Wind sprints interval or Circuit training	Full range of motion, high resistance, low repetitions	Isometric contraction at near maximum	Same as Isotonic strength Isokinetics	Calisthenics. Low resistance, high repetitions	Isometric contract, at low % of max.	Stretching exercises	Heredity	Overload muscles	Caloric expenditures vs. caloric intake	Heredity	Body attempts to keep fluids at a fairly constant % of total weight. Altered by sweating, fluid intake, etc.
Examples of sports requiring high levels	Long Distance Running, Swimming, Basketball, Soccer		Football, Ice Hockey, Wrestling		Football, Baseball, Field Events, e.g. Shot Put or Javelin			Gymnastics, Dance, Basketball		Diving, Gymnastics, Dance	Specific to sport and position. Each sport probably has an optimum range of height, weight, body fat and body type for each position				

Table 1. *The components of physical fitness.*

TESTING

a. Use ergometer such as treadmill, bicycle or step.
b. Progressively increase the work, e.g., successive increases in elevation of the treadmill or resistance on the bicycle ergometer.
c. Measure oxygen consumption (VO_2) at each work load.

```
                                    Work Load D
                                   | VO₂ = 3.0 liters
                      Work Load C
                     | VO₂ = 3.0 liters
          Work Load B
         | VO₂ = 2.5 liters
Work Load A
| VO₂ = 2.0 liters
```

d. At some point an increase in work is accompanied by no increase in VO_2.
e. Other criteria which indicate the person is at VO_2 max include maximal heart rates and blood lactates in excess of 70–80 mg/100 ml blood.
f. The VO_2 in liters/min is converted to ml/kg/min by dividing 1/min by body weight in kilograms.

Is it reliable? From classical studies (30, 43) to very recent studies (11, 12) the reported reliability of giving the test on successive days is very high.

Is it valid? It is valid because it is related to important physiological measures (2, 3, 30) such as cardiac output, maximal stroke volume, heart volume and A-VO_2 difference.

GENERAL CHARACTERISTICS:
SEX DIFFERENCES

Cross-sectional studies have shown that aerobic power is approximately 25–30% higher in males than females (3), although females have been reported with aerobic power levels 50–75% higher than the average male (11). In response to training, females improve in aerobic power at the same rate as males (8).

AGE DIFFERENCES

The age of maximal aerobic power is approximately 18–20 years in both sexes. The typical individual has an approximate 30% decrement in aerobic power from age 25–65.

HEREDITY

Through the study of identical versus fraternal twins, it has been well established that aerobic power is strongly influenced by heredity (29).

SPECIFICITY

Aerobic power is specific to the type of ergometer used. Usually higher scores will be elicited from ergometers causing the greatest muscle mass involvement, e.g., a treadmill will usually elicit a higher VO_2 max than will a bicycle ergometer.

FIELD TEST ESTIMATION

In well motivated individuals such as an athlete, the 12-minute run is an excellent measure of aerobic power as follows:

	Poor	Fair	Good	Excellent
12-Minute Run (miles)	1.25	1.5	1.75	2.00
Approximate VO_2 max (ml/kg. min − 1)	low 30's	35–45	45–55	55–65

Table 2. *Aerobic power: A summary.*

proved circulatory system.

In evaluating aerobic power, the coach or trainer should be able to understand that it is really a combination of two sub-abilities involving (1) the O_2 (oxygen) transport system and (2) the muscle itself. *The O_2 transport system,* involving the lungs, heart, blood and blood vessels, can be trained by any number of ways. Thus, the O_2 transport system is being helped for distance swimming and distance running. In contrast to the general nature of training the O_2 transport system, the *muscle* must be trained *specifically* for a given sport. Structures found in a specific muscle such as mitochondria and aerobic enzymes should be developed by a method as nearly identical to the given sport as possible. Thus, if you were to give advice to an ice hockey coach, you might indicate that prior to the season, running would help (since it develops the O_2 transport system) but not nearly so much as skating (since it does not develop the leg muscles in the specific movements of skating). The careful reader can now see the impropriety of terms such as cardiovascular and circulo-respiratory endurance. These terms imply only the O_2 transport system while the training of the individual *muscles* may be just as important.

As shown in the summary of aerobic power displayed in Table 2, this ability is influenced by heredity, age and sex. The ability can be decreased by long periods of inactivity such as can occur to the injured athlete or to the individual who likes to sit around the pool or beach all summer. As a matter of fact, Saltin et al (41) showed a 27 percent decrease in aerobic power as a result of a 20-day period of bed rest. It took 2-3 weeks of training to return their subjects to pre-bed rest levels of aerobic power.

Aerobic power is particularly important for performance in sports that require sustained periods of activity such as soccer, basketball, wrestling and, of course, distance running and swimming. Less obviously, it has been hypothesized by authorities that this ability may make the crucial difference between high level performers in sports of repeated bouts of high intensity such as football (49) or ice hockey (23) in which the primary energy source for the activity is anaerobic (a discussion of anaerobic power will follow) but performance is also based on recovery which is aerobic in nature.

The most commonly accepted criterion measure for aerobic power is the maximal oxygen intake test (VO_2 max). In this test (see Table 2) the individual works harder and harder on some type of ergometer such as a treadmill or stationary bicycle until there is an increase in work but no increase in oxygen intake. Age adjusted maximal heart rates and high blood lactic acid levels are also used to show that the individual has achieved VO_2 max. The score is commonly expressed in liters of O_2 per minute and ml of O_2 per kilogram of body weight per minute. The second measure is preferred in comparing between individuals since the first measure is affected by the individual's body weight. The test is quite reliable and has been shown to correlate well with several measures relating to circulatory health such as maximal cardiac output and stroke volume (2, 3, 31).

Luckily, you don't have to take your athlete to a sophisticated laboratory to determine his/her aerobic power. Assuming that the athlete is properly motivated you can get a very accurate assessment of aerobic power by finding out the distance he/she can cover in twelve minutes. Based on research in healthy young men (9) you will note the approximate estimation of aerobic power from the 12-minute run in Table 2.

If aerobic power is important, then what can we do about training this ability? In a recent review article, Pollock (36) indicates that aerobic power can be increased in healthy young males by about 5-10 percent. Hultgren and Burke (26) found that most authorities recommend training levels for healthy adults equivalent to 70-85% of $\dot{V}O_2$ max. Fardy (18) recommends higher intensities for young athletes. This means that the young athlete aged 15-25 should be working at heart rates of approximately 160 to 200. Their perception of effort should be that the exercise is "hard" to "very hard" as opposed to "moderately hard." Large-muscle exercise should be carried on fifteen minutes to an hour, 4–5 days per week, to insure adequate levels of aerobic power. Even longer durations of activity are needed in sports such as distance running and swimming.

Maintenance and improvement of aerobic power during practice sessions is of particular importance in sports where the actual playing of the sport is not sufficient to elicit a training effect. For example, in contrast to the playing of basketball or soccer the actual playing of football games may not be sufficient to elicit a training effect. This author has witnessed major college football players who couldn't run 1.5 miles in twelve minutes. Clearly, their performance on the field had to be hampered by such low levels of aerobic power.

This section of the paper has attempted to describe the importance of adequate levels of aerobic power for the overall well-being of the athlete. Perhaps the single most important point to be made is that the trainer or coach has the ability to measure the athlete's aerobic power. Athletes should be given pre-season and in-season goals such as a definite distance to be covered in twelve minutes. It is my personal recommendation that coaches demand minimum twelve-minute distances of 1.6 miles for females and 1.75 miles for their male athletes.

ANAEROBIC POWER

Anaerobic power refers to an ability characterized by movement of the body or body part at such high intensity that the predominant source of energy cannot be supplied aerobically. Activities which require a maximal effort in one minute or less depend primarily upon anaerobic power. The underlying physiological mechanisms at work are found within the muscle fiber and can be classified into two distinct systems: (1) the ATP-CP (alactate) System and (2) the Lactic Acid System. Regarding the ATP-CP System you should realize that the muscle has an ability to store these high energy compounds; however, supplies are used up in all-out activities of approximately 10 seconds. Clearly this ability is crucial to the football player or dash runner. The alternative anaerobic mechanism involves the breakdown of glucose to pyruvic acid and hence to lactic acid. This ability referred to as the Lactic Acid System is important to the 400-meter runner, the 200-meter swimmer or ice hockey player.

Anaerobic power is developed by all-out exercise. Traditionally, football coaches have used wind sprints to develop this ability. More recently, interval training (21) has been shown to be an effective method of improving anaerobic power. Strength training of the type to be subsequently described may also have implications for anaerobic power development.

Unlike aerobic power, there is no universally accepted measure of anaerobic power. I would recommend that each trainer/coach develop a test based on the precise needs of his/her sport. For instance, basketball consists of a series of all-out bursts of energy, consisting of stops and changes of direction lasting from 20-30 seconds. At Ithaca College, head basketball Coach Darryl Lehnus closes out most of his practice sessions with a series of 3-5 "suicide drills." A "suicide drill" is a commonly used basketball training technique in which the player is required to sprint to various sites on the basketball court with changes of direction. This "all-out" drill takes about 26-34 seconds. In the early pre-season, the quick guards are expected to run 30-second suicides while the taller players are timed at 32-34 seconds. As the pre-season and season progresses (as anaerobic power improves) times are progressively dropped. Objective assessment provides motivation, a base for future improvement and an easy way of determining who is not "putting out."

Training to develop anaerobic power should be as specific to actual game conditions as possible. Every trainer/coach should, with a little imagination, develop a training technique complete with objective assessment to develop this important ability. Perhaps more than any of the other components of physical fitness, anaerobic power separates the true athlete from those who really want to be spectators.

STRENGTH

Strength may be defined as the ability of a muscle or muscle group to apply force in a single maximal contraction. It is important to athletes because performance is frequently predicated on one of two general types of ability: (1) the ability to "push the other guy around" and (2) the ability to move the body or some body part "powerfully." Examples of individuals displaying the first ability are the ice hockey player who consistently comes out of the corners with the puck or the football lineman who opens up holes "you could drive a truck through." The second ability is manifested by the 9.5-second 100-yard dash man or the tennis player with the "big serve."

In order that we more fully understand the implications of strength to the athlete, two principles of physics should be briefly explained: momentum and power. *Momentum* is defined as the product of mass and velocity. When two bodies collide, the one with greatest momentum will push the other back. Thus, if we have two individuals of the same size (mass) then the individual who can move the fastest (attain greatest velocity) should be able to "knock the other guy back." Man's ability to move fast is predicated to a great extent on the force which can be applied by the skeletal muscles. Clearly, there are other factors affecting speed which we can do nothing about such as: length of the bones, attachment of tendons and ligaments, and fiber type of muscles. Flexibility which will be discussed later is another important factor in speed which you can help the athlete to improve upon. Dintiman (17) authored an interesting paper showing that a combination of strength and flexibility training could increase speed while programs of "only strength" or "only flexibility" did not improve speed.

Power is another parameter of great importance to the athlete. Power is defined as the product of force and velocity ($P = F \times V$). Thus, if we hold velocity constant (and we might be able to improve it with high speed isokinetic training), we can see that power is increased as one improves his/her force production capacity (strength).

Of course, strength has special implications for the athletic trainer. Injuries are often a result of: (1) a body part with relatively weak musculature (2) a relatively weak individual colliding with a stronger individual or (3) the inability of a muscle or muscle group to withstand the force of a blow, resulting in the stretching or tearing of tendons at a joint. At this point, it should be clear that strength is important for the athlete, but how is it best developed?

As an introduction to strength training principles perhaps we should briefly discuss the types of muscular contractions and their implications for training. *Concentric* contractions are those that result in a shortening of muscle fibers while *eccentric* contractions result in a lengthening of muscle fibers. When an individual curls a dumbbell, the biceps are concentrically contracted. If the effects of gravity are resisted in the extension of the arms then there is an eccentric contraction of the biceps. While the individual may be able to cope with greater resistance during eccentric exercise (sometimes called negative work), the two methods appear to have similar strength training effects (24, 27). A clear disadvantage of eccentric exercise is the muscle soreness commonly reported.

Most authorities now refer to three types of strength training: (1) isometric (2) isotonic and (3) isokinetic. A description of each with possible advantages and disadvantages will follow.

ISOMETRIC TRAINING

Isometric strength training occurs when the muscle or muscle group is put on near maximal contraction with no consequent movement of the body part employed. Isometric training may be helpful in a field situation such as occurs during football season (37). It is well established that strength will occur (21, 32, 36, 37) as a result of this type of training but these strength gains may be limited primarily to the angle at which the force was applied (22, 33, 37). Isometrics may also be criticized because of the difficulty in seeing improvements, thus decreasing the athlete's motivation to continue in the program.

Isometric strength training is particularly appropriate in the rehabilitation of an injured body part, e.g., the knee where the range (plane) of motion is limited. Specific weak angles of motion may be strengthened while minimizing the possibility of injury reoccurrence during rehabilitation.

Most experts (See Spackman, Page 43) recommend 4-6 second near maximal contractions, repeated 1-5 times per session with 2-3-minute rests between efforts. Training can be conducted daily but once adequate strength is achieved (equal to the non-affected body part) strength can be maintained with once per week training.

ISOTONIC TRAINING

Isotonic training consists of muscular contractions taken through a full range of motion. At present, this is by far the most commonly employed method of strength training and for several good reasons. Since most athletic events consist of muscle contractions through a range of motion, isotonics can be used to closely approximate a specific contraction needed for a given skill. Isotonic training provides built-in motivation since the individual is continually being reinforced by the usual steady improvement. Finally, isotonic training needn't involve any great investment of money. While it is true that certain strength training systems (consisting of racks of weights on pulleys with a series of stations for contractions of different muscle groups) cost several thousand dollars, a similar result can be obtained from free weights (barbells) costing only $100.

Thanks in large part to the original research of De Lorme (15, 16) and subsequently Berger (4, 5) it is commonly accepted (33) that isotonic strength training should be conducted along the following guidelines:

1. Every contraction should be made through the full range of motion. If this is done, far from the myth that weight training will cause "muscle boundness," there is an abundance of research to show that flexibility will be improved (33).

2. Almost any systematic overload (increased tension) procedure will result in improved muscle strength (4, 5, 15, 16). Based primarily on the work of Berger (5, 6), perhaps the most efficient method is for the athlete to work at a resistance equal to or greater than his/her 6RM (maximal repetitions). By this it is meant that the weight lifted should be so heavy that the individual is incapable of lifting it more than six times consecutively.

3. Each of these 2 to 6RM sessions is a set. Three to four sets should be done each training day. Allow five-ten minutes between sets for a given muscle group.

4. As the athlete becomes able to lift a given resistance more than six times, increase the resistance 5–10 lbs. for men; 2½ to 5 lbs. for women.

5. Make your training as nearly identical to the desired sport skill as possible.

6. A corollary to 5 is to emphasize that the athlete continue to practice the given skill during the strength-training period.

7. Train a given set of muscles on an every other day basis.

Traditional isotonic strength training may be criticized on two counts. First, the effects of gravity and the ballistic nature of the weight are such that the force needed to make a movement will vary through the range of motion. If we assume that near maximal tension should be applied to elicit greatest strength gain, we must conclude that a certain angle of a given movement, the muscle is not being strengthened as efficiently as possible. To look at it another way, the athlete is limited by the maximal weight capable of being lifted at the weakest angle of skeletal leverage. A second criticism may be that to develop maximal power the individual should contract the muscle through the range of motion at high velocity (14). This could cause injury to muscles and ligaments if there were no means of decreasing the resistance with the onset of fatigue.

RECENT TECHNOLOGY AND THE PRINCIPLE OF ISOKINETICS

Modern technology has provided us with several new mechanical devices which may be of value in overcoming some of the weaknesses of traditional isotonic training. Recently, a *unilateral lifting system* has been developed in which each limb is contracted against a different resistance in a given exercise such as the bench press. The unilateral lifting system involves two independent twin weight stocks which enable each body part to work independently at its own maximum resistance and speed. This is an apparent advantage but still shares the other criticisms of isotonic training.

Rope friction devices have been developed in which the subject pulls on a rope with the resistance applied by a cylindrical device which can be adjusted according to the load desired. These machines appear to be a combination of isometric and isotonic contraction through a full range of motion. They are inexpensive and can be adapted to a wide variety of movements and therefore can be used to simulate many sports skill. Equal speed of contraction is not possible, however, unless the rope is controlled by another individual at the end. This type of training is also quite boring and therefore may be criticized on a motivational basis.

Several manufacturers now produce *variable resistance devices* which provide increased resistance as the "average individual's" skeletal leverage improves, e.g., maximal resistance as the individual fully extends the limb. These devices are an improvement over traditional isotonic machines but may be criticized since all skeletal frames are obviously not the same and the machine is incapable of taking this into account. Furthermore, the resistance cannot be reduced as the individual fatigues.

Of the modern technological changes in strength training perhaps the *cam devices* have received the greatest publicity. Through the use of a mechanical device called a cam, the radius of which is altered according to the force applied against it; the speed of contraction is kept fairly constant through the entire range of motion. The resistance rotates on a common axis via a bony body segment. These devices are particularly attractive to the athlete since the nature of the machine is such that the athlete is forced through a full range of motion and thus flexibility is assured. They also provide both concentric and eccentric training during the same exercise, i.e., during the curl the individual is forced into contracting eccentrically during extension. Counsilman (14) has made an effective argument that for athletes interested in the development of power, high resistance fast speed training is best. The cam devices may be criticized since they can only be used at fairly slow speeds. Finally, while the sophistication of these machines makes them psychologically pleasing, clear objective evidence of strength or power improvement cannot be seen by the athlete as in traditional isotonic training.

True *isokinetic* exercise refers to a process in which resistance is altered throughout the range of motion such that speed of contraction remains the same. Furthermore, this is true at high, intermediate and low speeds. Research is available which points to the superiority of isokinetic as opposed to isotonic exercise in the development of strength and power (35, 46). Because the resistance of the machine is equal to the force applied by the athlete, fatigue will result in lower force production and hence less resistance while speed remains constant. Thus, we see an important safety feature when speed of contraction is high. These devices usually have clear indications of power output giving the athlete a clear indication of improvement. Although these devices are usually quite expensive, they appear to be the ultimate in strength-training techniques at this time.

LOCAL MUSCLE ENDURANCE

Local muscle endurance (LME) refers to the ability of a muscle or group of muscles in a specific part of the body to work effectively over a period of time. With the exception of tension employed, all of the principles of strength training apply to the training of LME. In strength training, the individual applies such great force (muscle tension) that contraction can only be carried on for a small number of contractions or a short duration of time. In contrast, LME may be improved with lower levels of tension spread over many contractions or for longer time periods. In this regard, the body may be used as the resistance to be moved and thus many of the calisthenics described in Appendix B are appropriate to achieve improved LME.

FLEXIBILITY

Flexibility refers to the range of possible movement about a joint or a sequence of joints. Testing of flexibility and appropriate exercises are illustrated in Appendices A and B.

Flexibility has important implications for injury prevention, sport performance and aesthetic movement. The irony is that this component of physical fitness is among the easiest to improve and yet is commonly overlooked by the coach and trainer.

Two types of flexibility are commonly described. *Static* flexibility involves the range of motion at a particular joint while *dynamic* flexibility refers to the looseness/stiffness or "ease of motion" of a joint.

The trainer should be wary of the athlete with too much and too little flexibility. The "tight" athlete is commonly subject to frequent pulls and strains resulting from explosive activities such as running from home to first base in baseball or "running to daylight" in football. In contrast Nicholas (32) has shown an increased incidence of knee injuries in football players with "loose" knee ligaments. Tests of flexibility such as those developed by Lenox Hill Hospital (Appendix A) are easy to administer and may pay valuable dividends in reduced injury incidence if remedial measures are taken on those who fall outside the limits of "normal."

BODY COMPOSITION

Perhaps the easiest component of physical fitness to recognize is body composition. Due to the peculiar biomechanical needs of each sport, there are usually ideal body characteristics needed for maximal performance.

There are several ways of analyzing the body composition of humans. Height and weight are easy to measure, if fallible parameters. Another measure is *body type,* which in the present context refers to the arrangement and relative size of bones along with the relative predisposition to musculature and fat deposits. The *endomorph* has short thick bones with a tendency to have extra fat in the abdominal area. The *ectomorph* is usually low in fat and muscle with long thin bones, while the *mesomorph* is muscular with wide shoulders and narrow hips. In-

dividuals rarely have a body consisting of only one of these types of characteristics. Rather, they usually have tendencies toward each characteristic in varying degrees. Assessment of body type may be useful in predicting performance in a given sport but since these characteristics are heritable, they can't be altered by training.

Perhaps the most useful designation of body composition for the coach and trainer is the ratio of fat to lean weight in the body. Lean weight refers to that aspect of total weight containing muscle, bone and organs. Of these, muscle is most susceptible to alteration through training. The rest of the body weight is taken up by fat and expressed as a percentage of total weight, varies from five percent and less in marathoners and wrestlers to twenty percent (and higher) in some football players and weight lifters.

Lean weight is best measured by underwater weighing techniques; however, recent research has supplied the coach with simple easy to use techniques which can be effectively utilized to measure lean weight in football players (28), wrestlers (31), and a wide variety of athletes (20).

Too often, in sports such as football, coaches fail to see the relevance of measuring fat weight/lean weight ratios. We have already discussed the importance of muscle mass to the athlete. Excess fat may be considered as "extra baggage" that must necessarily reduce the athlete's speed and explosive power.

If the athlete is found to have too much fat weight, two methods of reduction are possible. First, the athlete can be put on a diet (41) in which he/she takes in less calories than are used. A 500 calorie deficit each day will result in a weight loss of one pound per week. Progressive resistance muscle training of the type described earlier may also be used to alter muscle/fat weight ratios. Holding calorie intake and expenditure constant, muscle hypertrophy must necessarily result in decreased fat stores.

Any discussion of body composition would be incomplete without an analysis of the fluid aspect of body weight and the special case of the competitive wrestler who has to "make weight." The body maintains approximately 70 percent of total weight in a fluid form. As a percent of total weight, these fluids are distributed: (1) in the cells of the body (intracellularly), approximately 40 percent (2) in the spaces between the cells (interstitially), approximately 25 percent and (3) in the fluid portion of the blood, 5 percent. The fluids, in delicate balance with the electrolytes (e.g., minerals such as sodium, potassium, etc.), provide the medium for a variety of vital body processes such as: nerve transmission, muscle metabolism, and the transport of energy sources and waste products. When fluid is lost, it is initially removed from the interstitial spaces and then from the blood, in an attempt to maintain the integrity of the cellular processes. With the loss of substantial amounts of fluid, studies have shown decreases in muscular strength (42), work performance (38) and in the efficiency (20, 39, 40) of the circulatory system.

As most people realize, weight classification systems have been set up in wrestling with the intent of insuring that no unfair advantage is obtained by size. Unfortunately, these weight classification systems have not taken into account the biological fact that humans are distributed in a fairly normal curve about an average weight which for high school boys is about 145 pounds (38). Since only one boy can participate in each weight classification in a given match and since there is such a gap between weight classifications, it is almost a certainty that some boys will be forced to participate below their "desired weight."

Frequently, the length of pre-season conditioning is four to six weeks. Often, the wrestler has just finished another sport such as football or soccer where there is a higher "desired weight." Thus, circumstances result in a tendency for wrestlers to "pull weight." The preferred method and the one which should be recommended by coaches, should be to lose fat weight. Through a proper diet (42) the athlete can lose 3-4 pounds of fat per week. Fat losses in excess of 4-5 pounds per week may result in an acidic condition known as ketosis. When the wrestler cannot lose sufficient fat weight, he is often compelled to lose weight through excessive sweating (rubber suits), fluid deprivation and even by laxatives, all resulting in dehydration.

What should be done about this problem? As a coach or trainer we must discourage the practice of dehydration prior to performance (1). Although Cooper (13) has pointed out that there have been few reports of adverse health implications due to this practice, the coach may be persuaded quickly on a pragmatic basis. The athlete simply cannot possibly perform at maximum. Incidentally, the lack of acute dehydration health problems associated with wrestlers and with marathon runners as opposed to the high incidence of problems seen in football players may be a function of the highly efficient nature of the former group of athletes' circulatory systems. Another fact which may be useful for the high school wrestling coach is the finding that champion high school wrestlers have fat ratios of about 5 percent of total weight (47). Tcheng and Tipton (45) have established an "easy to administer" set of measurements which can give the coach the total weight for each wrestler to achieve in approximating "ideal weight."

SUMMARY

In this paper, I have attempted to analyze physical fitness with special regard to those who are involved in the prevention and care of athletic injuries. If you asked me to pick out the highlights of the paper, they would be these:

1. Aerobic power has important health and performance implications for the athlete. It can be effectively measured by the 12-minute run.

2. Anaerobic power should be trained and tested in a manner as nearly identical to actual playing conditions as possible.

3. Strength can be developed in a variety of ways. Isokinetic training is the most efficient method of strength development followed by isotonic training. Isometrics have important implications for the development of strength in field conditions and for the rehabilitation of the injured athlete.

4. LME and flexibility are commonly overlooked, yet very important aspects of a good training program.

5. Body composition is best analyzed as the ratio of lean to fat weight. Improvements in body composition should be directed toward a reduction of fat weight and/or an increase in lean weight. Changes in body weight brought about through dehydration are to be vigorously opposed on both practical (performance) and ethical grounds.

REFERENCES

1. American College of Sports Medicine. Weight Loss in Wrestlers. *Sports Medicine Bulletin*, 11:1-2, 1976.
2. Astrand, P-O., et al. Cardiac output during submaximal and maximal work. *Journal of Applied Physiology*, 19:268, 1964.
3. Astrand, P-O. and Rodahl, K. *Textbook of Work Physiology*. New York, N.Y.: McGraw Hill Co., 1977.
4. Berger, R. A. Comparative effects of three weight training programs. *Research Quarterly*, 34:396-398, 1963.
5. Berger, R. A. Effects of varied weight training programs on strength. *Research Quarterly*, 33:329-338, 1962.
6. Burke, E. J. A factor analytic investigation into the validity of selected field tests of physical working capacity. Unpublished doctoral dissertation, Temple University, 1973.
7. Burke, E. J. Measuring the components of physical fitness in future physical educators. *NYSAHPER Journal*, 306, 1977.
8. Burke, E. J. Physiological effects of similar training programs in males and females. *Research Quarterly*, 48:510-517, 1977.
9. Burke, E. J. Validity of selected laboratory and field tests of physical working capacity. *Research Quarterly*, 47:95-104, 1976.
10. Burke, E. J. Work physiology and the components of physical fitness in the analysis of human performance. In: *Toward an Understanding of Human Performance*, Burke, E. J. (ed.). Ithaca, N.Y.: Mouvement Publications, 1977.
11. Burke, E. J. and Brush, F. Physiological and anthropometric assessment of successful teenage female distance runners. *Research Quarterly*. In press, 1978.
12. Burke, E. J., Jones, L. C. and Meade, T. J. Aerobic power, heart rate and perceived exertion during tethered swimming in male and female age-group swimmers. A paper presented at the AAHPER National Convention, Kansas City, April, 1978.
13. Cooper, D. L. Wrestling and weight fluctuations, *JACHA*, 21:451-454, 1973.
14. Counsilman, J. E. The importance of speed in exercise. *Scholastic Coach*, 46:94-99, 1976.
15. De Lorme, T. L., Ferras, B. G. and Gallagher, J. R. Effects of progressive resistance on muscular contraction time. *Archives of Physical Medicine*, 33:86-89, 1952.
16. De Lorme, T. L. and Watkins, A. L. Techniques of progressive resistance exercise. *Archives of Physical Medicine*, 29:263-273, 1948.
17. Dintiman, G. B. Effects of various training programs on running speed. *Research Quarterly*, 35:456-463, 1964.
18. Fardy, P. S. Training for aerobic power. In: *Toward An Understanding of Human Performance*, Burke, E. J. (ed.). Ithaca, N.Y.: Mouvement Publications, 1977.
19. Fleishman, E. *The structure and measurement of physical fitness*. Englewood Cliffs, N.J.: Prentice-Hall, 1964.
20. Forsyth, H. L. and Sinning, W. E. The anthropometric estimation of body density and lean body weight of male athletes. *Medicine and Science in Sports*, 5:174-180, 1973.
21. Fox, E. and Matthews, D. *Interval Training: Conditioning for Sports and General Fitness*. Philadelphia: W. B. Saunders Co., 1974.
22. Gardner, G. W. Specificity of strength changes of the exercised and nonexercised limbs following isometric training. *Research Quarterly*, 34:98-101, 1963.
23. Jetté, M. The physiological basis of conditioning programs for ice hockey players. In: *Toward an Understanding of Human Performance*, Burke, E. J. (ed.). Ithaca, N.Y.: Mouvement Publications, 1977.

24. Johnson, B. I., Adamezyk, J. W., Tennoe, K. O. and Stromme, S. B. A comparison of concentric and eccentric muscle training. *Medicine and Science in Sports,* 8:35-38, 1976.

25. Harris, M. L. A factor analytic study of flexibility. *Research Quarterly,* 40:62, 1969.

26. Hultgren, P. B. and Burke, E. J. Methodology for prescription of exercise. *Australian Journal of Sports Medicine,* 8:127-130, 1976.

27. Kearney, J. T. Resistance training development of muscular strength and endurance. In: *Toward an Understanding of Human Performance,* Burke, E. J. (ed.). Ithaca, N.Y.: Mouvement Publications, 1977.

28. Kelly, J. M., and Wiekkiser, J. D. For 'ideal football weight' assess fat, not poundage. *The Physician and Sports Medicine,* 3:38-42, 1975.

29. Klissouras, V. Heritability of adaptive variation. *Journal of Applied Physiology,* 31:338-344, 1971.

30. Michael, E. D. and F. I. Katch. Prediction of body density from skinfold and girth measurements of 17-year-old boys. *Journal of Applied Physiology,* 25:747-750, 1968.

31. Mitchell, Jere H., Sproule, B. J. and Chapman, C. B. The physiological meaning of the maximal oxygen intake test. *Journal of Clinical Investigation,* 37:538-546, 1958.

32. Nicholas, J. A. Injuries to knee ligaments relationship to looseness and tightness in football players. *Journal of the American Medical Association,* 212:2236-2239, 1970.

33. O'Shea, J. P. *Scientific Principles and Methods of Strength Fitness.* Reading, Mass.: Addison-Wesley Co., 1969.

34. Palmer, W. Selected physiological responses of normal young men following dehydration and rehydration. *Research Quarterly,* 39:1054-1059, 1968.

35. Pipes, T. V. and Wilmore, J. H. Isokinetic vs. isotonic strength training in adult men. *Medicine and Science in Sports,* 7:262-274, 1975.

36. Pollock, M. L. The quantification of endurance training programs. In: *Exercise and Sport Sciences Reviews Vol. 1,* Wilmore, J. H. (ed.). New York, N.Y.: Academic Press, 1973.

37. Reilly, M. and Burke, E. J. A comparison between a conventional and field method in the development of leg strength and power.

38. Ribisl, P. M. Rapid weight reduction in wrestling. *Journal of Sports Medicine,* 3, 1975.

Athletic Training, 11:75-78, 1976.

39. Saltin, B. Aerobic and anaerobic work capacity after dehydration. *Journal of Applied Physiology,* 1114-1118, 1964.

40. Saltin, B. Circulatory response to submaximal and maximal exercise after thermal dehydration. *Journal of Applied Physiology,* 19:1125-1132, 1964.

41. Saltin, B., Blomquist, B., Mitchell, J. H., Johnson, R. C., Wildenthal, K. and Chapman, C. B. Response to submaximal and maximal exercise after bed rest and training. *Circulation,* 38 Suppl. 7, 1968.

42. Smith, N. J. Gaining and losing weight in athletics. *Journal of the American Medical Association,* 236:149-151, 1976.

43. Taylor, H. L., Buskirk, E. R., Brozek, J., Anderson, J. T. and Grande, F. Performance capacity and effects of caloric restriction with hard physical work on young men. *Journal of Applied Physiology,* 10:421-427, 1957.

44. Taylor, H. L., Buskirk, E. and Henschel, A. Maximal oxygen intake as an objective measure of cardio-respiratory performance. *Journal of Applied Physiology,* 8:73, 1955.

45. Tcheng, T. K. and Tipton, C. M. Iowa wrestling study: Anthropometric measurements and the prediction of ''minimal'' body weight for high school wrestlers. *Medicine and Science in Sports,* 5:1, 1973.

46. Thistle, H., Hislop, H. J., Moffroid, M. and Lowman, F. W. Isokinetic contraction: A new concept of resistance exercise. *Archives of Physical and Medical Rehabilitation,* 48:279-282, 1967.

47. Tipton, C. M., T. K. Tcheng and E. J. Zambraski. Iowa Wrestling Study: Classification Systems. *Medicine and Science in Sports,* 8:101-104, 1976.

48. Ward, J. E. and Fisk, G. H. The difference in response of quadriceps and the biceps brachii muscle to isometric and isotonic exercise. *Archives of Physical and Medical Rehabilitation,* 45:614-620, 1964.

49. Wilmore, J. H., Parr, R. B., Haskell, W. L., Costill, D. L., Milburn, L. J., and Kerlan, R. K. Football pros' strengths and weakness — charted. *The Physician and Sports Medicine,* 4:45-54, 1976.

Nutrition and Athletic Performance*

National Dairy Council * *

SUMMARY

Optimal nutrition is one of the basic conditions necessary to maintain top physical performance. Contrary to common beliefs, the question of nutrition for the athlete is perfectly straightforward and involves little if any mystique. The optimum diet for athletes, like non-athletes, must supply adequate water, calories, protein, fats, carbohydrates, minerals, and vitamins in suitable proportions. By virtue of his high energy expenditure, the athlete in training requires a greater caloric intake than the more sedentary person to maintain body weight. However, excessive caloric intake above the daily energy expenditure may lead to obesity and is, therefore, not recommended. When the caloric intake of the athlete is increased, his protein intake is proportionately increased and may be more than he actually needs. Inasmuch as protein is an expensive and inefficient source of energy, the athlete, like the non-athlete, relies on fats and carbohydrates for fuel for his working muscles. The possible risks accompanying the practice of carbohydrate loading to increase endurance are presented as well as the aspects of vitamin and mineral supplementation and fluid replacement. Areas of special concern which are discussed include the use of liquid meals to relieve pre-game nervous tension, the hazards of total starvation alternated with semi-starvation to make lower weights, and food fads and misinformation relative to the athlete's diet.

One of the basic conditions necessary to maintain top physical efficiency and performance is optimal nutrition. This concept has been defined, not as the consumption of excessive calories which would result in obesity, but as the nutrient intake necessary to maintain man in maximal physical condition for athletic or other performance (1). This *Digest* will present scientific evidence relating the role of nutrition in athletic performance. Emphasis will focus on additional needs of athletes imposed by the type or amount of physical activity involved and on the effect nutrient supplementation of the diet may have on performance.

*An article published in *Dairy Council Digest* 46, March-April 1975, ISSN 0011-5568. Appreciation for the article is extended to the National Dairy Council, 111 North Canal Street, Chicago, IL 60606.
**The National Dairy Council assumes the responsibility for writing and editing this publication. However, we would like to acknowledge the help and suggestions of the following reviewers in its preparation: C. F. Consolazio, Chief of Bioenergetics Division, Department of Nutrition, Letterman Army Institute of Research, Presidio of San Francisco, California; T. T. Craig, Ph.D., Secretary, Committee on the Medical Aspects of Sports, American Medical Association, Chicago, Illinois; and L. M. Hursh, M.D., Director of Health Services, University of Illinois, Urbana, Illinois.

NUTRITIONAL NEEDS

It is rather difficult to assess the effect of a single food component on physical performance because of the interference of such variables as motivation, differences in experimental conditions, types of work performed, and the wide range of individual responses (2). However, the performance of an athlete is largely dependent upon a ready supply of nutrients needed by his working tissues (3). Contrary to common beliefs, the question of nutrition for the athlete is perfectly straightforward and involves little if any mystique (4). Although relatively little investigation has been done into the special problems of athletes, the best available evidence to date suggests that the optimum diet for athletes, as for non-athletes, must supply adequate quantities of water, calories, protein, fats, carbohydrates, minerals, and vitamins in suitable proportions (1,4).

Calories. In general, by virtue of his high energy expenditure, the athlete in training will require a greater caloric intake than the more sedentary person (4,5). Whereas the recommended daily allowance of calories for the average man is in the order of 2,700 to 3,000 according to the National Research Council's RDA (6), a vast majority of athletes undergoing training may require more than 3,000 kilocalories per day, depending on the athlete's size and the energy demands of the particular sport (1,5,7,8,9). The athlete's greatly increased caloric expenditure automatically increases his appetite, with the result that he ingests more food. Although it is unlikely that an athlete in heavy physical training will gain weight, excessive caloric intake above the daily energy expenditure is not recommended, as it results in an increase in fat deposition (obesity) with a subsequent increase in body weight, which may present a greater workload to the heart (1). The increased caloric requirements should be provided by increasing food intake across the board without in any way significantly altering the proportions of the micro- and macronutrients of the diet (4). There are no special food sources which supply extra reserves of energy that are not supplied by other foods with the same nutrients. An adequate guide on which an athlete should base his food selection is the basic food groups.

Protein. The major role of proteins in the body is the construction and preservation of the integrity of body tissues (5). The minimum protein lost by a 70-kg man consuming no protein has been estimated to be 23 g/day or 0.33 g/kg of body weight (6). Thus, the protein allowance of 0.80 g/kg of body weight recommended by the National Research Council (6) should provide the protein an athlete needs for peak performance. Furthermore, since the athlete's caloric intake is increased, a nutritionally adequate diet of normal foods will usually provide a protein intake at least twice as high as that of the moderately active non-athlete, and this is probably more than the athlete needs (1,2,10).

Astrand (10) cited data revealing that the combustion of protein was no higher during heavy exercise than during rest. Even after glycogen depots have been depleted, continued exercise does not cause a significant increase in the amount of protein metabolized (8,10). Thus, the customary preference of athletes for high-animal protein diets, commonly provided in the form of steak, is due to psychological rather than physiological factors (1, 8,10-13). It has been noted that an increased protein intake also increases the water requirement since 1) additional fluid is required to eliminate the nitrogen by-products in the urine, and 2) as muscle contains 72% water, each gram of protein retained as muscle requires three grams of water. In addition, an excessive protein intake serves only as an expensive and inefficient source of energy because of an increased specific dynamic activity (1).

Fats and Carbohydrates. Inasmuch as the aforementioned reasons exclude the protein from consideration as a major source of fuel for working muscles, attention is focused on fats and carbohydrates. Carbohydrate has been traditionally regarded as the exclusive fuel for skeletal muscles. However, Astrand (10,11) concluded, based on early experiments by muscle physiologists, that the intensity of work in relation to the athlete's maximal aerobic power affects the proportion of nutritional energy derived from fat and that contributed from carbohydrates. It has been reported that fat supplied about 50 to 60 per cent of the energy in subjects engaged in light to moderate aerobic exercise. Also, in prolonged aerobic work, fat contributed in an increasing amount — up to 70 per cent — to the energy fuel. On the other hand, in more strenuous exercise where anaerobic metabolic processes were involved, carbohydrates became the main energy source (14). Thus, the utilization of carbohydrates varies inversely with the oxygen supplied to the working muscle. The more inadequate the oxygen supply (due to increased metabolic requirement during prolonged and heavy exercise), the higher the carbohydrate utilization. High-carbohydrate diets (70% of the kilocalories) have been reported to increase work performance in heavy exhausting exercise as they appear to give the best energy yield per liter of oxygen compared to high-fat and high-protein diets (1). However, there is still no direct explanation for the value of carbohydrate as an important substrate for skeletal muscle during very heavy physical exercise.

Based on recent studies, Astrand (10,11) also noted that different diets appear to markedly influence glycogen stores in the muscles. The higher the glycogen stores, the better the performance. The importance of a high initial level of muscle glycogen is that it enables the athlete to maintain his optimal pace from start to finish (15). A dietary manipulation, known as carbohydrate loading, has been reported to increase glycogen stores in the muscles and, thus, to improve performance during endurance events exceeding 30-60 minutes (10,11, 16). Basically, this practice involves exercising the muscles one week in advance to exhaust glycogen stores. The diet is then modified to be almost exclusively fat and protein for about three days to keep the glycogen content of the exercising muscles low. As the competition day nears, large quantities of carbohydrates are added to the previous diet.

The use of this dietary regime is, however, not without possible risks (17,18). Glycogen retains water and both may be deposited in the muscle to such an extent that a feeling of heaviness and stiffness is experienced. The resulting weight increase due to water retention may reduce the ability of the athlete to take up oxygen maximally (15,19). Carbohydrate loading designed to increase endurance has also been reported to produce cardiac pain and electrocardiographic abnormalities in an older marathon runner (18). The effect of this practice on heart function is worrisome enough to caution all athletes against its use without expert advice from competent physicians.

Vitamins and Minerals. The common belief that "if enough is good, more is better" has probably been largely responsible for the continued use of massive doses of vitamins and minerals to improve athletic performance. The rather limited information on the effect of vitamin and mineral supplementation on athletic and physical performance has been reviewed by several investigators (1,2,17,20). These reviews cite increased demands for B-complex vitamins because of their important role in many biochemical reactions which make energy available for muscular work. While there is no doubt that B-complex vitamin deficiencies decrease athletic performance (1,2), whether or not excess levels derived from supplementation are of significant value may be debatable (8).

Most investigators do not advocate vitamin supplementation for athletes for several reasons. It is a fact that excess water-soluble vitamins cannot be stored in the body and, thus, are rapidly excreted in the urine once tissue levels are saturated (1,2, 13). Recent studies have also revealed that vitamin C supplementation had negligible effect when compared to that of a placebo on endurance performance and rate, severity, and duration of athletic injury (13,21). In addition, vitamin C supplementation may increase biochemical reactions in the body that destroy vitamin B^{12} (22). The fat-soluble vitamins are retained and stored in the body, and daily supplementation of large quantities of vitamin A has been known in some instances to be very toxic and even fatal (1,7,13,17). Thus, although it may be deemed advisable to increase vitamin intake for the athlete in training, this need may be met simply when the total caloric content of a nutritionally-balanced diet is increased (1,2,9).

An important change in mineral metabolism caused by physical exertion is the loss of salt in the sweat (20) which contains 20 to 30 meq of sodium per liter (6). Excessive sweating from heavy physical activity and exercise can lead to sodium losses of as much as 350 meq/day (or more in the non-acclimated individual) (6), an amount more than enough to disturb homoestasis. A total sodium deficiency results in diuresis since the body is unable to retain water (1).

Because of high concentrations that can be lost in sweat, the salt (sodium chloride) intake of athletes should be more than that of the usual American adult intake of 6 to 18 g/day, which contains 100 to 300 meq of sodium (6). Excessive salt intakes, however, are to be avoided as they increase water requirement and could result in greater water retention, which could likewise impair the athlete's efficiency during training (1,2). The need varies with sweating in the proportion of two grams salt per liter of extra water lost (6); however, there is no actual need for salt in excess of that lost in sweat. Salt may be replaced at the end of the day by salting foods. The use of salt tablets should be avoided since gastrointestinal disturbances have been known to occur (1).

Water. Whereas man can live without food for 30 days, he will die in five to six days if deprived of water. Water serves as the principal vehicle for transporting substances and heat within the body. It is the only means of dissipating body heat effected by evaporation of sweat. Since body heat production is greatly accelerated during physical exercise, water for perspiration must be replaced. Otherwise, body temperature increases beyond normal and may eventually lead to heat stroke. It is imperative to increase fluid intake to maintain fluid balance as the work level and environmental temperature increase (23).

The recent statement of the Food and Nutrition Board, NRC-NAS (23) emphasized that there is no basis for restricting water intake of athletes during contests, nor is there any evidence that man can adapt to tolerate water intake lower than his daily losses. Rather, scientific evidence strongly supports the practice of replacing water loss by intermittent fluid intake.

The manner of replacing fluid and accompanying mineral losses during exercise is still controversial in the sports community. The merits and demerits of natural foods, plain water, water plus salt tablets, saline solutions, and glucose or glucose and salt solutions for the above purpose have been discussed but, to date, no agreement on the optimal course of action has been reached (1-3,7,9,12,13, 24,25). The mid 1960's witnessed the introduction of isotonic solutions, more popularly called electrolyte ades. Tremendous publicity from the sports community was accorded several versions of these ades—®Gatorade, ®Sportade, and ®Bike Half Time

Punch. These ades differed in their electrolyte concentration but they basically contained sodium, potassium, and carbohydrates (26). Despite numerous claims in favor of these ades as well as their wide acceptance in athletic circles, there is yet no conclusive evidence of their physiological advantage over water, saline solutions, or glucose syrup drinks in improving performance.

SPECIAL CONCERNS

In addition to the obvious need for adequate nutrient intake by the athlete, the psychological aspects of eating are of equal importance. It is important that meals be palatable and presented at appropriate and suitable times (4). It has been suggested that athletes should have at least three meals a day, or perhaps more frequent light meals especially if the sport concerned requires long hours of effort (24). Sports of shorter duration and less demanding in energy should not require any drastic modification of the pattern of meal distribution except that, from the point of view of digestion, the pre-game meal should be scheduled three hours prior to an athletic contest (3,4,24). The rationale behind this practice is that as the blood supply is compromised between the working muscle and digesting food, one or both functions may suffer (4,13).

The problem of providing the athlete with a nutritionally adequate diet is complicated by the emotional tension that so often accompanies competition (5). Indigestion caused by pre-game nervous tension has resulted in the current popularity of the liquid pre-game meal, claimed to cut down nervous indigestion during athletic contests (5,13,27-29). Liquid meals, consisting of the recommended daily dietary proportions of nutrients, have reportedly eliminated nausea, vomiting, and abdominal and localized cramps (5,13,28). It was also the opinion of the authors that strength and endurance were improved although no data were offered to substantiate this observation. However, the explanation for these beneficial effects does not lie in any special food contained in the fluid diet. The fluid form is simply easier to digest since it eliminates the liquefaction process in the stomach under nervous conditions (13,27-29).

A nutritional practice which is harmful and thus must be strongly discouraged is total starvation alternated with semi-starvation and dehydration (2,17). This is routinely practiced by boxers and wrestlers in order to make lower weight classifications. Total starvation does more than dehydrate the body. The accompanying weight loss also involves loss of protein, glycogen, minerals, enzymes, and other important cell constituents. These responses diminish body reserves for athletic demands and, in the young competitor, could affect normal growth response (17). Significantly abnormal electrocardiograms have also been observed in six healthy adults during a ten-day starvation period (30). This practice has been condemned by the American Medical Association as it serves the ethics of sportsmanship no better than it does the health of the athlete (31).

Food faddism and ignorance are more prominent in the area of athletics than in any other sphere of nutrition (24,32). Special dietary schemes and ergogenic aids have been advocated by trainers and coaches to improve performance and endurance. Common examples of these schemes include wheat germ oil supplementation (as a potent source of vitamin E and polyunsaturated fatty acids) as well as the addition of gelatin (as a source of glycine), phosphate, and alkalinizing agents to the athlete's diet (2,11,24). Similarly, certain foods have been restrained (3,9). For example, milk has been withheld on the contention that it 1) causes "cotton mouth", 2) curdles in the stomach, and 3) lowers the respiratory quotient, hence decreasing efficiency (33). Although these dietary schemes may have some kind of psychological advantage for the athlete, they have neither sound physiological nor nutritional basis (1) but, rather, they are based mainly on older traditions and superstitions. Numerous other nutritional misconceptions relative to athletes' diets have been discussed in the light of scientific data (12,34).

A recent study conducted to determine the nutritional knowledge of physical education students demonstrated that students who ranked college courses as the primary source of knowledge scored significantly higher than those who ranked their parents or coaches (35). This study reveals the need for better nutrition education for coaches and trainers, who actually have greater influence on habits of athletes on account of their close contact and association. Coaches and trainers should discourge athletes from seeking "super" or "wonder" foods or drugs to substitute for hard work in training (4) and adequate nutrition.

REFERENCES

1. Consolazio, C.F. Nutrition and Athletic Performance. In: *Progress in Human Nutrition, Vol. 1.* Margen, S. (Ed.) Westport, Connecticut: AVI Publishing Co., 1971, pp. 118-131.
2. Bullen, B., J. Mayer, and F.J. Stare. Am.J.Surg. *98*:343, 1959.
3. Turco, S.J.P., and A.A. Savastano. R.I.Med.J. *52*:325, 1969.
4. Williams, J.G.P. Practitioner *201*(Suppl.):324, 1968.
5. Cooper, D.L., B. Bird, and J. Blair. Okla.State Med. Assoc.,J. *55*:484, 1962.
6. Food and Nutrition Board. *Recommended Dietary Allowances,* 1974. National Research Council—National Academy of Sciences, Washington, D.C., 8th ed., Publ. 2216.
7. National Athletic Trainers Association. Principles of Athletic Fitness. In: *Fundamentals of Athletic Training:* a joint project of the National Athletic Trainers Association, the Athletic Institute, and the Medical Aspects of Sports Committee of the American Medical Association. Chicago: American Medical Association, 1971, pp. 13-54.
8. Parizkova, J. Borden's Rev.Nutr.Res. *29*:1, 1968.
9. Upjohn, H.L., J.A. Shea, F.J. Stare, and L. Little. J.A.M.A. *151*:818, 1953.
10. Astrand, P. Fed.Proc. *26*:1772, 1967.
11. Astrand, P. Nutr. Today *3*:9, 1968.
12. Darden, E. Sch.Coach *42*:88, 1972.
13. Anonymous. Nutrition. In: *Comments in Sports Medicine.* Craig, T.T.(Ed.). Chicago: American Medical Association, 1973, pp. 131-136.
14. Astrand, P. Nutrition and Physical Performance. In: *World Review of Nutrition and Dietetics, Vol. 16.* Rechcigl, M. (Ed.). Washington: S. Karger, 1973, pp. 59-79.
15. Karlsson, J., and B. Saltin. J.Appl.Physiol. *31*:203, 1971.
16. Bergstrom, J., and E. Hultman. J.A.M.A. *221*:999, 1972.
17. Nelson, R.A., and C.F. Gastineau. Nutrition for Athletes. In: *The Medical Aspects of Sports:15.* Craig. T.T. (Ed.). Chicago: American Medical Association, 1974, pp. 19-21.
18. Mirkin, G. J.A.M.A. *223*:1511, 1973.
19. Anonymous. Nutr.Rev. *30*:86, 1972.
20. Keller, W.D., and H.A. Kraut. Work and Nutrition. In: *World Review of Nutrition and Dietetics, Vol. 3.* Bourne, G.H. (Ed.). London: Pitman Medical Publishing Co., Ltd., 1962, pp. 69-81.
21. Gey, G.O., K.H. Cooper, and R.A. Bottenberg. J.A.M.A. *211*:105, 1970.
22. Herbert, V., and E. Jacob. J.A.M.A. *230*:241, 1974.
23. Food and Nutrition Board. *Water Deprivation and Performance of Athletes.* A Statement of the Food and Nutrition Board. National Research Council—National Academy of Sciences, 1974.
24. Mayer, J. Atl.Mon. p. 50, 1961.
25. Brooke, J.D. Proc.Nutr.Soc. *33*:12A, 1974. (Abstr.)
26. Balakian, G. Med. Times *99*:202, 1971.
27. Johnson, R.D. J.Med.Assoc.State Ala. *36*:1283, 1967.
28. Rose, K.D., P.J. Schneider, and G.F. Sullivan. J.A.M.A. *178*:30, 1961.
29. Hirata, I.J.Sch.Health *60*:409, 1970.
30. Consolazio, C.F., R.A. Nelson, H.L. Johnson, L.O. Matoush, H.J. Krzywicki, and G.J. Isaac, Am.J.Clin.Nutr. *20*:684, 1967.
31. American Medical Association. A.M.A. News p. 2, 1959.
32. Durnin, J.V.G.A. Can.Med.Assoc.J. *96*:715, 1967.
33. Van Huss, W.D., G. Mikles, E.M. Jones, H.J. Montoye, D.C. Cederquist, and L. Smedley. Res.Q. *33*:120, 1962.
34. American Association for Health, Physical Education, and Recreation. *Nutrition for Athletes. A Handbook for Coaches.* Washington, D.C., 1971.
35. Cho, M., and B.A. Fryer. J.Am.Diet.Assoc. *65*:30, 1974.

Anabolic Steroids in Sport: A Biophysiological Evaluation

John P. O'Shea, Ed.D.

The first reported use of male steroids to improve performance is said to have been in World War II, when they were administered to German SS troops before battle to enhance aggressiveness. Following the war, steroids were given to the survivors of German concentration camps to rebuild strength and body weight. Unconfirmed rumors in 1954 had the Russian weight lifters receiving doses of testosterone, the male sex hormone. The first widespread reported use of synthetic anabolic steroids by strength athletes came about the time of the 1964 Tokyo Olympic Games. For the most part the stories were based upon rumors and hearsay and not much notice was paid to them by the sports medicine community or sports officials. Starting in 1965, however, world records in strength events such as Olympic lifting, discus, hammer and shot put were broken and rebroken with remarkable regularity. The era of the "steroid" athlete had begun.

Strength athletes in the "dark" on this new wonder pill or who refused to take it because of either medical or ethical considerations soon found themselves at a decided disadvantage. By denying themselves of whatever advantage steroids could provide they were effectively eliminating themselves from national and international competition. For as the qualifying standards for competition kept rising only those willing to assume the risks involved in taking steroids were able to meet them. Paradoxically, the governing bodies of the various sports who declared themselves against steroids, kept raising the qualifying standards so that only the athletes on the pill could meet them. If too many qualified for the competition the next time around the meet officials set the standards higher. This forced the athlete on the steroid to take a higher dose . . . and so a vicious cycle was set in motion that continues to this day.

Who is to blame for the present mess with anabolic steroids? Certainly the athletes can't be held responsible for all of it. Steroids are a prescription drug requiring a physician's signature. Meanwhile, coaches cooperated with the physicians by ignoring the entire situation.

To combat the widespread use and abuse of anabolic steroids in competitive sport, the American Medical Association, the National Collegiate Athletic Association Committee on Competitive Safeguards and Medical Aspects of Sport, and the International Olympic Committee (IOC) have totally condemned the practice. Steroid administration is now considered "DOPING" by the AAU and the IOC which in effect means they are illegal to take at any time under any circumstance. To enforce this ban biochemical testing procedures have been established to detect steroids users. If caught the penalty can be quite severe for the guilty athlete.

Physicians comprising the various national and international sports medicine associations have continually pointed out the potential dangers involved in anabolic steroid usage: they may cause precocious puberty or premature epiphyseal closure in adolescents, testicular shutdown, decreased libido, acute liver problems, prostatic hypertrophy, and increase the risk of heart disease. Sports medicine physicians have also emphasized that long-term usage may result in irreversible pathological damage.

Current clinical research literature in anabolic steroid treatment is not in total agreement with the position taken by sports medicine physicians. For example, Dr. Anthony A. Albanese (1) an internationally known hormone researcher has stated, that based upon his findings present day synthetic anabolic steroids are almost entirely free of androgenic, hepatoxic and salt retention effects and that the problems of long-term administration have been greatly reduced. Also, their application in sport does not necessitate prolonged use.

While the chemistry of anabolic steroid agents is beyond the scope of this paper, its purpose is to examine objectively current scientific data concerning the safety, dangers, and the effectiveness of this drug on human physical performance and health.

STEROID BACKGROUND

Natural steroids are hormones secreted by the body to control various metabolic functions. The body's hormone system is concerned principally with: controlling the rates of chemical reactions in the cells, the transport of substances through cell membranes, and other aspects of cellular metabolism such as body growth. Most hormones are catalysts in that they do not initiate a reaction but serve to modify rate processes in the body although the change in rate may be remarkably great. The biochemical pathways by which hormones control or influence the body's internal environment are relatively unknown at this time.

Genetic factors, nutrition, and hormones all influence the growth process. Growth in terms of linear change and body weight is primarily influenced by (1) the pituitary growth hormone, (2) thyroid hormone, (3) androgens, (4) estrogens, and (5) corticosteroids. There are many aspects of growth to be considered but the prime concern here is the influence of androgen hormones on muscular growth and development.

The typical androgen has both ANDROGENIC-ANABOLIC effects. The ANDROGENIC effects may be described as development of the secondary male characteristics or virilizing effects such as enlargement of the external gentitalia and accessory sex organs, growth of facial and body hair, and deepening of the voice.

The ANABOLIC effect promotes growth and development and increases protein synthesis through greater nitrogen retention.

Sources and Production of Androgens

Androgens are derived from two sources: the interstitial cells of the testis, and the adrenal gland. Androgens from the testis and the adrenal gland are excreted in part as 17-ketosteroid, and the measurement of urinary 17-ketosteroid serves as an index of androgen production. The adult male excretes an average of 14 mg. of ketosteroids per day. Of this amount, about 9 mg. are believed to be derived from the adrenal gland. The adult women excretes about 8-10 mg. per day.

Children under seven years of age excrete little if any 17-ketosteroid. Talbot (42) found that the excretion of 17-ketosteroid begins to increase at approximately the eighth or ninth year, with the rise continuing through the fifteenth or eighteenth year. There is no significant difference in excretion between sexes before puberty. Further, the ketosteroids excreted before puberty are generally thought to be derived from adrenal androgens. The greater increase in 17-ketosteroid excretion that occurs in males, as compared to females after puberty, is attributed to the added output from the testis.

Androgens and Epiphyseal Cartilage

As androgens are first formed and secreted in significant amounts by the testes and adrenal glands, the growth response is augmented. Then, as the output of androgens reaches a peak during the end of adolescence, epiphyseal fusion occurs. Whether or not the endogenous supply of androgen is sufficient to account for the epiphyseal closure at this time has not been determined. At least, such a mechanism of action does exist. Drill (12) believes that androgens may influence epiphyseal closure either by (a) direct action on the epiphyseal cartilage or by (b) inhibiting the secretion of growth hormones. In any case, anabolic steroids should never be administered to any adolescent 21 years of age and under except under close medical supervision.

Androgens and Growth

From the data collected by Howard (19), Talbot, Soble, and Burke (43), and Talbot and Soble (44) there is sufficient evidence demonstrating that testosterone and related steroids increase growth rate (height) in children of subnormal level to normal or above normal levels. They found that androgens also accelerated the rate of skeletal maturation during the treatment period. Further, the androgens did not increase linear growth after fusion of the skeletal epiphyses had occurred.

Testosterone

Androgenic hormones are secreted mainly by the testis, but small amounts are produced by the adrenal glands and the ovary. Testosterone is the principal androgen produced by the Leydig cells of the testis. Testosterone has long been known for its anabolic effects, but its androgenic properties has limited its usefulness for this purpose.

Anabolic Effects of Testosterone

It has been known for centuries from observation of eunuchs castrated before puberty, that the general body build, musculature, and strength of the human male has a close relationship to testicular function. In a young boy with an over active adrenal cortex, the so-called infant "Hercules" syndrome is produced which is evidenced by the precocious arrival of puberty-adult genitalis, a full beard, and the musculature of a grown man. This same condition in a young girl results in hypertrophy of the clitoris, masculine hirsutism, acne, rapid growth, and heavy musculature.

SYNTHETIC STEROIDS

Early attempts (beginning about 1938) were made to utilize the anabolic action of testosterone for underweight patients and those recovering from debilitating illnesses. However, the androgenic potencies of this compound limited its usefulness. During the past decade, a number of compounds with favorable anabolic-androgenic activity have been developed and employed to affect excessive protein deterioration in body tissue arising from many clinical conditions. The results of laboratory and clinical tests appear to indicate that a wide separation of anabolic and androgenic effects has been achieved (31). Drill and Saunders (13) produced a synthetic steroid which proved to have only six percent of the androgencity of testosterone, while retaining anabolic effects equal to testosterone. The compound produced nitrogen retention at the rate equivalent to that obtained with testosterone in a variety of clinical situations.

Nitrogen Retention

Kochakian (26) found that one of the effects of anabolic steroids is to bring about a positive nitrogen balance by offsetting excessive protein deterioration through a slowdown of the catabolic processes of the body. Kochakian and Murlin (27) demonstrated the nitrogen retention effects of anabolic steroids in castrated dogs after injection of testosterone. However, the mechanism by which steroids influence protein metabolism is not yet clearly understood. Nathan, Cahill, and Gardner (32) have characterized testosterone as a protein and glucose sparing agent rather than an active protein builder. There is substantial evidence that the degree of nitrogen retention produced by anabolic agents depends on both caloric and protein intake; when either is restricted these agents cannot be expected to induce a positive nitrogen balance.

The laboratory evaluation of one of the new steroids, methandrostenolone, indicates it possesses potent anabolic effects as demonstrated by increase in body weight in low doses, by hypertrophy of the levator ani muscle and increase in kidney weight, and by counteracting cortisone-induced growth inhibition (52). Androgenically this drug is very weak, having an activity of about 1/150 to 1/250 testosterone propionate, 1/70 to 1/30 norethandrolone, and 1.70 methyltestosterone. In clinical tests by Albanese (2), methandrosterolone was shown to have a lower Steroid Protein Activity Index (SPAI) rating than other oral synthetic compounds. The SPAI affords a means of estimating dosage ranges of anabolic steroids which could be expected to offset the protein-catabolic effects of exercise, illness, or clinically indicated cortiosteroids. It permits the examination of the protein-metabolic effects of steroids under conditions of self-selected food intake. SPAI measures the effects of steroid agents on protein metabolism more systematically in terms of nitrogen balance to nitrogen intake ratios rather than in terms of nitrogen output or balance per se (17). In other words, it gives a quantitative measure of the beneficial efficiency of anabolic steroid on protein metabolism. To determine the relative numerical value of the effects of steroid agents on protein metabolism the Steroid Protein Activity Index is obtained from the following equation:

$$SPAI = \frac{\frac{NBSP}{NISP}}{\frac{NBCP}{NICP}} \times 100$$

where:

NBSP = nitrogen balance in steroid period;
NISP = nitrogen intake in steroid periods;
NBCP = nitrogen balance in control period; and
NICP = nitrogen intake in control period.

This treatment of the data affords the advantage of compensating for changes in nitrogen intake which may be induced by the steroid.

In this frame of reference, anabolic agents will have a positive SPAI, corticosteroids a negative SPAI, and the magnitude of the value is directly proportional to the metabolic effect.

The data in Table 1 shows that the anabolic steroids have a positive SPAI, and corticosteroids have a negative SPAI of varying magnitude.

Highest SPAI values are obtained with those hav-

TABLE I

STEROID PROTEIN ACTIVITY INDEX (SPAI) OF SOME NEWER ORAL STEROIDS

Therapeutic agent	Number of assays	Dosage range (mg./day)	Average SPAI
Anabolic Steroids:			
Testosterone propionate	12	10-25	+ 6
19-Nortestosterone	14	25-75	+ 9
Norethandrolone	10	30-60	+ 8
Oxandrolone	27	10-20	+20
4-OH MT	14	15-45	+11
Methandrosterolone	16	5-30	+16
Stanozolol	10	6-12	+29
BAS-71	9	15-25	+30
Norbolethone	11	7.5	+33
Corticosteroids:			
Prednisone	4	30	-38
Prednisolone	7	30	-33
Triamcinolone	8	12-24	-17
Dexamethasone	7	2.25	-11
Haldrone	13	6	- 8
Celestone	4	3.60	-19

ing a negative nitrogen balance. Albanese (2) has found SPAI averages as high as +100 with one patient having +66, +97, and +74, successively, in three weeks following a single 50 mg. injection of stanozold. O'Shea and Winkler (34) in administering 10 mg. of oxandrolone for a six-week period to competitive swimmers and weight lifters found SPAI averages as high as +82 for a three-day period.

Nitrogen Retention and Protein Metabolism

The body loses nitrogen through the so-called "wear and tear" of tissue protein, but cannot produce its own. It must be received through the ingestion of protein food. As previously indicated, the anabolic action of androgens is to increase nitrogen-retention in the form of protein tissue (lean muscle tissue). Nitrogen-retention accelerates the rate of protein synthesis and decreases the rate of catabolism of amino acids resulting in a progressive gain in weight. For this to be a gain in muscular strength, the subject must be engaged in severe muscular activity such as weight training. Commenting on this factor the British Medical Journal (49) stated: "Anabolic steroid administration combined with a high protein diet might have an anti-catabolic effect under conditions of severe muscular exercise and hence produce an increase in physical performance." Some investigators (10 and 15) have questioned the need of supplementing the diets of subjects being administered anabolic steroid. In the biochemical process of developing dynamic muscle strength however, increasing nitrogen retention seems to be a critical factor. O'Shea (33), in a steroid study involving competitive swimmers in which a protein supplement was not fed, found no change in body weight or performance. In a subsequent study where a protein supplement was included a significant increase in body weight and nitrogen retention was produced (34 and 36). In these studies lean body tissue was not assayed. However, since all of the subjects were competitive athletes in hard training one might believe that the gain in body weight was not due to the accumulation of adipose tissue or water retention. The work of Ward (46) supports this belief. Celijowa and Homa (11) found Olympic weight lifters often are in negative nitrogen balance, and hence an anabolic steroid and a protein supplement would be of value in preventing the loss of lean muscle. As a result of his work, Torizuka (45) believes that anabolic steroid not only inhibits catabolism, but also directly accelerates protein synthesis which is highly desirable in strength building. Additional support is presented by Albanese (2) who demonstrated that anabolic steroid induced a significant and consistent improvement in protein utilization in almost all of 50 subjects.

During steroid administration the SPAI is also affected by the level of food intake in terms of both calories and protein. It has long been established from animal experiments that the efficacy of anabolic steroids may be reduced significantly by a poor diet. Administration of anabolic steroids can only improve the utilization of protein nitrogen; it cannot create protein nitrogen.

Duration of treatment will also affect the SPAI. In general, there is a tendency for the SPAI to decline with prolonged administration of the steroid. This is especially true with doses greater than optimal.

STEROIDS AND STRENGTH DEVELOPMENT

Investigations to determine the effects of anabolic steroid administration on strength development in normal healthy individuals have produced conflicting results. This may be attributed to differences in: drug and or dosage, treatment duration, diet, age of the subjects, type and intensity of the training program, the experience and strength level of the subjects, and the knowledge and experience of the investigator relating to dynamic strength training methods and procedures.

Studies that have found anabolic steroids to effect no positive influence on the acquisition of dynamic or static strength have been reported by Fowler et al. (14), Fahey and Brown (15), Casner and Early (10), and Golding et al. (17). The main failings of these studies in not producing a significant increase in strength may be attributed to the low quality and intensity of the training program.

They did not reflect the type of program undertaken by a strength athlete preparing for national or international competition. Too, the majority of these studies did not deal with the critical question of nitrogen retention and protein intake. As previously indicated, research has shown that a positive nitrogen balance and a high protein diet seem to play a critical function in developing muscular strength.

Anabolic steroid studies that have produced a positive increase in dynamic strength have been reported by Johnson and O'Shea (22), O'Shea and Winkler (34), Johnson et al. (23), Ward (46), O'Shea (35), Ariel (3), and O'Shea (36). These studies lend strong support to the theory that anabolic steroid administration when accompanied by a high protein intake and an isotonic exercise program of severe muscular stress significantly increases muscular strength. This is graphically illustrated in Figures 1, 2, and 3, which present a comparative summary of two studies by O'Shea (35 and 36). Such a comparison is possible as both studies employed identical research protocol. Extrapolating these results over a longer period of time one can only surmise as to when there would be a diminishing effect of the steroid on increasing strength and body weight.

Following a review of the forementioned studies one may conclude that the use of anabolic steroids as an erogenic aid does enhance dynamic strength levels in trained strength athletes. Validity of this statement however, is largely dependent upon the type and quality of both the training program and the diet which the athlete is following.

SIDE EFFECTS OF STEROID ADMINISTRATION
Short-Term Effects

A review of the medical research literature relating to the short-term side effects of anabolic steroid administration report that no serious irreversible physiological or biochemical changes occurred in any of the studies. By short-term administration we are referring to three to six weeks of drug treatment. Albanese (4) in administering 20 mg. of nor-

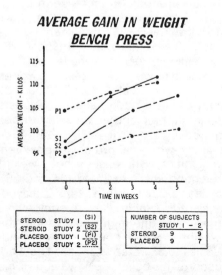

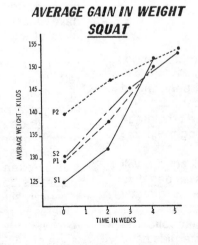

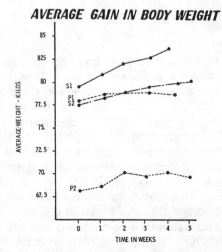

Figures 1–3. *A summary of two studies (35, 36).*

bolethone per kilogram of bodyweight per day in mature dogs for one year produced no significantly abnormal changes in the enzymes SGPT and SGOT, blood urea nitrogen, or sodium retention. In a subsequent study Albanese (2) found that following administration of an anabolic steroid for a four-week period there was no indication of any measurable hemoglobin or hepatic effects or appreciable alterations of electrolytes — sodium, potassium and chloride. There was however, significant decreases in blood cholesterol, total lipid and free fatty acids.

In a study involving competitive swimmers and weight lifters, O'Shea and Winkler (34) in administering 10 mg. of an oral synthetic steroid for six weeks produced no toxic side effects such as edema or changes in electrolyte balance. Significant alterations were noted in LDH, the LDH isoenzyme fractions of LD1 and LD5, CPK, urea nitrogen, and iron. Elevation of the serum enzyme levels may be associated with increased protein metabolism. The mechanism by which this takes place is not clearly understood at this time. It does indicate though that the body is responding biochemically to the "wear and tear" of training.

The response to anabolic steroid treatment seems to be dose and time related. In this frame of reference the data contained in the reports of (5, 18, 28 and 29) has shown that large doses of testosterone suppress the secretion of gonadotropin and may cause atrophy of the tubules and interstital tissue of the testes. The mechanism through which this action takes place can be seen in Diagram 1. Several hypophyseal (pituitary) hormones — adrenocorticotropic (ACTH) and gonadotropins — act on peripheral endocrine glands. The activity of the hypophysis is itself regulated by yet another hormone, so that there exists a hierarchy of hormone glands, which comprise three levels. Certain centers of the midbrain elaborate a neurosecretion that travels through the pituitary stalk to the anterior lobe of the hypophysis, where it stimulates the release of glandotropic hormones. Gonadotropin is itself a glandotropic hormone that stimulates the Luteinezing hormone which in turn acts on the Leydig Cells of the testes to produce testosterone. Testosterone is released in the urine as androsterone and androgenicly is very strong. Androsterone was the first androgen to be isolated in pure form.

The growth promoting effects of androgens may be seen in the prostate, with prostatic hypertrophy an occasional side effect in middle-aged and older men. Prolonged overdoses of anabolic steroids could result in this condition in younger men. A lesser condition sometimes observed in younger men following continuous overdoses of steroid is inflammation of the prostate gland and seminal vesicles.

In measuring adrenal function during five weeks of anabolic steroid administration, O'Shea (36) found no significant changes in the urinary excretion of 17-OH corticosteroid and 17-Ketosteroid. This indicates there was no suppression effect of anabolic steroid on adrenal cortical function. While

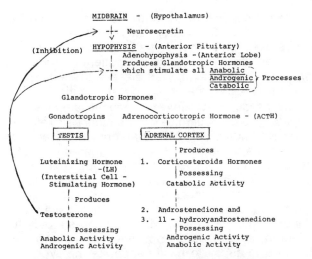

A feedback system controls the master gland, the hypophysis, in that its activity is adjusted by the amount of circulating peripheral hormone; an increase of the level of testosterone inhibits the activity of the hypophysis. High doses of androgens depress the secretion of pituitary gonadatropins and may result in hypogonadism, this is inadequate androgen secretion by the testis and deficient spermatogenesis.

Diagram 1. *Central role of the master gland — the pituitary gland (hypophysis).*

urinary neutral 17-Ketosteroids do not represent a direct measurement of adrenal activity as do 17-OH, they are a reflection of the androgenic function, particularly testicular hormone production; mainly, the excretion of metabolic derivatives from the endocrine secretion of the gonads and the adrenal cortex (20).

"It would probably require . . . discovery of a particularly damaging side effect to shake athletes from their attachment to steroids." Nicholas Wade (47)

Long-Term Effects

In clinical studies relating to long-term anabolic steroid therapy there seems to be a direct association between these agents and peliosis hepatis and heptocellular carcinoma, both potentially fatal disorders. By long-term therapy we are referring to an intake of 10-25 mg./day for a period of nine months and longer.

The most common reported side effects are hepatic, with mild to marked alterations in liver function found in 80 percent of 69 patients treated with steroids in one series (39). These changes ranged from a slight elevation of blood serum protein, or mild elevation of other liver function test without symptoms of liver disease, to the histological findings of cholestasis (40). They appeared benign and reversible upon withdrawal of the steroid (41).

Two other liver lesions — peliosis hepatis and hepatocellular carcinoma — have been also associated with long-term steroid administration with increasing frequency (6, 7, 16, 24 and 50). Peliosis hepatis is characterized by the presence of dilated, blood-filled cystic spaces within the liver. Although originally thought to be found in patients with pulmonary tuberculosis (51), five reports have now documented the association between this postmortem hepatic finding and the use of anabolic steroids (6, 8, 40, and 51). These reports record 17 cases in which peliosis hepatis followed the use of oral steroids. Seven of these patients all without previous evidence of liver disease preceding the administration of steroids, died of hepatic failure.

The association between anabolic steroids and hepatocellular carcinoma (liver cancer) is a relatively recent finding. In 1965 an autopsy revealed liver cancer in a patient who had been treated with anabolic steroids (38). At the time though, no association was made between the two. Speculation that such an association might exist was made in 1971 in a case report of a 20-year-old man with Fanconi anemia treated with anabolic steroids for 10 months who died from liver failure and was found at autopsy to have cancer of the liver, and peliosis hepatis (7). Following this, four other subjects with aplastic anemia treated with high doses of synthetic anabolic steroids were found to have developed symptoms characteristic of liver cancer (24). Since this report in 1972, seven further cases documenting such an association have been reported (16, 21, 30 and 50). The association between the administration of steroids and the appearance of liver problems decreases with time (25).

Whether these lesions were truly malignant can be questioned on the basis that although they resembled liver cancer, histologically no instance of metastatic spread has ever been reported (24). Too, in studies by O'Shea and Winkler (34) and O'Shea (36), in which athletes received low doses of steroid for five weeks, assessment of liver function revealed an increase in the blood serum level of LDH which returned to normal following withdrawal of the drug. SGOT activity is relatively greater in liver than in other tissues and its measurement is useful in diagnosis and study of acute hepatic disease. These two studies (34 and 36) lend support to the theory that most adverse effects associated with steroid therapy are dose and time related.

Another highly dangerous potential side effect of anabolic steroid treatment is the accelerated development of atherosclerosis which leads to heart disease, stroke and peripheral vascular disease. In a study by Wynn (48), anabolic steroids were found to exert profound effects on lipid metabolism; hypertriglyceridaemia and hypercholesterol — which have been identified as being risk factors predisposing to the development of ischaemic heart disease (reduced oxygen flow to the heart). Increased triglyceride production distrubs the metabolism of cholesterol and in heart disease-prone individuals this may well lead to elevated cholesterol levels and atherosclerosis.

The following table of oral anabolic steroids indicates the ones most frequently taken by strength athletes. These particular steroids have been identified as being associated with pathological side effects and hence should be considered life-threatening when large doses are taken for prolonged periods of time.

TABLE 2

ORAL ANDROGENIC ANABOLIC STEROIDS ASSOCIATED WITH SIGNIFICANT SIDE EFFECTS (25).

Chemical Name	Trade Name	Dosage	Duration (months) in Affected Patients	Side Effects
Oxymetholone	Ora-Testyl Adroyd Anapolon Androl 50	10-250mg/day	10-51	Peliosis Hepatis Hepatoma Acute Myelogenous Leukemia
Methyltestosterone	Oreton Methyl Metandren Android	20-50mg/day	1-165	Hepatoma
Stanazolol	Winstrol	12mg/day	18	Hepatoma
Methandrostenolone	Dianabol	10-15mg/day	12-80	Hepatoma
Fluoxymesterone	Halotestin Ultandren Ora-Testryl	15-80mg/day	4-16	Peliosis Hepatis
Norethandrolone	Nilevar	20-30mg/day	1.5-9	Peliosis Hepatis

DETECTION OF ANABOLIC STEROIDS BY RADIOIMMUNOASSAY

The synthetic anabolic steroids have structural features which distinguish them from the natural steroid hormones. It is therefore possible to detect the taking of these substances by testing for their presence in either blood or urine. At present suitable techniques include gas chromatography, mass spectrometry and radioimmunoassay. For practical and psychological reasons urine tests are preferred although, as with the natural steroid hormones, only a small proportion of the steroid usually undergoes minor chemical modification before being conjugated with glucuronic or sulphuric acids and is then excreted in the urine. It is this larger conjugated fraction which is usually used in gas chromatography and mass spectrometry methods. Because of the great sensitivity of the radioimmunoassay technique it has been used only with the unconjugated steroid (9).

Although studies of the metabolism of anabolic steroids are incomplete at present, it is possible however to detect their metabolites in urine. For example, Dianabol can be detected in the small amount of urine obtained from athletes and it is only a matter of time when the metabolites of other steroid agents can be detected in an analogour fashion (9).

CONCLUSIONS AND RECOMMENDATIONS

The purpose of this paper was to deal with the problem of anabolic steroids in an objective scientific manner. A survey of the medical and scientific literature does not permit us to make the specific statement that anabolic agents can or should be administered to mature athletes. While there seems to be no serious toxic side effects associated with short-term treatment (3-5 weeks), long-term usage and overdoses must be considered life-threatening.

This then brings us to the question as to what grounds the administration of anabolic steroids can or should be justified. We know that the taking of steroids can be condemned on the following moral and ethical grounds:

1) the use of steroids by a competitor to improve performance constitutes a violation of sportsmanship — the ethic of FAIR PLAY — by providing an unfair-advantage over opponents not taking them.
2) the use of steroids deliberately falsifies the results of human performance.
3) it is wrong to give a drug to a healthy person just to produce a high level of performance.

On the other hand, these objections can be answered as follows:

1) anabolic steroids are reputed to be universally used by athletes at national and international levels; not to take them is to submit to an unfair disadvantage.
2) steroids are an ergogenic aid like vitamins and other food supplements. They can not

directly improve performance [   ] panied by an intense high [   ] training program. Under these [   ] athlete is not falsifying h[   ] achievements but earning th[   ]

3) almost every strength athlete [   ] to obtain the drug, legally or [   ] take it. With this fact in mind, it would be better to make steroids available to athletes and have them taken under medical supervision.

An intelligent approach in the application of steroids would be to establish a practical screening procedure to ascertain the metabolic status of the athlete prior to anabolic treatment. Assessment of the individual's physical state would be based upon a blood chemistry profile test and a urinary nitrogen balance test. The latter test would determine the protein state of the individual.

In administering anabolic steroids to athletes under medical supervision a number of factors must be given strict attention if the most desirable effects are to be realized. These factors are:

1) During the steroid period, weekly nitrogen checks employing a Steroid Protein Activity Index are necessary to determine the changes in protein utilization thus permitting adjustments in the steroid dosage. High SPAI values have been obtained with the administration of as little as 2.5 mg. per day, with the most effective anabolic response obtained with 7.5 mg. per day.
2) The second factor influencing the efficacy of steroid therapy is the duration of administration. During one year, three five-week periods spaced three months apart are recommended. In general, but not always, there is a tendency for the SPAI to decline with prolonged use. Research indicates this to be especially true with doses greater than the optimal.
3) A third factor frequently affecting the SPAI of the steroid agent is the level of food intake in terms of calories and protein. The efficiency of anabolic steroids may be reduced significantly by inadequate food intake. Administration of anabolic steroids can only improve the utilization of protein nitrogen, it cannot create protein nitrogen. Significant responses are obtained with diets providing a minimum of 1.5 Gm. of high quality protein and from 40 to 50 calories per kilogram of bodyweight per day.
4) The fourth and final factor is that the training program must be severe enough to create a demand for greater protein synthesis. Through the application of the overload principle of training a condition is created that not only justifies but demands an increase in protein intake to offset the catabolic effects of exercise on tissue protein (37). By creating a positive SPAI ratio, the athlete, theoretically, should be able to re-

over more rapidly between strenuous workouts and train at capacity or near capacity with greater frequency. As the quality of workouts improve, so will strength and performance.

In the final analysis, while steroid administration seems to produce no serious adverse side effects and may be valuable in enhancing athletic performance, this writer strongly feels that the moral and ethical objections still stand. To permit the present uncontrolled use of anabolic steroids to continue is allowing our young athletes to play Russian Roulette with their health. We must continue to seek ways to effectively stop their usage on a world-wide scale. Anything less would be self-defeating.

REFERENCES

1. Albanese, A. A. Director, Nutrition and Metabolic Research Division, The Winifred Materson Burke Relief Foundation. Personal communication. White Plains, New York, December 13, 1969.
2. Albanese, A. A. Nutritional and Metabolic effects of some newer steroids V. New York State Journal of Medicine, 68:2392, 1968.
3. Ariel, G. Prolonged effects of anabolic steroid upon muscular contractile force. Medicine and Science in Sports, 6:62, 1974.
4. Albanese, A. A. Anticatobolic application of newer anabolic steroids. Medical Times, 9:871, 1968.
5. Bogdanove, E. M. Direct gonad-pituitary feedback: an analysis of effects of intracranial estrogens depots on gonadotripin secretin. Endrocrinology, 73:696, 1963.
6. Bagheri, S. A. and J. L. Boyer. Peliosis hepatis associated with androgenicanabolic steroid therapy. American Internal Medicine, 81:610, 1974.
7. Bernstein, M. S. et al. Hepatoma and peliosis hepatis developing in a patient with Franconi's anemia. New England Journal of Medicine, 284:1135, 1971.
8. Burger, R. A. and P. M. Marcus. Peliosis hepatis, report of a case. American Journal of Clinical Pathology, 22:569, 1952.
9. Brooks, R. V. et al. Detection of anabolic steroids by radioimmunoassay. British Journal of Sports Medicine, 9:89, 1975.
10. Casner, S. W. and R. G. Early. Anabolic steroid effects on body composition in normal young men. Journal of Sports Medicine, 11:98, 1971.
11. Celojowa, I. and M. Homa. Food intake, nitrogen and energy balance in Polish weightlifters during a training camp. Nutrition & Metabolism, 12:259, 1970.
12. Drill, V. A. Steroids and Growth, in Zarrow, M. X. Editor, Growth in Living Systems. New York, Basic Books Inc., 1961.
13. Drill, V. A. and E. J. Saunders, Androgenic and Anabolic Action of Testosterone Derivatives, in Hormones and Aging Process. New York, Academic Press, 1956.
14. Fowler, W. M. et al., Effects of an anabolic steroid on physical performance of young men. Journal of Applied Physiology, 20:1038, 1969.
15. Fahey, R. and H. Brown. Effects of anabolic steroids plus weight training on normal males — a double blind study. Medicine and Science in Sports, 4:54, 1972.
16. Farrell, G. C. et al., Androgen-induced hepatoma. Lancet, L:430, 1974.
17. Golding, L. A. et al. Weight size and strength unchanged with steroids. The Physician and Sports Medicine, 2:39, 1974.
18. Gersten, B. E. and B. L. Baker, Local action of intrahypophyseal implants of estrogen as revealed by straining with peroxydase-labeled antibody. American Journal of Anatomy, 128:1, 1970.
19. Howard, J. E. et al. The metabolic and growth effects of various androgens in sexually immature dwarfs. Association of American Physicians Transactions, 57:212, 1942.
20. Harper, H. A. Review of Physiological Chemistry. Lang Medical Publications. Los Altos, California, p. 50, 1971.
21. Henderson, J. T. et al. Androgenic-anabolic steroid therapy and hepatocellular carcinoma. Lancet, 1:934, 1972.
22. Johnson, L. and J. P. O'Shea, Anabolic steroid: effects on strength development. Science, 164:957, 1969.
23. Johnson, L. et al. Anabolic steroid: effects on strength, body weight, oxygen uptake and spermatogenesis upon mature males. Medicine and Science in Sport. 4:43, 1972.
24. Johnson, F. L. et al. Association of androgenic anabolic steroid therapy with development of hepatocellular carcinoma. Lancet, 2:1273, 1972.
25. Johnson, F. L. The association of oral androgenic-anabolic steroids and life-threatening diseases. Medicine and Science in Sports. 7:284, 1975.
26. Kochakian, C. D. The protein anabolic of steroid hormones. Vitamins and Hormones, 4:255, 1946.
27. Kochakian, C. D. and J. R. Murlin. The effects of male hormone on the protein and energy metabolism of castrate dogs. Journal of Nutrition, 10:437, 1935.
28. Kingsley, T. and E. M. Bogdanove. Direct androgen-pituitary feedback. Federation Proceedings, 30:253, 1971.
29. Muhlen, A. and J. Koberling, Effects of testosterone on the LH and FSH release induced by LH-releasing factor (LRF) in normal men. Hormone and Metabolic Research, 5:266, 1973.
30. Meadows, A. T. et al. Hepatoma associated with adrogen therapy for aplastic anemia. Journal of Pediatrics, 84:109, 1974.
31. New Drugs. American Medical Association, Chicago, p. 401, 1967.
32. Nathan, D. G. et al. The effects of large doses of testosterone on the body fat of elderly men. Metabolism, 12:850, 1963.
33. O'Shea, J. P. The effects of anabolic steroid treatment on blood chemistry profile, oxygen uptake, static strength, and performance, in competitive swimmers. Doctoral Thesis, University of Utah, 1970.
34. O'Shea, J. P. and W. Winkler. Biochemical and physical effects of anabolic steroids in competitive swimmers and weight lifters. Nutrition Reports International, 2:351, 1970.
35. O'Shea, J. P. The effects of an anabolic steroid on dynamic strength levels of weight lifters. Nutrition Reports International, 4:363, 1971.
36. O'Shea, J. P. A biochemical evaluation of the effects of Stanozola on adrenal, liver and muscle function in humans. Nutrition Reports International, 10:381, 1974.
37. O'Shea, J. P. Scientific Principles and Methods of Strength Fitness. Addison-Wesley Publishing Co. Boston, 1976.
38. Recant, L. and P. Lacy, Editors, Fanconi's anemia and hepatic cirrhosis. Clinicopathologic Conference. American Journal of Medicine, 39:464, 1965.
39. Sanchez-Medal, L. et al. Anabolic androgenic steroids in the treatment of acquired aplastic anemia. Blood, 34:283, 1969.
40. Sherlock, S. Diseases of the Liver and Bilary System. 4th edition. F. A. Davis Co. Philadelphia, p. 371, 1969.
41. Shahidi, N. T. Androgens and erythropoiesis. New England Journal of Medicine. 289:72, 1973.
42. Talbot, N. B. Panel discussion on the adrenal gland in health and disease; physiology of adrenal cortex. American Academy of Pediatrica, 3:515, 1949.
43. Talbot, N. B. et al. Dwarfism in healthy children; its possible relation to emotional nutritional and endocrine disturbances. New England Journal of Medicine. 263:783, 1947.
44. Talbot, N. B. and E. H. Sobel. Endocrine and other factors determining the growth of children. Levin, S. Z. editor. Advances in Pediatrics. Vol. 2, Interscience, New York, 1947.
45. Torizuka, K. The effects of anabolic steroids upon protein metabolism studies by the isotye method. Metabolism, 12:11, 1963.
46. Ward, P. The effects of an anabolic steroid on strength and lean body mass. Medicine and Science in Sports, 15:277, 1973.
47. Wade, N. Anabolic steroids: doctors denounce them, but athletes aren't listening. Science, 176:1399, 1972.
48. Wynn, V. Metabolic effects of anabolic steroids. British Journal of Sports Medicine, 9:60, 1975.
49. Body building by drugs. British Medical Journal, 4:310, 1967.
50. Ziegenfuss, J. and R. Carabasi, Androgens and hepatocellular carcinoma. Lancet, 1:262, 1950.
51. Zak, F. G. Peliosis hepatis. American Journal Pathology, 26:1, 1950.
52. Wyeth Laboratories, Medical Division. Investigational Compounds — WY 3475, "New Orally Active, Totally Synthetic Anabolic Steroid," Philadelphia, 1967.
53. Anabolic Steroids in Sport. The Proceedings of an International Symposium held at the Royal Society of Medicine, London, 14th February, 1975. British Journal of Sports Medicine, July 1975.

Special Considerations for Optimal Performance

Edmund J. Burke, Ph.D.

Human performance can sometimes be affected by factors and considerations outside the individual's heredity and physical efforts. Substances or phenomena which may alter human performance in a positive way may be properly classified as *ergogenic aids*. In most sports, and especially in the elite athlete, the margin between success and failure is quite small. Thus, the athlete in search of that "extra edge" will often come to you with questions concerning the merits of various agents and procedures purported to improve human performance. It is of great importance therefore that all those involved in the prevention and care of athletic injuries have quick and informed answers for their athletes.

Over the centuries, numerous myths have grown concerning the benefits of certain agents in augmenting human performance. The reported benefits of the steak pregame meal dates back to the ancient Greeks, while vitamin supplementation for improved performance is a product of the twentieth century. In the present paper, an attempt will be made to describe and analyze some of the commonly discussed means of augmenting human performance. The reader is also directed to the excellent review presented by O'Shea in the present volume, for a complete analysis of the potential ergogenic merits and drawbacks of the anabolic steroids.

CARBOHYDRATE LOADING

Prior to a discussion of carbohydrate loading, perhaps we should say a few words about the fuels which we burn during exercise. As you know, we take in three basic categories of food (alcohol excluded): carbohydrates (breads, macaroni, potatoes, sugar, etc.) fats (milk, fatty meat, butter, pie crust, etc.) and proteins (lean meat, fish, beans, etc.). As it turns out, fats and carbohydrates are the predominant fuel burned during exercise. Fuel for short all-out activities such as a 400-yd. run or a 100-meter swim is almost totally carbohydrate but as the event becomes longer and longer, fats play a greater and greater role. In the marathon run, fats may be responsible for 75 percent of the fuel used. For optimal efficiency in events of 45 minutes or greater it is preferable to use as high a percentage of carbohydrate as possible, since less O_2 is needed for each calorie of expenditure (26). Furthermore, when the carbohydrates have been used up in the muscle fibers responsible for performance, i.e., slow twitch leg muscle fibers in long-distance runners, then the athlete is always at exhaustion!

The basic problem with carbohydrates as fuel is that we have only a very limited supply. The liver and the muscles have an ability to store approximately 1200 calories in the form of glycogen; however, long duration events such as the marathon run can involve expenditure of 20 calories/minute for three hours! The idea is to increase the pre-event glycogen stores so that the athlete is able to work longer and more efficiently. The hypothesis that increases in pre-event glycogen stores in the working muscles would bring about an increased endurance potential has been confirmed by several research studies (4, 31). Carbohydrate stacking works and is used widely by distance athletes (44, 47, 49). As a means of improving working capacity, in events of some duration (at least 45 minutes), the technique has the endorsement of several prominent exercise physiologists (2, 8).

Briefly here's how it works. Approximately one week before the "big event" the athlete should exercise to exhaustion, using the same muscles as needed in the big event. For the next few days the athlete should participate in only mild exercise while consuming a diet of almost exclusively fats and protein. Approximately 3 days before the "big event," the athlete should take part in a one-hour all-out work session. From this time until the "big event" the diet should be almost totally carbohydrate. The most important time for stacking is during the 10 hours following that one-hour all-out work load. This is due to an increased activity of the enzyme glycogen synthetase during this period. This enzyme is responsible for the stockpiling of glycogen.

Before leaving this discussion, a few words are in order. There have been some reports of chest pain and at least one abnormal ECG associated with this process (42). Furthermore, some individuals have experienced nausea and diarrhea as a result of the technique. Obviously, it is best to have an experienced physician supervise the process (42, 44). It should be noted that glycogen is stored with water, so the individual can expect to be a little heavier than normal as a result (44). Finally, research has shown that it only works about once every two months so some planning is needed (43).

PREGAME MEAL

Before talking about the pregame meal we ought to make a brief review of what digestion is all about. In the body, we have a long tube, beginning in our mouth and throat, entering into our stomach, passing into a long coiled tube, the small intestine, and then to the large intestine from where food wastes are emptied during excretion. The main purpose of digestion is to break down our food from large complex molecules such as starch into small simple molecules such as glucose. Much of this process takes place in the stomach from where the food is passed into the small intestine for entry into the circulatory system. The main issue for us relative to the pregame meal is that some types of food take longer to digest than others. Meals high in fats or protein take longest, perhaps as long as five to six hours. Meals high in carbohydrates might take two to three hours while liquid meals, high in carbohydrate may be digested in less than two hours.

Over the centuries, dating back to the ancient Greeks, steak has become the traditional course for the pregame meal of the athlete. Actually, as you now see, you couldn't find a worse food. Steak, of course, is high in protein and fat. Protein is not used as fuel for exercise while all of us have a plentiful supply of fat for fuel. In one rather interesting study, four University of Nebraska football players were fed a typical steak dinner five hours before a game. X-ray analysis before and after the game revealed that much of the meal was still in the stomach after the game. Apparently, athletes will get just as much physiological benefit from a steak pregame meal by strapping the steak around their waist as by eating it three to four hours before the athletic event!

There is rather widespread agreement that in considering the pregame meal, care should be given not so much as to how it can help the athlete but rather in preventing the meal from hurting the athlete. Only in events of longer than 45 minutes is there any problem with regards to the availability of carbohydrates. An exception to this rule may be in the tournament situation where the athlete is asked for all-out performances on consecutive days. The main purpose in most sporting events should be to make sure that the meal is quickly digested while being psychologically pleasing to the athlete. If the athlete believes that some type of food is preferable it may be detrimental to performance to suddenly cause a dramatic change in behavior; rather, the athlete should be educated over a period of time. A number of coaches and trainers have gone to liquid pregame meals such as nutrament or nutrameal. These liquid diets are high in carbohydrates, are easily digested and when chilled can be quite tasty.

We shouldn't leave this topic without a brief analysis of the practice of taking sugar pills just before a basketball or soccer game. Since glycogen is not a limiting factor in such games and since it takes quite a while for the sugar to be absorbed into the bloodstream, this practice can't have any significant effect on performance from a physiological sense. Furthermore, taken 30 to 40 minutes,

prior to performance, sugar pills may stimulate the formation of insulin which in turn may reduce the ability of the muscles to use fats. This can cause mild hypoglycemia (as sugar is pulled out of the blood to be used by the muscles) and will almost certainly *decrease* performance.

In summary: (1) the pregame meal should be light and contain as high a percentage of carbohydrates (breads, macaroni, pancakes, potatoes, etc.) as is practicable (2) it should be consumed at least 3 hours before the event, longer if it is high in protein or fat, possibly shorter if its a chilled, liquid, "carbohydrate meal."

To this point in this paper, we have, based on available research, been able to make some fairly clear "statements of fact." For the rest of this paper, such "statements of fact" will be harder to find. Research into the effectiveness of the ergogenic aids (presented alphabetically) to be discussed, has not for the most part yielded clear and consistent findings. Possible causes (16) of these apparent ambiguities may be as follows:

1. Often the research design has been faulty. Sometimes this has been due to poor research techniques such as the lack of double blind procedures, i.e., where neither the subject nor the person administering the supposed ergogenic aid knows exactly what is being given to the subject. More often, however, the design has been faulty due to an inability to randomly sample. Because of obvious ethical considerations, these experiments must of necessity be on a volunteer basis.

2. The external validity (applicability to the real world) has often been poor, since the drug doses given are less than those taken by athletes. Furthermore, the laboratory setting does not adequately simulate "game conditions."

3. For the most part, there have been a lack of studies with too few subjects in most studies. Because of the important individual differences between subjects this may have lead to results which are based solely on the sample studied as opposed to all of humanity.

AMPHETAMINES

Amphetamines are perhaps the most widely used drugs taken by the athlete for the purpose of improving performance (23). Perhaps the most commonly used amphetamine goes by the trade name Benzedrine. These drugs which are related to epinephrine, act as sympathetic nervous system stimulants, thus causing increased cardiac output, vasoconstriction of blood vessels, elevated blood pressure, increased metabolism, increased mental alertness and decreased fatigue.

Careful research into the effects of amphetamines seems to support the premise that they may be useful in improving short duration all-out strength type performance (28, 29, 36, 50). However, no beneficial effects have been found for endurance performance (24, 32, 48). Interestingly, long-distance cyclists are among the most common misusers of these drugs in attempting to combat fatigue.

The detrimental effects of amphetamines are clear. Several athletes have either died or experienced circulatory collapse while using these drugs (53). During hot, humid weather, the drug may hide the symptoms of impending heat stroke (41). Amphetamines are highly addictive and the athlete soon develops a tolerance for the drug, resulting in the need for greater and greater doses to experience the same psychological effect. While the drug undoubtedly will cause a heightened emotional arousal prior to a game, it is questionabne to what extent the normal "psyched up" athlete needs such inducement. Golding (23) has also discussed the phenomenon of athletes "high" on amphetamines needing barbiturates for sleep resulting in a "barbiturate to stimulant" cycle. The possible negative effects of amphetamines far overshadow their possible limited value in strength type events. These drugs must be condemned and banned from sport.

ALKALINIZERS

As lactic acid is formed as a result of intensive exercise, the blood pH (index of acid/base balance) drops. One of the causes of fatigue therefore is a low pH (high acidity). As described by deVries (14) alkalinizers are purported to work on the principle that if blood pH begins from a higher than normal level, i.e., prior to performance the blood is alkaline, then the athlete will be able to make more lactic acid prior to exhaustion and presumably be capable of greater work output.

The technique involves the ingestion of alkaline salts such as sodium citrate, sodium bicarbonate or potassium citrate following meals for two days prior to and following performance. Several early studies (12, 13, 15) found possible benefits from this technique. However, Karpovich and Sinning (34) describe how the Springfield College swimming team used the formula of Dennig (12) and found no beneficial effect. Furthermore, Dawson (11) described an athlete who could not complete a long race following ingestion of sodium bicarbonate. In the most recent study found on the topic, Johnson and Black (30) found no significant effect of alkalinizers in highly-trained athletes. In summary, the possible benefits of this ergogenic aid seem suspect and cannot be recommended without further research.

ASPARTATES

It is well known that blood ammonia levels rise as a result of heavy exercise. It is thought that these high blood ammonia levels are a possible factor in fatigue. Blood ammonia is reduced to normal levels through the urea cycle in the liver. Furthermore, it appears that one of the rate limiting factors in the production of urea from ammonia is aspartic acid. It has been hypothesized that increased levels of aspartic acid may be able to improve the capability of the liver in changing ammonia to urea and hence one of the factors in fatigue could be reduced. Animal studies have been reviewed by Golding (23) which seem to be prom-

ising regarding the effectiveness of this procedure. Unfortunately, the research on human performance has been limited and contradictory. While Ahlborg et al (1) found an increased endurance performance, Consolazio et al (6) found no reduction in all-out run fatigue. The literature is simply too contradictory and sparse to make any judgment concerning the merits of aspartates.

CAFFEINE

Caffeine clearly acts as a stimulant for both the cardiovascular and nervous systems. A glass of cola contains about one-third and a cup of tea only slightly less caffeine than a cup of coffee. Karpovich and Sinning (34) reviewed some early studies which indicate that caffeine may have a positive effect on endurance but not sprint performance. Based on his review of the literature, deVries (14) noted that caffeine can interfere with carbohydrate and protein metabolism and decrease blood chloride, thus adversely affecting cardiovascular function. Obviously, the research on the possible benefits of caffeine is confusing and little can be said about its possible merits.

BLOOD DOPING

Stemming from the rumors and hearsay at the Montreal Olympics concerning the great distance runner Lasse Verin, the topic of blood doping has become one of considerable controversy. Blood doping involves the removal and subsequent reinfusion of blood. Blood doping might consist of the following procedures: (1) about four weeks prior to the "big event" (endurance) approximately one pint of blood is removed from the athlete (2) the red blood cells are then stored (3) the athlete goes back into training and in the intervening weeks the system restores the lost blood and (4) a short time before the "big event" the red blood cells are then reinfused. The technique is based on the well-known fact that blood volume and red blood cells are increased as a result of training and since these structures are so important in oxygen transport, the reinfusion should provide for an instantaneous "training effect."

Unfortunately, the few research studies which have investigated the merits of this technique have not been in agreement. Although Ekblom et al. (17) found a significant increase in VO_2 max. as a result of blood doping, neither Robinson et al. (45) nor Williams et al. (52) were able to find significant alterations in physiological and performance parameters. Apart from the ethical considerations of obtaining an "unfair advantage," blood doping should be discouraged because its inevitable use by nonmedically trained personnel could result in: (1) infection (2) blood poisoning and (3) intravascular blood clotting (35).

OXYGEN

It is well documented that the ability of the body to transport and use oxygen is the critical limiting factor in man's capacity for endurance exercise. By increasing the oxygen breathed, it might be hoped to favorably increase performance. The oxygen concentration in the inspired air can be altered by increasing: (1) the concentration from the usual twenty-one (20.93) percent up to one hundred percent (2) the compression of normal air or (3) by a combination of these procedures. The net effect of these procedures might be expected to improve two important components of the oxygen transport system: (1) the diffusion of oxygen from the alveoli of the lungs into the blood and (2) the diffusion of oxygen from the blood into the muscle tissue. The use of oxygen prior to, during and after performance will be discussed.

PRE-EVENT

The technique of breathing pure oxygen prior to performance first gained attention when the Japanese swimmers seemed to improve their performance in the 1932 Olympics as a result of this practice. Subsequently, studies (18, 33) have found improved performance in short all-out events as a result of pre-event oxygen inhalation. Karpovich (33) concluded that pre-event oxygen inhalation would improve swimming performance in events greater than the 50-yard swim and less than the 400-yard swim, if the time between oxygen inhalation and the onset of performance was two minutes or less. The effect may be similar to that experienced by swimmers when they hyperventilate (blow off CO_2) (38). Two studies (18, 39) have been unable to find significantly improved performance in exercise of longer than two minutes.

DURING PERFORMANCE

Oxygen breathing during exercise is clearly beneficial to performance (3, 25, 27, 39). In Wilmore's (54) review of the literature, he noted that the breathing of 100 percent oxygen may result in a six-fold increase in partial pressure of oxygen (pO_2) in the blood. This greatly elevated pO_2 is an important factor in the diffusion of O_2 from the blood to the active tissues. The practical value of breathing O_2 during performance is rather limited however.

POST-EXERCISE

Professional athletes are commonly seen inhaling oxygen on the sidelines during breaks in performance. Wilmore (53, 54) has indicated that post exercise oxygen breathing may have some limited value although several research studies (5, 18, 25, 39) have been unable to show beneficial physiological effects of the practice. Wilmore (54) points out that the practice may possibly be of value following all-out work when the player has to quickly return to the game. In contrast, Matthews and Fox (38) have concluded that although there may be possible psychological advantages from the practice, there is no physiological benefit from the use of oxygen during recovery.

In summary, it appears that: (1) preevent O_2 inhalation may have benefit for short all-out events of about 30 seconds to two minutes duration if the oxygen is administered within two minutes of performance (2) oxygen breathing during work will improve performance (3) any benefits of oxygen inhalation following exercise appear to be primarily psychological rather than physiological.

VITAMINS

Vitamin supplementation is a popular practice among athletes. Certain facts are known about vitamins, namely: (1) the B-vitamins which act as coenzymes in the body form vital links in the metabolism of fats and carbohydrates (2) Vitamin C is a key link during the oxidative phosphorylation phase of aerobic metabolism (3) Vitamin E plays a role in creative excretion (4) although deficiencies in Vitamin E are rare, vitamin deficiencies in the B-vitamins and in Vitamin C will clearly lead to reduced human performance. Based on these facts, researchers have set out to determine if possible benefits may accrue to the athlete who takes large doses (megadoses) of these important vitamins. Golding (23) reports that no controlled laboratory studies have been able to show an ergogenic effect of the B-vitamins or of Vitamin E. While early work with Vitamin C yielded similar results, more recent studies (3, 53) have shown a possible ergogenic effect for Vitamin C. In a recent discussion of their world class athletes (47), Parizkova of Czechoslavakia, Rogozkin of the Soviet Union and Drake of New Zealand recommended Vitamin C supplementation (300-500 mg.) for their elite athletes. Reasons offered included possible increased resistance to infection and possible avoidance of stress related connective tissue injuries. Costill (8) has noted that although Vitamin C is necessary in building collagen, a substance which aids in the healing of muscle and tendon injuries, there has been no evidence that Vitamin C will reduce the likelihood of injury.

In summary, there may possibly be merit (unproved) in the supplementation of the athlete's normal diet with 300-500 mg. of Vitamin C. As Parizkova (47) pointed out, such supplementation can do no harm. Assuming a balanced diet, with the increased caloric intake consistent with training, no other vitamins seem worthy of supplementation at this time.

WARM-UP

The practice of "warming-up" the athlete has several bases in theory: (1) elevated temperature may allow for higher metabolic activity of muscle cells (2) certain enzymes become more efficient with increases to resting body temperature (3) hemoglobin more freely releases oxygen at higher temperatures (4) there may be increased "ease of movement" with decreases in the viscosity of muscle and (5) performance of skills may be easier when the primary means of energy production is aerobic as opposed to the anaerobic activity characteristic of the early minutes of exercise. Warm-up may be classified in several ways. *Identical* warm-up occurs when the basketball player warms up by taking practice shots as opposed to *indirect* warm-up characteristic of the football team taking calisthenics prior to the game. *Active* warm-up takes place when the individual warms the muscle through contraction during some form of exercise as opposed to *passive* warm-up characteristic of a hot shower or hot compress.

Unlike most of the other ergogenic aids discussed, warm-up has been widely researched. In a thorough review of the literature, Franks (20) found that about one-half of the studies show beneficial effects of warm-up while most of the rest show no effect on performance with a few concluding warm-up to be detrimental. Warm-up may be of greatest advantage in activities that require sudden demands on the heart and circulation (35). Furthermore, identical warm-up may have benefits in establishing important nervous system patterns needed for the optimal performance of skills.

The application of cold may be another ergogenic aid. The application of cold will result in the constriction of skin blood vessels, with a possible reflex dilation of muscle blood vessels, thus providing more blood for the working muscle. According to Falls (19), cold application may have greatest implications during long-distance endurance exercise. Furthermore, athletes may recover faster in sports such as lacrosse or soccer by the application of cold packs or cold towels between work periods. Passive warm-up on the other hand may be an advantage in "anaerobic" short all-out type activities.

In summary, it may be noted that the warm-up literature is rather unclear. Since the overwhelming majority of athletes take part in warm-up and since only a very few studies have shown any disadvantages, the practice of warm-up is to be recommended. Furthermore, in preparation for complex skill oriented activities, identical warm-up is to be preferred. Passive cold applications may be useful as a means of improving performance in endurance exercise and in recovering from all-out work while passive warm-up may be useful in all-out strength activities.

WATER AND ELECTROLYTES

Water and electrolyte replacement are not commonly classified as ergogenic aids. Costill (9) however has prepared a superb review of the literature in which he documents their possible effects on performance. Since water and electrolytes such as salt are lost during exercise it follows that either their storage or replacement may alter performance. The reader is referred to the earlier paper in this volume by Burke for a brief discussion of the negative effects of dehydration.

The following summary of the ergogenic effects of water and electrolyte replacement is based on the recommendations of Costill (8, 9):

1. Excess water ingestion prior to performance has no effect if the performance is short term.
2. Water ingestion of 13-20 ounces approximately 30 minutes prior to endurance performance (at least 50-60 minutes) especially during hot, humid weather, may have a significant beneficial effect by reducing body temperature and dehydration.
3. Ingestion of extra salt prior to exercise can lead to reduced performance by causing excessive potassium losses and reduced sweating.
4. During performance, especially in a hot, humid environment, voluntary water replacement does not fully restore water supplies. Therefore, performance may be improved by 3-6-ounce ingestions of water, every 15 minutes. Improved performance is probably due to a lowered body temperature (10).
5. Salt replacement during exercise is only needed under the hottest and most humid of conditions as may occur in mines.
6. Water administration following exercise can rapidly make up for any circulatory impairment due to dehydration.
7. Fluids taken following exercise should be low in sugar and electrolytes, and chilled to insure fastest absorption into the circulatory system.
8. Needs for salt replacement can easily be met by sprinkling extra salt on food at the dinner able. Other electrolytes can be replaced by a glass of orange or tomato juice.

OTHER ERGOGENIC AIDS AND A SUMMARY

With the exception of the anabolic steroids described earlier by O'Shea, the present paper has now completed discussion on most of the commonly discussed ergogenic aids. There are, however, other ergogenic aids which the author feels are of such dubious merit as not to add significantly to this paper. The reader is directed to the sources listed for a description of the ergogenic merits of: alcohol (34, 35, 53), cocaine (34), fruit juices (34), gelatin and glycine (34, 35), hormones (23, 34, 35), hypnosis (35, 40, 53), lecithin (34), marijuana (35), mental practice (7, 53), music (35, 37), Pavlovian procedures (14), phosphates (34), tobacco (34, 35), ultraviolet rays (34), and wheat germ oil (14).

An attempt has been made to summarize for the reader the available knowledge concerning some of the various agents and methods commonly purported to improve work performance. In closing, it should be noted that no attempt has been made to justify the use of any of these agents on an ethical basis. The writer feels that such decisions are better left to national and international governing bodies on an informed basis. And beyond such laws and rules the athlete in tune with his/her conscience in the final arbiter.

REFERENCES

1. Ahlborg, B., Ekelund, L. G. and Nilsson, C. G. Effect of potassium — magnesium — aspartate on the capacity for prolonged exercise in man. *Acta Physiol. Scand.*, 74:238–245, 1968.
2. Astrand, P. O. and Rodahl, K. *Textbook of Work Physiology* (2nd ed.). New York: McGraw Hill, 1977.
3. Bannister, R. and Cunningham, D. The effects on the respiration and performance during exercise of adding oxygen to the inspired air. *J. Physiol. Lond.*, 125:118–137, 1954.
4. Bergstrom, J., Hermansen, L., Hultman, E. and Saltin, B. Diet, muscle glycogen and physical performance. *Acta Physiol. Scand.*, 71:140–150, 1967.
5. Bjorgum, R. K. and Sharkey, B. J. Inhalation of oxygen as an aid to recovery after exertion. *Research Quarterly*, 37:462–467, 1966.

6. Consolazio, C. F., Nelson, R. A., Matoush, L. O. and Isaac, G. J. Effects on aspartic acid salts on physical performance of men. *Journal of Applied Physiology,* 19:257–261, 1964.

7. Corbin, C. B. Mental practice. In: *Ergogenic Aids and Muscular Performance,* Morgan, W. P. (ed.). New York: Academic Press, 1972.

8. Costill, D. L. Nutritional requirements for endurance athletes. In: *Toward an Understanding of Human Performance,* Burke, E. J. (ed.). Ithaca, N.Y.: Mouvement Publications, 1977.

9. Costill, D. L. Water and electrolytes. In: *Ergogenic Aids and Muscular Performance,* Morgan, W. P. (ed.). New York: Academic Press, 1972.

10. Costill, D. L. Cote, R., Miller, E., Miller, T. and Wynder, S. Water and electrolyte replacement during repeated days of work in the heat. *Aviation, Space, and Environmental Medicine,* 46:795–800, 1975.

11. Dawson, P. M. *The Physiology of Physical Education.* Baltimore: Wilkins Co., 1935.

12. Dennig, H. Ueber Steigerung der korperlichen leistungsfahigkeit durch eingriffe im den Saurebasenhaushalt. *Deutsch Medizinische Wochenschrift,* 63:733–736, 1937.

13. Dennig, H., Talbot, J. H., Edwards, H. T., and Dill, D. B. Effect of acidosis and alkalosis upon capacity for work. *Journal of Clinical Investigation,* 9:601–613, 1931.

14. de Vries, H. A. *Physiology of Exercise for Physical Education and Athletics.* Dubuque, W. C. Brown Co., 1974.

15. Dill, D. B., Edwards, H. T. and Talbott, J. H. Alkalosis and the capacity for work. *Journal of Biological Chemistry,* 97:58–59, 1932.

16. Eddington, D. W. and Edgerton, V. R. *The Biology of Physical Activity.* Boston: Houghton Mifflin Co., 1976.

17. Ekblom, B., Goldbord, A. and Gullbring, B. Response to exercise after blood loss and reinfusion. *Journal of Applied Physiology,* 33:175–180, 1973.

18. Elbel, E., Ormond, D. and Close, D. Some effects of breathing O_2 before and after exercise. *Journal of Applied Physiology,* 16:48–52, 1961.

19. Falls, H. B. Heat and cold applications. In: *Ergogenic Aids and Muscular Performance,* Morgan, W. P. (ed.). New York: Academic Press, 1972.

20. Franks, B. D. Physical warm-up. In: *Ergogenic Aids and Muscular Performance,* Morgan, W. P. (ed.). New York: Academic Press, 1972.

21. Fowler, W. M. The facts about ergogenic aids and sports performance. *JOHPER,* 40:37–42, 1969.

22. Ganslen, R. V. Doping and athletic performance. In: *Exercise Physiology,* Falls, H. B. (ed.). New York: Academic Press, 1968.

23. Golding, L. A. Drugs and hormones. In: *Ergogenic Aids and Muscular Performance,* Morgan, W. P. (ed.). New York: Academic Press, 1972.

24. Golding, L. A. and Barnard, R. J. The effects of d-amphetamine sulphate on physical performance. *J. Sports Med. Phys. Fit.,* 3:221–224, 1963.

25. Hagerman, F., Bowers, R., Fox, E. and Ersing, W. The effects of breathing 100 percent oxygen during rest, heavy work and recovery. *Research Quarterly,* 39:965–974, 1968.

26. Horstman, D. H. Nutrition. In: *Ergogenic Aids and Muscular Performance,* Morgan, W. P. (ed.). New York: Academic Press, 1972.

27. Hughes, R., Clade, M. Edwards, R., Goodwin, T. and Jones, N. Effect of inspired O_2 on cardiopulmonary and metabolic responses to exercise in man. *Journal of Applied Physiology,* 24:336–347, 1968.

28. Hurst, P. M., Radlow, R. and Bagley, S. K. The effects of d-amphetamine and chlordiozepoxide upon strength and estimated strength. *Ergonomics,* 11:47–52, 1968.

29. Ikai, M. and Steinhaus, A. H. Some factors modifying the expression of human strength. *Journal of Applied Physiology,* 16:157–163, 1961.

30. Johnson, W. R. and Black, D. H. Comparison of effects of certain blood alkalinizers and glucose upon competitive endurance performance. *Journal of Applied Physiology,* 5:577–78, 1953.

31. Karlsson, J. and Saltin, B. Diet, muscle glycogen and endurance performance. *Journal of Applied Physiology,* 31:203–206, 1971.

32. Karpovich, P. Effect of amphetamine sulphate on athletic performance. *JAMA,* 170:558–561, 1959.

33. Karpovich, P. The effect of oxygen inhalation on swimming performance. *Research Quarterly,* 5:24, 1934.

34. Karpovich, P. V. and Sinning, W. E. *Physiology of Muscular Activity.* Philadelphia: W. B. Saunders, 1971.

35. Lamb, D. R. *Physiology of Exercise.* New York: Macmillan Co., 1978.

36. Lovingood, B. W., Blyth, C. S., Peacock, W. H. and Lindsay, R. B. Effects of d-amphetamine sulfate, caffeine and high temperature on human performance. *Research Quarterly,* 38:64–71, 1967.

37. Lucaccini, L. F. and Kreit, L. H. Music. In: *Ergogenic Aids and Muscular Performance,* Morgan, W. P. (ed.). New York: Academic Press, 1972.

38. Matthews, D. K. and Fox, E. L. *The Physiological Basis of Physical Education and Athletics.* Philadelphia: W. B. Saunders Co., 1976.

39. Miller, A. Influence of oxygen administration on the cardiovascular function during exercise and recovery. *Journal of Applied Physiology,* 5:165–168, 1952.

40. Morgan, W. P. Hypnosis and muscular performance. In: *Ergogenic Aids and Muscular Performance,* Morgan, W. P. (ed.). New York: Academic Press, 1972.

41. Murphy, R. J. The problem of environmental heat in athletics. *Ohio State Medical Journal,* 59:799, 1963.

42. Nelson, R. A. Exceptional nutritional needs of the athlete. Paper presented at the 15th national conference on the medical aspects of sports, Anaheim, California, December, 1973.

43. Olsson, K. and Saltin, B. Diet and fluids in training and competition. *Scandinavian Journal of Rehabilitation Medicine,* 3:31–38, 1971.

44. Osternig, L. B. Carbohydrate loading: a boon or a bone? *Athletic Training,* 11:22–23, 1974.

45. Robinson, B. et al. Circulatory effects of acute expansion of blood volume. *Circulation Research,* 19:26–32, 1966.

46. Ronzoni, E. The effect of exercise on breathing in experimental alkalosis by ingested sodium bicarbonate. *Journal of Biological Chemistry,* 67:25–27, 1926.

47. Round Table Discussion: Mann, G. V., Parizkova, J., Rogozkin, V. A. and Drake, L. Nutritional practices in athletics abroad. *Physician and Sports Medicine,* 33–44, January, 1977.

48. Ryan, A. J. Use of amphetamines in athletics. *JAMA,* 170:562, 1959.

49. Slovic, P. Eating way precious minutes. *Runners World,* 9:34–35, 1974.

50. Smith, G. M. and Beecher, H. K. Amphetamine sulfate and athletic performance. *JAMA,* 170–542–557, 1959.

51. Williams, M. Blood doping — does it really help athletes? *The Physician and Sports Medicine,* January, 1975.

52. Williams, M., Goodwin, H., Perkins, R. and Bocrie, J. Effect of blood reinjection upon endurance capacity and heart rate. *Medicine and Science in Sports,* 5:181–185, 1973.

53. Wilmore, J. H. *Athletic Training and Physical Fitness.* Boston: Allyn and Bacon, Inc., 1977.

54. Wilmore, J. H. Oxygen. In: *Ergogenic Aids and Muscular Performance,* Morgan, W. P. (ed.). New York: Academic Press, 1972.

The Need for a Certified Athletic Trainer in the Junior-Senior High Schools*

E. James Kelley, Ed.D.
Sayers J. Miller, Jr., M.S., R.P.T., A.T.C.

Athletic trainers, like other professionals in today's society, live in an environment which is undergoing constant change. New treatment information is being generated so rapidly that it has become extremely difficult for one to keep abreast of new developments in the field. Therefore, since present skills and knowledge will not enable individuals to operate effectively in tomorrow's world, those in specialized fields are constantly faced with the danger of becoming obsolete.

It was within this context of change that a recent study was conducted at The Pennsylvania State University to determine the extent of knowledge obsolescence among non-certified junior-senior high school athletic trainers.* The study was designed to assess the extent the sample population (N = 128) understood current knowledge in the area of athletic training and conditioning. The subjects, teachers employed in Pennsylvania public schools completed an instrument composed of twenty multiple choice items developed by nationally recognized athletic training and conditioning experts. The items dealt with such topics as the care and treatment of athletic injuries — conditioning programs, diet, drugs and heat exhaustion, each of which was deemed essential to the implementation of athletic training and conditioning programs and care of athletic injuries. Based on the established standard of competency used in previous studies (70% correct answers), the results indicated that 85% of the respondents could be considered obsolete in their understanding of current knowledge.

Earlier studies on training and conditioning conducted by Kelley involving male physical educators (1) and coaches (2,3) produced similar findings. A comparison of the results of the three groups can be seen in Table 1.

As shown in Table 1, 85% of the athletic trainers sampled would be considered obsolete in their understanding of current knowledge. The performance of the athletic trainers was somewhat lower than that achieved in an earlier study (1) involving

TABLE 1
COMPARISON OF STUDIES INVOLVING
MALE PHYSICAL EDUCATORS, COACHES AND TRAINERS

Population Sample	Number of Respondents	% of Sample Who Did Not Meet Established Criteria
Male Physical Educators	1024	77%
Coaches	292	86%
Athletic Trainers	128	85%

*Answer 70% of the items correctly.

male physical educators which estimated that 77% of this group were not aware of current information. The study involving coaches (2,3) found 86% of this group falling below the established criteria. The fact that the athletic trainers did not score highest among the three groups completing the instrument is cause for concern. Since the items contained in the instrument pertained exclusively to athletic training and conditioning, one would expect that those individuals working in this specific area would be the most knowledgeable. Since this was not the case, one might assume that many individuals assigned the responsibility of the athletic trainer in public schools have not had the needed professional preparation in athletic training and physical education or the opportunity for updating. The very similar obsolescence rates for coaches and athletic trainers would lend support to the belief that many high school athletic trainers are primarily coaches, appointed to carry out this role. The study indicates a definite need for persons involved in athletic training to have more information relating to anatomy, physiology, care and treatment of athletic injuries and related subject matter.

An examination of the items contained in the instrument indicated obsolescence in understanding questions related to diet. For example, an item pertaining to the type of diet which would favor the

*An article published in Athletic Training, 11:180, 182-183, Winter, 1976. Reprinted with permission of the publisher.

most efficient performance on the part of the athlete revealed that 85% of the group were unaware that a pre-game meal should be high in carbohydrate, moderate in protein and low in fat. This type of response indicates that many persons serving in the role of athletic trainer at the junior-senior high school level do not have sufficient knowledge concerning proper nutrition. This is one of the contributing factors for fads and fallacies in the diet of the athletes.

The sampled population was asked to respond to an item identifying numerous athletic catastrophies and select the one which could be prevented. Possible choices included: (1) cerebral concussion, (2) blisters, (3) shin splints, (4) heat stroke, and (5) hamstring pulls. The fact that only 53% of the respondents correctly identified heat stroke as a preventable catastrophy reflects a lack of knowledge regarding specific injuries and illnesses. Unfortunately, results such as this further support the feeling that many individuals assigned the role of "the athletic trainer" have not been selected on the basis of their professional preparation.

Items relating to heat stroke prevention and the use of modalities were answered correctly by nearly 70% of the respondents. However, it is expected that information such as this would be understood by all persons involved in athletic training. Those individuals identifying themselves as athletic trainers in this study were also asked to identify a variety of injuries. For example, if a player complains that his arm has no feeling and he cannot move it, or has little or no strength in it, what are the possible dangers? Only slightly more than half of the responding group answered this correctly by indicating that he may have fractured a cervical vertebrae. This incorrect response on the part of so many further reflects a poor anatomical background of the respondents. In addition, they have indicated a lack of ability in recognizing signs and symptoms of particular injuries. Anatomy and clinical signs (symptoms) are the two weakest points in the professional preparation of these athletic trainers.

Further evidence that many of the athletic trainers in this study needing more education is revealed in their response to items related to recurring straining of the groin muscles. Less than 50% of the group realized that this type of injury is frequently associated with tight hamstring muscles. The natural response of the untrained individual to a question such as this would be to associate the groin with the nearest anatomical landmark.

One of the greatest dangers to an athlete who has an unsuspected case of mononucleosis and is still engaging in sports practices or competition is the rupture of the spleen. Only 24% of the responding group answered this correctly. The uninformed athletic trainer would naturally relate the symptom, excessive fatigue, to mononucleosis rather than the complication of a rupture of the spleen. Unfortunately, many individuals involved in athletic training are not familiar with the pathol-

ogy and complications which may develop if the athlete continues to engage in sports activity.

Items related to heat exhaustion were answered correctly by a significant portion of the population. A fundamental precept in preventing heat exhaustion is to provide liquids without restriction. Seventy percent agreed that players should be permitted free access to water at all times during practice and games. Off the field, heat adaptation can best be maintained by generously salted food and maintaining fluid intake of about two quarts daily. Less than 30% responded correctly to this item.

DISCUSSION

An analysis of the examination indicates that a large proportion of those individuals assigned to the role of athletic trainer are in need of updating. While the degree of obsolescence varied according to the areas of knowledge, the general performance of the group was low.

Based on the results of the study, it was concluded that the individuals assigned to the role of athletic trainer have to be made aware of the many changes that have occurred in the field during the past several years. These are the people who have many responsibilities which include making decisions on the purchase and selection of athletic equipment and the development and implementation of conditioning programs.

Another important aspect that should be noted is that in the absence of an attending physician, athletic trainers are frequently the first to attend injured athletes, to render a judgment of the severity of the injury, and to administer appropriate primary care. In addition, it's not uncommon for athletic trainers to make suggestions on the athlete's diet and to establish policies on the use of water and salt while engaging in sports activity.

This poses a very important question: Are the individuals making such decisions competent and familiar with current knowledge? The results of this study indicate that a large majority are not aware of the most current information.

TERMINOLOGY VS. PRACTICE

It should be pointed out, however, that it's possible for a person to be obsolete in terms of recent developments and still fulfill his responsibilities. To illustrate: An athletic trainer may know that he should apply ice to a person who has just suffered an ankle sprain, but may not be able to answer a question on the use of "cryotherapy." Since cryotherapy is the use of ice, a person unfamiliar with the term could be considered obsolete in terms of current terminology, yet be up to date from the practical or functional standpoint. Nevertheless, a lack of knowledge as extensive as that indicated appears to justify concern.

IMPLICATIONS

The study has professional implications. It implies that daily, hundreds of decisions, ranging from the planning and implementation of training and conditioning programs to the care and treatment of injuries, are being made by individuals without adequate preparation and training.

A POSSIBLE SOLUTION

The results of this study have provided a basis for the development of a program of studies designed to update non-certified athletic trainers assigned to this role by their high school administration. Dr. E. James Kelley, Assistant Dean for Continuing Education and Mr. Sayers Miller, Assistant Professor of Health Education at The Pennsylvania State University, have developed a program of instruction which, upon successful completion, will provide certification as a trainer for interscholastic sports. The program was designed to improve competency in the area of training and conditioning techniques for those responsibilities on the care and prevention of injuries related to sports activities. The certification program offered by Penn State and submitted for endorsement by the N.A.T.A. consists of studies in first aid, recognition of injuries, athletic training techniques, injury management, rehabilitation of athletic injuries, injury prevention, and administration of athletic training programs. Upon satisfactory completion of the 24 credits, a certificate stating that a person has met the requirements and is qualified to serve as an athletic trainer for interscholastic sports is awarded. In addition, this program would also assist the student to meet Section III of the N.A.T.A. procedures.

CONCLUSION

In this era of knowledge explosion, stagnant prac-

titioners pose a major challenge to professional educators. Fortunately, in today's society, opportunities for updating are extensive. It is imperative professionals be aware that these opportunities exist and realize it is not necessary for them to experience a decline in competency. Firstly, if athletic trainers, as other professionals, are to function at a high level of efficiency, it is essential that they continue their education, for learning is a lifelong process.

Secondly, school and athletic administrators must not condone the practice of assigning a coach or staff member to the role of athletic trainer who lacks the professional preparation or is obsolete in his or her knowledge in the field. The appointment of an unprepared individual to care for the health of athletes will only breed many more legal and medical problems in the future. Consequently, the wise administrator would be the one that hires a teacher on his faculty that is also qualified to carry out the duties and responsibilities of an athletic trainer or requires the individual assigned this position to become professionally prepared to carry out his or her role of athletic trainer. In other words, make sure that your athletic trainer *is* or *becomes* a certified athletic trainer.

BIBLIOGRAPHY

1. Lindsay, Carl A., Morrison, James L., and Kelley, E. James. Professional Obsolescence: Implications for Continuing Professional Education. *Adult Education — A Journal of Research and Theory.* 25:3-22, November 1974.
2. Kelley, E. James, and Kalenak, Alexander. Knowledge Obsolescence: The Need for Sports Medicine Education among Physical Educators and Coaches. *The Journal of Sports Medicine.* 3: 277-281, November/December 1975.
3. Kelley, E. James, and Kalenak, Alexander. Knowledge Obsolescence. *The Scholastic Coach.* 45: 19, 83-85, January 1976.

Legal Responsibilities in Athletic Injuries *

*George Elliot Moss ,
J.D., Attorney at Law*

Sports accidents are an all too frequent occurrence and unfortunately the resulting injuries are usually extremely serious. We should wish that broken bones and sprains would be the only injuries athletes would suffer; however, the gridiron, ski slope, ball park, and boxing ring have all produced their share of quadriplegics and deaths.

Five areas of liability exist within the sports domain, with the responsibility within each area resting on a different party.

Assumption of Risk — Such a concept generally means that an individual with knowledge of the attendant risks, voluntarily enters into some relation which will necessarily involve that risk, and so is regarded as tacitly or impliedly agreeing to take his own chances. Thus, those who participate or sit as spectators at sports and amusements may be taken to assume all the known risks of being hurt by roller coasters, flying baseballs, golf balls, or wrestlers.[1]

A 1962 Oregon case brings home the devastating injuries one can suffer. During a football game between Vale and Nyssa High Schools young Louis Vendrell was seriously hurt, resulting in his neck being broken and him becoming a paraplegic. On the issue of assumption of risk, the court held "The playing of football is a body contact sport. The game demands that the players come into physical contact with each other constantly, frequently with great force. The linemen charge the opposing line vigorously shoulder to shoulder. The tackle faces the risk of leaping at the swiftly moving legs of the ball-carrier and the latter must be prepared to strike the ground violently. Body contacts, bruises, and clashes are inherent in the game. There is no other way to play it. No prospective player need be told that a participant in the game of football may sustain injury. That fact is self-evident. It draws to the game the manly; they accept its risks, blows, clashes, and injuries without whimper."[2] Justice Cardozo summarized all this quite neatly: "The timorous may stay at home."[3]

Equipment — An open range of liability exists in the area of faulty equipment. Product liability cases have flooded the courts in recent years with automobile design cases in the forefront. American law has moved away from the traditional (or more

correctly — vintage) caveat emptor — let the buyer beware, to a concept of placing responsibility for defective chattels on the party who could have and should have prevented or discovered the defect. An athlete need not wear a football helmet "hoping" that the helmet will not split apart, nor must the gymnast "hope" that parallel bars will withstand calisthenics. Current negligence law and the Uniform Commercial Code[4] have put sellers on notice that they warrant that goods are fit for the particular purpose of the buyer and that the goods are of merchantable quality.

It is not just the purchaser who the seller is responsible to for faulty equipment, but all those who fall within the zone of liability. The limits of this zone of liability are incapable of precise definition, and each case must be decided on its own particular set of facts; though if the harm caused was the natural and probable result of the defendant's negligent act, liability may be thrust on a defendant. An illustration is in order. Widget Baseball Bat Company delivers to the North Carolina Pioneers defective baseball bats, which Widget has manufactured. During a baseball game, a bat splits open and part of it hits an opposing player on the field, and part hits a spectator. To whom, if anyone is Widget liable; and is assumption of risk a valid defense against the opposing player or spectator? Where does the zone of liability end — should Widget be responsible to anyone who may have been hit by a splinter of the bat? Widget should know of the presence of opposing players, but is Widget responsible to all the spectators. These probing questions are incapable of easy answers and have provided courts and legal writers with mountains of briefs.

Treatment — California[5] and New Jersey provide interesting cases on treatment of injured persons. A football play popularly known as the quarterback sneak, starting with the T-formation, resulted in damage to the spinal cord of plaintiff Welch and him becoming a permanent quadriplegic. After the tackle, the team doctor who was 20-25 feet away from the injury did not go over to see Welch till he was removed to the sidelines. Eight boys, four on each side of Welch carried him to the sidelines. Certainly at least a litter was available to transport the injured boy off the field, and some medical attention should have been given to the injured boy on the field. The California courts held that "the

*The following article, authored by George E. Moss, is a copyrighted feature of *Emergency Product News,* and is reprinted with their written authorization. The article was published in April, 1975.

doctor and coach were negligent in the removal of the plaintiff from the field to the sidelines; the coach in failing to wait for the doctor and the doctor in failing to act promptly after the injury."[6]

New Jersey's contribution to the treatment issue illustrates the outer bounds of medical assistance in an emergency. As in the preceding situation, high school football is the culprit. After a tackle, young Frank Duda's "shoulder came out of place." The boy was properly removed from the field, his arm placed in a sling and escorted home by a classmate. He wore the sling for three days, thereafter, at home and in the presence of his parents and did not miss a day of school. In a suit against the teachers for failing to obtain medical assistance the Superior Court of New Jersey held "in no way was there an immediate pressing necessity for medical aid for the boy before he went home and the decision to obtain such aid could await his parent's consideration. He was suffering pain from the injury, but was fully possessed of his faculties, was able to walk unattended the 125 yards from the field to the clubhouse and after changing clothes, to walk home. In these circumstances the facts do not reasonably permit opposing conclusions by fair-minded men as to whether or not the boy was then in urgent need of medical attention."[7]

Transportation — Just what should be used to transport injured persons is answered by use of an ambulance. But where the injury is in an isolated area and inaccessible to normal transportation, reasonable transportation facilities will suffice. Where an individual was injured on a bobsled run the State's (which operated the bobsled run) obligation rested on reason and common sense, and transportation of the injured party in a dump truck or pickup truck, was reasonable in light of the special circumstances. These special circumstances were: (a) injury on a mountainside, (b) no showing of unnecessary delay, (c) hospital eight miles away.[8] Conspicuous by its absence is the lack of discussion on whether the injured party should have, when the dump truck reached the highway, been then transferred to a waiting ambulance. Inasmuch as frostbite was one of the injuries, prudence and sound medical care dictate that the injured party be transferred to a waiting ambulance; however, this was absent from the Court's opinion.

Causation — Who caused the plaintiff's injuries? The time span between injury and final treatment is so short that to separate the negligent parties in relation to the amount of damage each one caused is a problem not unlike coming to grips with the Holy Ghost. New York has solved the problem, by appointing damages caused, among all the defendants. Hypothetically, where an Emergency Medical Technician, and a doctor are both found to be negligent though each in different amounts, the damages will be apportioned between them. This modern approach recognizes that one party may not be entirely negligent, yet may not be wholly free from negligence, and attempts to be fair in assessing liability.

As Justice Cardozo stated "the timorous may stay at home." Sports injuries are a common occurrence and with competition in schools and colleges increasingly emphasized, it is the athlete who after the team has won a game or championship and the partying is over, is left with permanent scarring. Placing fault is difficult, for both athlete, coach, parent and spectator have a hand in producing the injury. One can only strive for quick and capable responses — and for this all concerned must salute the EMT.

REFERENCES

1. Prosser, *Law of Torts* 3rd Ed. 67.
2. Vendrell v. School District No. 26 C Malheus County, 1962, 376 Pgs. 406, 411, 412.
3. Prosser *Law of Torts* 3rd Ed. 67 Murphy v. Steeplechase Amusement Co. 1929 250 NY 479, 166 N.E. 173.
4. Uniform Commercial Code Sections 2-313 2-314 2-315.
5. Welch v. Dunsmuir Joint Union High School District 1958, 326 P. 633.
6. *Ibid.*
7. Duda v. Gaines 1951 79 2d 695, 696.
8. Clark v. State 1949 276 App. Div. 10.

APPENDIX A.
Simple Tests of Flexibility*

Lenox Hill Hospital

The following tests of flexibility were developed with the belief that a particular pattern of flexibility may be advantageous for certain athletic activities and at the same time, predispose the athlete to injury in other endeavors. Preliminary findings indicate that females are generally more flexible than males, that individuals lose flexibility with age and that there are specific flexibility patterns for professional athletes in different sports. (1,2)

The following simple testing protocol may be useful for the coach in determining the athlete's flexibility. Based on this determination, the coach may find Appendix B useful in improving flexibility in the "tight" athlete. Alternatively, the "loose jointed" athlete may be referred to appropriate strength training procedures.

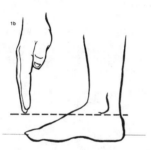

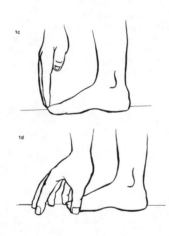

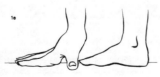

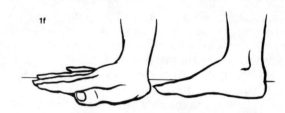

Figure 1. PALMS TO THE FLOOR

(a) *Keep knees and feet together.*
(b) *Do not bend at the knees.*
(c) *Slowly, attempt to place palms on the floor in front of feet in one movement.*
(d) *Do not bounce to gain a greater range.*
(e) *If subject can't perform this, have him attempt to touch the most distal point he can reach on his legs.*
(f) *Keep knees fully extended (straight) throughout motion.*

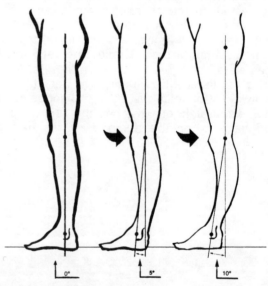

Figure 2. RECURVATION

(a) *Keep knees and feet together, have subject stand erect.*
(b) *Maintain knees in most backward position (Tester should push knees back.)*
(c) *Locate greater trochanter; Locate lateral femoral candyle; Locate lateral malleolus.*
(d) *Observe angle between the line through the greater trochanter and lateral condyle to the floor and the line through the lateral malleolus lateral condyle.*

*These tests were developed by the Institute of Sports Medicine and Athletic Trauma at Lenox Hill Hospital, 130 East 77th St., New York, NY 10021, and are reprinted with their permission.

128

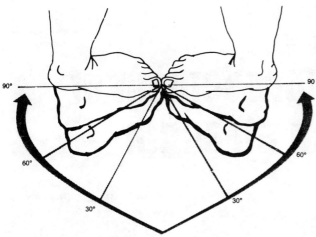

Figure 3. TOES INWARD

(a) *Keep knees locked, fully extended.*

(b) *Keep toes together and swing heels forward as far as possible. Do not let any part of the foot off of the ground.*

(c) *Use any support for balance.*

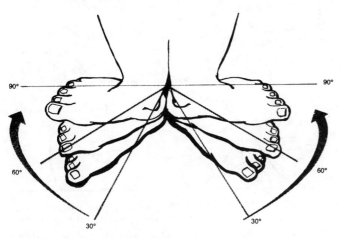

Figure 4. TOES OUTWARD

(a) *Same conditions as above but keep heels together as well as knees and rotate feet outward.*

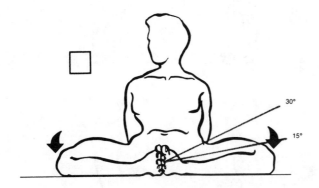

Figure 5. LOTUS

(a) *Sit on floor.*

(b) *Place feet flat against each other.*

(c) *Bring feet close to body.*

(d) *Place hands on feet, relax.*

(e) *Tester should lightly attempt to push knees to the floor.*

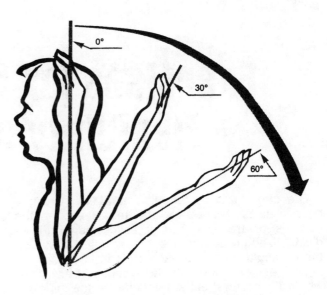

Figure 6. HUMERAL EXTERNAL ROTATION

(a) *Position dominant arm with 90 abduction at the shoulder, 90 flexion at the elbow.*

(b) *Relax all muscles and stand straight.*

(c) *While supporting the humerus, tester should grasp the wrist and rotate the humerus externally (backward).*

(d) *Make sure there is no scapular rotation or elevation.*

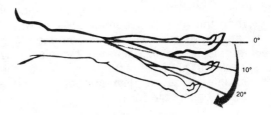

Figure 7. ELBOW EXTENSION

(a) *Hold arm at 90 of abduction.*

(b) *Relax muscles in arm, supinate the forearm.*

(c) *Fully extend the dominant arm at the elbow.*

(d) *While supporting the humerus, the tester should push down on the forearm to achieve maximum extension.*

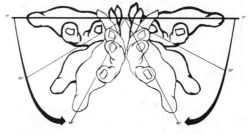

Figure 8. WRIST TURN-OUT

(a) *Place arms parallel to the ground in front of subject.*

(b) *Completely extend and lock the arms at the elbow and wrist.*

(c) *Supinate the palms.*

(d) *Grasping the wrists, the tester should hyper-supinate.*

REFERENCES

1. Nicholas, J.A. Risk factors, sports medicine and the orthopedic system: an overview *Journal of Sports Medicine.* 3:243—259, 1975.

2. Nicholas, J.A. Injuries to knee ligaments relationship to looseness and tightness in football players. JAMA 212:2236—2239, 1970.

APPENDIX B.

Exercises for Improvement of Flexibility and Strength

The importance of strength and flexibility has been well established for athletes. Based on the coach's or trainer's careful assessment, an individualized program can be constructed based on the particular needs of each athlete. In the following pages you will be offered a series of exercises which the editors feel are optimal for the improvement of strength (S) and flexibility (F) in each part of the body. In general, all flexibility exercises should be done slowly, held for at least 5 to 10 counts and repeated several times. For strength exercises, the athlete should be taught to make each contraction through the FULL RANGE OF MOTION, 3 sets a day, every other day. The weight (resistance) lifted should be such that more than 6 repetitions are impossible (high resistance/low reps). When the athlete becomes capable of more than 6 repetitions, the weight is increased. While some marginal strength gains will be elicited with "low resistance/high repetition" exercises, these may be primarily used to develop local muscle endurance and or muscle tone.

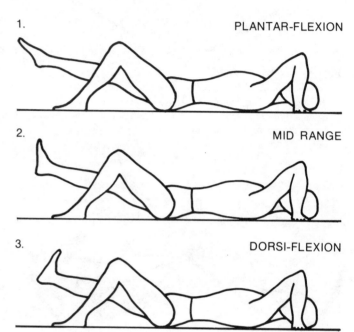

Figure 2 (F). *Lower leg stretch. From a supine position with one leg flexed and the other fully extended and off the ground; the foot is pointed down (plantar flexed) and held, then pointed up (dorsiflexion) and held. Hold each position for 7 counts.*

Lower Leg

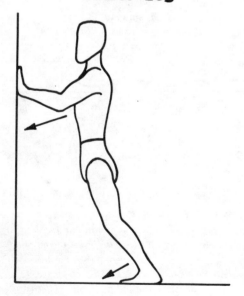

Figure 1 (F). *Heel cord stretch. With the arms outstretched, the hands against the wall and the heels flat on the floor, the elbows are bent to allow the body to gradually lean forward. This stretch should be held for 15 to 20 counts and repeated several times.*

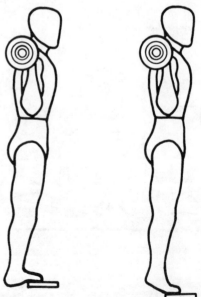

Figure 3 (S). *Heel lifts. Standing with the heels over a board and a weight resting on the shoulders, the athlete raises as high onto the toes as possible, then lowers. This will develop the calf musculature.*

Thigh and Hamstring

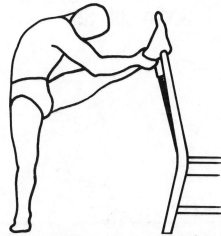

Figure 4 (F). *Thigh and shoulder stretch. From a face lying position the athlete reaches back with both hands and clasps onto the ankles. The legs are lifted off the ground to form a cradle and this position is held.*

Figure 7. (F). *Hamstring stretch. From a standing position, one leg is placed on a support at least as high as the waist while the other leg is straight. The ankle of the elevated leg is grasped and the trunk is bent toward this leg.*

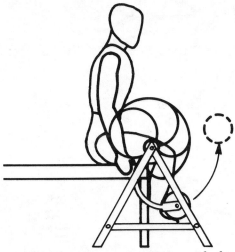

Figure 5 (F). *Leg extension. Sitting with the knee bent, the resistance is lifted while the leg is fully extended. Increased strength in the quadriceps femoris muscle group will result.*

Figure 8 (F). *Hamstring stretch. Sitting in a V-position with the knees fully extended, the toes are alternately touched with hand of the opposite arm.*

Figure 9 (F). *Hamstring stretch. From a long sitting position, one leg is elevated as high as possible, grasped at the ankle and pulled toward the head. The stretch should be held for 10 counts and both legs should be stretched.*

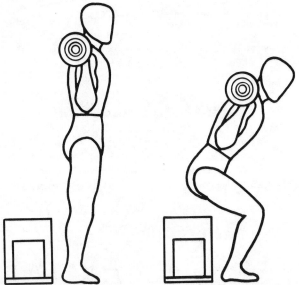

Figure 6 (S). *Squats. Standing straight with the barbell resting on the shoulders behind the neck, the athlete squats approximately half way into a knee bend. A bench should be placed under the athlete's buttocks to restrain the athlete from going beyond parallel with the floor. Also, the back should be kept straight to prevent injury. The thigh musculature will be strengthened with this exercise.*

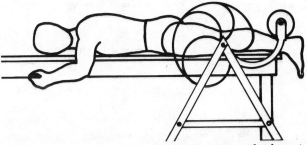

Figure 10 (S). *Leg curl. From a prone position the knee is bent or flexed against a resistance. This exercise is used for the development of strength in the hamstring muscle group.*

131

Groin and Hip

Figure 11 (F). *Groin stretch. Sitting, the athlete gently pushes down on his knees to stretch the muscles of the groin region. This stretch should be held for several counts and repeated.*

Figure 12 (F). *Groin and hip flexor stretch. From a forward stride position with both feet pointing directly forward, a slow stretch is placed on the leg that is extended back to stretch the adductors, the foot of the extended leg is turned to the side.*

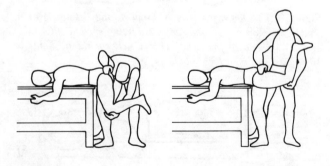

Figure 13 (F). *Hip flexor stretch. With the athlete standing on one foot with the trunk bent and supported on a table, the athletic trainer gently stretches the opposite knee. The knee should be bent, the low back should be stabilized, and the exercise should be repeated several times.*

Figure 14 (F). *Hip flexor stretch. From a back lying position, the knee is pulled toward the chest. The opposite leg should be kept in a straight position.*

Figure 15 (F). *V-stretch. From a seated position with the legs straight and straddled as far apart as possible, the ankle is reached for and grasped. The hamstrings, groin and back will be stretched.*

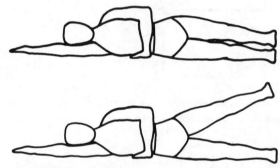

Figure 16 (S). *Straight leg raises (abduction). From a side lying position the top leg is lifted straight upward. This will develop the lateral hip and this musculature.*

Trunk and Abdomen

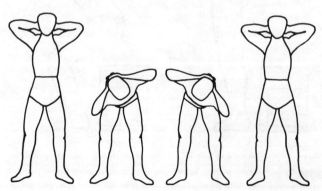

Figure 17 (F). *Trunk twister. From a standing position with hands held behind the neck, the low back and trunk muscles are stretched by rotating the trunk to the right and left.*

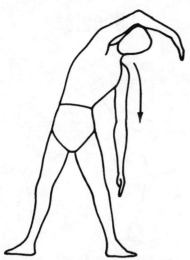

Figure 18 (F). *Side stretch. From a standing position with the feet spread apart, the athlete slowly bends sidewards at the waist and holds in the stretched position.*

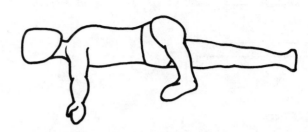

Figure 22 (F). *Single leg crossovers. From a supine position with arms out to the sides, one leg is raised and crossed over toward the opposite hand. There is a return to the starting position and alternated. The low back, the lateral thigh and hip musculature will be stretched with this exercise.*

Figure 19 (S). *Clean and press. Squatting; the weight is "cleaned" or lifted to the chest while the legs are straightened. The weight is then pressed straight overhead. The arms, shoulders and chest are developed with this exercise.*

Figure 23 (F). *Legs up and over. From a position lying on the back the legs are held straight and pulled over the head until the toes touch the ground. If this is done slowly the hip flexors and abdominal muscles will be strengthened while the hamstrings and back are stretched.*

Figure 20 (S). *Bent knee sit-up. From a lying position with the knees bent and with the hands behind the neck, the trunk is flexed forward. The bent knees prevent low back strain and the exercise develops the musculature of the abdominal region.*

Figure 21 (S). *V-up. From a sitting position with the knees straight, the legs are lifted up to touch the finger tips. This exercise will develop the musculature in the abdominal region.*

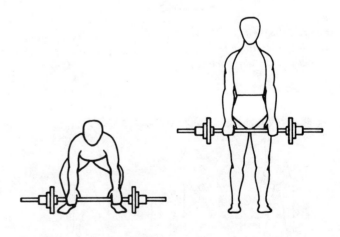

Figure 24 (S). *Dead lift. From a position with the feet flat and the knees bent, the athlete lifts the weight until the body is erect. The spine should be kept straight to prevent a lower back strain. This exercise strengthens the low back and thigh musculature.*

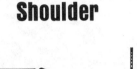

Shoulder

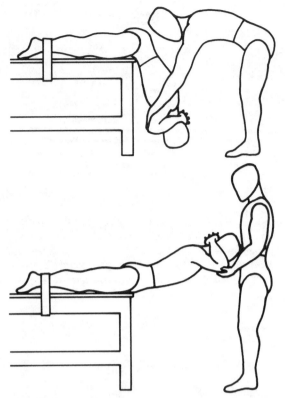

Figure 25 (S). *Back extension. From a face lying position with the feet stabilized and the trunk over the table, the torso is lifted until the back is fully extended. Assistance may be used and the exercise will develop strength of the back muscles.*

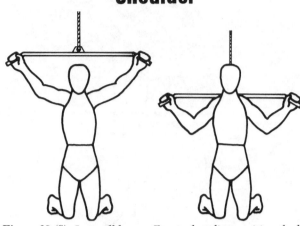

Figure 28 (S). *Lat pulldowns. From a kneeling position the bar is pulled down to the back of the neck. This will develop strength specifically in the latissimus dorsi muscle.*

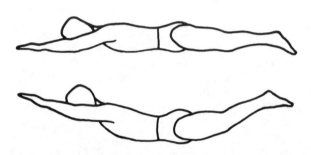

Figure 26 (S). *Prone arch. From a face lying position, the arms and legs are lifted by arching the back. This will develop strength of the low back musculature.*

Figure 29 (F). *Shoulder stretch. From a long sitting position, the hands are edged behind the athlete as far as possible to stretch the anterior aspect of the shoulder.*

Figure 30 (F). *Shoulder and upper arm stretch. From a standing position with the arms extended overhead, the athlete holds his opposite wrist and stretches slightly backwards.*

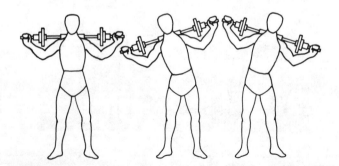

Figure 27 (S & F). *Side bends. From a standing position with the feet spread and the weight held behind the neck, the athlete bends as far to the side as possible. Muscle strength is increased in the abdominal and low back regions.*

Figure 31 (F). *Shoulder and upper arm stretch. From a standing position with the elbow bent, and the arms overhead, the opposite hand is used to pull the elbow slowly behind the head.*

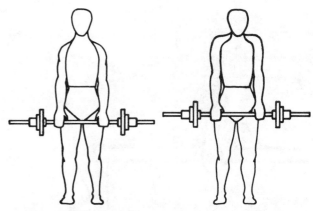

Figure 34 (S). *Shoulder shrug. From a standing position with the knees, back and arms straight the shoulders are shrugged to lift the weight. The upper back, especially the upper fibers of the trapizius muscle, are strengthened.*

Figure 32 (F). *Shoulder and chest stretch. From a standing position the fingers are interlocked behind the athlete's back and the arms are slowly lifted upward. The stretch should be held for 10 counts and repeated several times.*

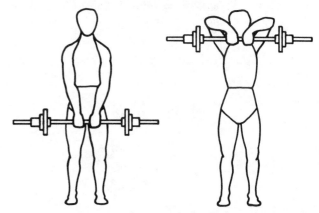

Figure 35 (S). *Upright rowing motion. Standing straight with the weight held across the upper thigh, the weight is pulled toward the chin. This exercise will develop the strength of the muscles of the shoulders and upper back.*

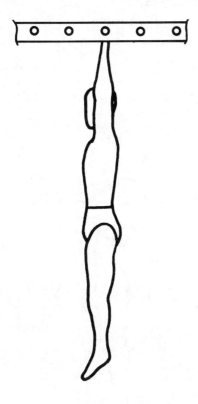

Figure 33 (S & F). *Bar hang. With the arms straight overhead, the athlete holds his/her body off the ground for at least 10-15 counts and repeats the exercise several times. The shoulder girdle and the back musculature will be stretched.*

Figure 36 (S). *Military press. Standing with the legs apart and the knees and back straight the weight is lifted straight overhead from the chest. Development of strength will occur to the muscles of the anterior part of the shoulder and chest.*

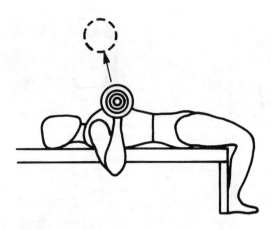

Figure 37 (S). *Bench press. From a lying position with the knees bent and the feet flat on the floor, the weight is pushed straight upward. The buttocks should remain in contact with the bench and the back should not arch. This will strengthen the muscles of the chest.*

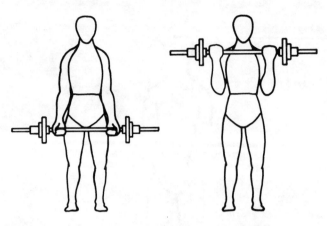

Figure 39 (S). *Arm curls. Standing straight with the arms extended, the weight is lifted toward the chest by flexing the arms at the elbows. Strength development is greatest to the biceps muscle.*

Forearm and Wrist

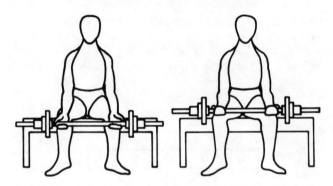

Figure 40 (S). *Wrist curls. From a sitting position with the elbow flexed at a right angle, the weight is lifted from a position of full flexion. This exercise develops the flexor muscles of the wrist and forearm.*

Upper Arm

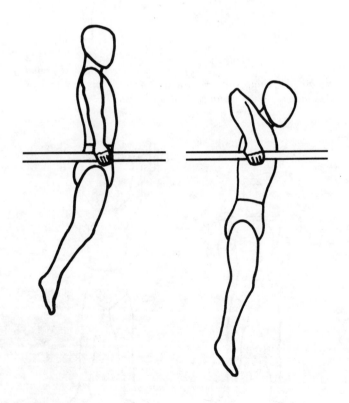

Figure 38 (S). *Dips. With the arms extended straight on the parallel bars or a dip station, the body is lowered and raised. The strength of the triceps muscle and shoulder muscles will increase with this exercise.*

Figure 41 (S). *Wrist rolling. The arms are extended and parallel with the floor and the weight is rolled up. If it is done with both an overhand grip and an underhand grip the entire forearm musculature will be developed.*

Selected Taping Procedures

The following illustrations represent selected techniques of taping and wrapping used by many people involved with athletic medicine today. This is not intended to cover all of the techniques that may be used, but it covers several basic procedures that are often needed by the coach or athletic trainer. There are many successful techniques for almost every taping or wrapping procedure. The most important points that one should remember when taping or wrapping are that the technique should be anatomically sound, functional, and it should offer support to the intended area.

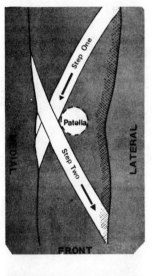
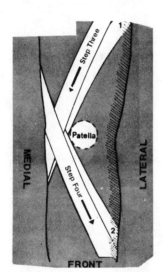
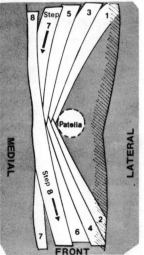
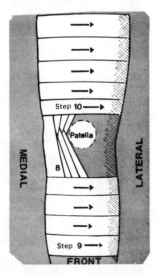

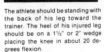

The athlete should be standing with the back of his leg toward the trainer. The heel of his injured leg should be on a 1½" or 2" wedge placing the knee in about 20 degrees flexion.

Initial strips of diagonal basketweave should be 1½" wide adhesive tape, each strip running from midcalf to midthigh (see illustration).

The strapping should be anchored by 3" wide ELASTIKON Tape covering the entire basketweave, but not covering the patella.

Figure 2. *Techniques of knee taping — hyperextension of cruciate ligament strain. From: Athletic Uses of Adhesive Tape. Reprinted with permission of Johnson and Johnson Co., New Brunswick, N.J.*

Figure 1. *Techniques of knee taping. From: Techniques of Taping. Reprinted with permission of Kay Laboratories. San Diego, California.*

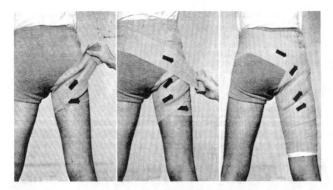

Figure 3. *Wrap for the hamstring pull deep in the hip. This particular wrapping technique gives the best possible support and the greatest degree of pressure for a hamstring pull deep in the hip. From: The First Aider, December, 1974. Reprinted with permission of Cramer Products, Inc.*

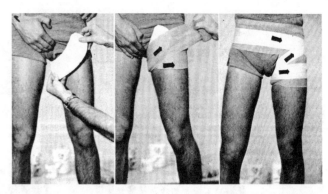

Figure 4. *Spica Wrap technique. The best treatment for groin strains includes a compression bandage utilizing the Spica Wrap technique illustrated above. From: The First Aider, December, 1974. Reprinted with permission of Cramer Products, Inc.*

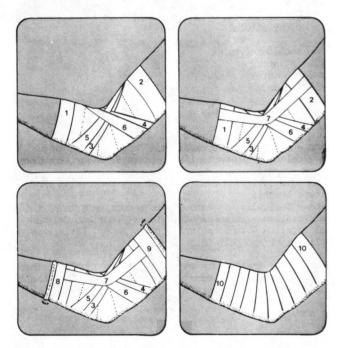

Figure 5. *Hyperextension of the elbow joint. From: Techniques of Taping. Reprinted with permission of Kay Laboratories. San Diego, California*

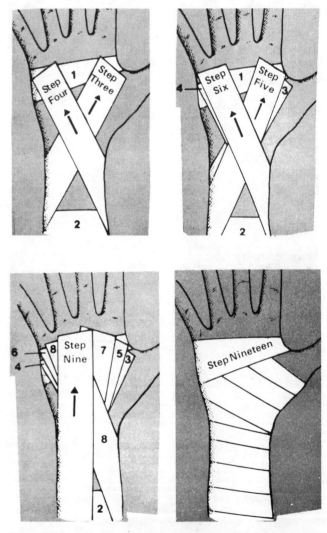

Figure 6. *Taping the wrist. From: Techniques of Taping. Reprinted with permission of Kay Laboratories. San Diego, Cal*

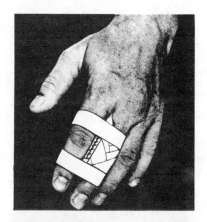
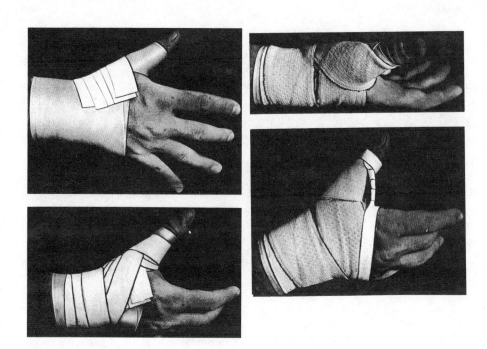
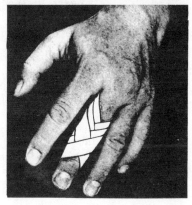

Figure 7. *Taping of the hand and fingers. From: Athletic Uses of Adhesive Tape. Reprinted with permission of Johnson and Johnson Co., New Brunswick, N.J.*

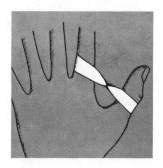

Figure 8. *Taping of the fingers and thumb. From: Techniques of Taping. Reprinted with permission of Kay Laboratories. San Diego, California.*

EPIDURAL. above the dura.

EVERSION. a turning of the foot outward.

EXOSTOSIS. a bony growth projecting outward from the surface of the bone.

EXTENSION. the reverse of flexion, or movement that moves a joint toward a straight position.

EXTERNAL. situated on the outside or on the surface.

FASCIA. a sheet or band of fibrous connective tissue, often found between areas of more specialized tissue such as muscle.

FLEXION. act of bending at a joint.

FRACTURE. a rupture or break in the continuity of a bone.

HEAT TRANSFER (COOLING) MECHANISMS:

(1) CONDUCTION. the transfer of heat from direct contact of one body or structure to another, e.g., conduction of heat from a football player to his pads and vice versa.

(2) CONVECTION. cooling by means of circulating air, e.g., a breeze will cool the body.

(3) EVAPORATION. loss of heat from the body as a liquid (sweat) is passed from the liquid to the gaseous state; rate of cooling is based on the amount of liquid (humidity) present in the air, the higher the humidity the lower the cooling rate.

(4) RADIATION. a mechanism of cooling the body whereby electromagnetic waves are given off to the environment (region of lower concentration), e.g., body heat is radiated into a cool room; cooling is based on the thermal gradient, i.e., the difference between body heat and heat of the environment.

HEMATOMA. a pooling of blood within tissue as a result of a damaged blood vessel.

HEMORRHAGE. escape of blood from the vessels; bleeding.

HOMEOSTASIS. a tendency toward stability in the normal body internal (fluids) environment.

HYPOXIC. where there is a lack of oxygen either in the inspired air or in the tissues.

HYPERTENSION. to have high blood pressure.

HYPOTENSIVE. to have low blood pressure.

HYDROCULATOR COLPAKS. an agent containing a gell-like substance; used to apply cold to injuries.

INFERIOR. near the bottom or lower end of the body.

INFLAMMATION. the condition into which tissues enter as a reaction to injury; the classical signs are pain, heat, redness, swelling, and sometimes function loss.

INTERNAL. situated or occurring within or on the inside.

INVERSION. a turning inward of the foot.

JOINT CAPSULE. a sac-like ligamentous envelope which encloses the cavity of a synovial joint.

LACERATION. a wound made by a tearing of the skin.

LATERAL. meaning further from the midline of the body.

LESION. a discontinuity or loss of function of a tissue.

MALLEOLUS. a rounded process on either side of the ankle joint.

MEDIAL. pertaining to the middle or closer to the midline of the body.

MENINGES. the membranes covering the brain and spinal cord.

METABOLISM. energy transfer in the body. The body converts chemical energy in food to the chemical energy in ATP which in turn is used for (1) the work of the cells (2) heat (3) fat if there is not enough work performed.

NEUROGENIC SHOCK. loss of peripheral circulatory system control originating in the nervous system. It is often characterized by complete collapse following an injury.

NYSTAGMUS. an involuntary rapid movement of the eyeball.

PALPATION. to touch or feel with the hand.

PERIOSTEUM. a specialized type of connective tissue which covers all bones of the body; it contains bone formation material.

PLANTARFLEX. bending of the foot such that the toes point downward.

POSTERIOR (DORSAL). referring to the back surface or behind part.

PRONATION (FOREARM). medial rotation turning the palm backward.

PROXIMAL. designates nearness to a point of reference.

PUNCTURE. a piercing wound made by a pointed instrument.

QUADRIPLEGIA. paralysis of both arms and legs.

RDA. (recommended dietary allowances) food allowances judged by the National Research Council to be adequate for nearly all healthy people and generous for most.

RANGE OF MOTION (ROM). the amount of movement at a specific joint.

RETROGRADE AMNESIA. loss of memory for recent events prior to trauma or disease; following a violent blow.

ROENTGENOGRAM. a film produced from photography by means of roentgen rays. In this process detailed images are produced in a predetermined plane of the body while blurring or eliminating images in other planes of the body (an x-ray).

ROTATION. a movement of the body part about its own longitudinal axis.

SLING PSYCHROMETER. an apparatus in which atmospheric moisture is determined by the difference in readings from a dry bulb and wet bulb thermometer; for measurement, the thermometers are swung through the air to increase the evaporation from the wet bulb.

SOLAR PLEXUS. (celiac plexus) a network of nerves that control certain internal organs.

SPASM. an involuntary contraction of a muscle or a group of muscles.

SPRAIN. a stretch, or partial or complete tear of joint ligaments (mild, moderate, or severe).

STRAIN. a stretch, or partial or complete tear of muscle fiber or tendon (mild, moderate, or severe).

SUBLUXATION. an incomplete or partial dislocation.

SUBDURAL. below the dura.

SUPINATION. lateral rotation of the forearm turning the palm upward.

SUPERFICIAL. pertaining to or situated near the surface.

SUPERIOR. near the top or upper end of the body.

SYNCOPE. a sudden loss of strength or consciousness; to faint.

SYNOVITIS. inflammation of a synovial membrane.

SYNOVIAL FLUID. a viscous fluid that provides lubrication in synovial joints, bursa, and tendon sheaths.

TENDONITIS. inflammation of a tendon.

TENOSYNOVITIS. inflammation of a tendon sheath.

TUMOR. a swelling or mass of new tissue which persists independently of the surrounding structures.

USRDA. (United States recommended dietary allowance) the amounts of protein, vitamins, and minerals used as standards in nutrition labeling; in most cases higher than RDA.

VENTRICULAR FIBRILLATION. a rapid, uncontrolled beating heart in which almost no blood is pumped, and death is imminent.